C# Cookbook
Modern Recipes for Professional Developers

Joe Mayo

Beijing · Boston · Farnham · Sebastopol · Tokyo

C# Cookbook

by Joe Mayo

Published by O'Reilly Media, Inc., 1005 Gravenstein Highway North, Sebastopol, CA 95472.

O'Reilly books may be purchased for educational, business, or sales promotional use. Online editions are also available for most titles (*http://oreilly.com*). For more information, contact our corporate/institutional sales department: 800-998-9938 or *corporate@oreilly.com*.

Acquisitions Editor: Amanda Quinn
Development Editor: Angela Rufino
Production Editor: Katherine Tozer
Copyeditor: Justin Billing
Proofreader: Piper Editorial Consulting, LLC

Indexer: WordCo Indexing Services, Inc.
Interior Designer: David Futato
Cover Designer: Karen Montgomery
Illustrator: Kate Dullea

October 2021: First Edition

Revision History for the First Edition
2021-09-29: First Release

See *http://oreilly.com/catalog/errata.csp?isbn=9781492093695* for release details.

978-1-492-09369-5

[LSI]

Table of Contents

Preface

Why I Wrote This Book

In the course of a career, we collect many tools. Whether concepts, techniques, patterns, or reusable code, these tools help us get our job done. The more we collect, the better, because we have so many problems to solve and applications to build. *C# Cookbook* contributes to your toolset by providing you with a variety of recipes.

Things change over time, including programming languages. As of this writing, the C# programming language is over 20 years old, and software development has changed during its lifetime. There are a lot of recipes that could be written; this book acknowledges the evolution of C# over time and the fact that modern C# code makes us more productive.

This book is full of recipes that I've used throughout my career. In addition to stating a problem, presenting code, and explaining the solution, each discussion includes deeper insight into why each recipe is important. Throughout the book, I've avoided advocacy of process or absolute declarations of "you must do it this way" because much of what we do in creating software requires trade-offs. In fact, you'll find several discussions of what the consequences or trade-offs are with a recipe. This respects the fact that you can consider to what extent a recipe applies to you.

Who This Book Is For

This book assumes that you already know basic C# syntax. That said, there are recipes for various levels of developers. Whether you're a beginner, intermediate, or senior developer, there should be something for you. If you're an architect, there might be some interesting recipes that help you get back up to speed on the latest C# techniques.

How This Book Is Organized

When brainstorming for this book, the entire focus was on answering the question "What do C# developers need to do?" Looking at the list, certain patterns emerged and evolved into chapters:

- One of the first things I do when writing code is to build the types and organize the application. So I wrote Chapter 1 to show how to create and organize types. You'll see recipes dealing with patterns because that's how I code.

- After creating types, we add type members, like methods, and the logic they contain, which is a natural category of recipes for Chapter 2.

- What good is code unless it works well? That's why I added Chapter 3, which contains recipes that help improve the quality of code. While this chapter is packed with useful recipes, you'll want to check out the recipe that shows how to use nullable reference types.

While Chapters 1 through 3 follow the "What do C# developers need to do?" theme, from Chapter 4 to the end of the book I break away, taking a technology-specific focus:

- Many people think of Language Integrated Query (LINQ) as a database technology. While LINQ is useful for working with databases, it's also excellent for in-memory data manipulation and querying. That's why Chapter 4 discusses what you can do with the in-memory provider, called LINQ to Objects.

- Reflection was part of C# 1, but dynamic programming came along later in C# 4. I think it's important to discuss both technologies in Chapter 5 and even show how dynamic programing can be better than reflection in some situations. Also, be sure to check out the Python interop recipes.

- Async programming was a great addition to C# and seems straightforward, on the surface. Chapter 6 covers async with recipes that explain several important features you might not be aware of.

- All apps use data, whether securing, parsing, or serializing. Chapter 7 includes several recipes covering different things you want to do with data. It focuses on some of the newer libraries and algorithms you might want to use for working with data.

- One of the largest transformations of the C# language occurred over the last few versions in the area of pattern matching. There are so many that I was able to fill Chapter 8 with only pattern-matching recipes.

- C# continues to evolve and Chapter 9 captures recipes dedicated to C# 9. We'll look at some of the new features and discuss how to apply them. While I provide insight in the discussion, remember that sometimes new features can become more integral to a language in later versions. If you're into the cutting edge, these recipes are pretty interesting.

Conventions Used in This Book

The following typographical conventions are used in this book:

Italic
Indicates new terms, URLs, email addresses, filenames, and file extensions.

`Constant width`
Used for program listings, as well as within paragraphs to refer to program elements such as variable or function names, databases, data types, environment variables, statements, and keywords.

`Constant width bold`
Shows commands or other text that should be typed literally by the user.

`Constant width italic`
Shows text that should be replaced with user-supplied values or by values determined by context.

This element signifies a tip or suggestion.

This element signifies a general note.

This element indicates a warning or caution.

Using Code Examples

Supplemental material (code examples, exercises, etc.) is available for download at *https://github.com/JoeMayo/csharp-nine-cookbook*.

If you have a technical question or a problem using the code examples, please send email to *bookquestions@oreilly.com*.

This book is here to help you get your job done. In general, if example code is offered with this book, you may use it in your programs and documentation. You do not need to contact us for permission unless you're reproducing a significant portion of the code. For example, writing a program that uses several chunks of code from this book does not require permission. Selling or distributing examples from O'Reilly books does require permission. Answering a question by citing this book and quoting example code does not require permission. Incorporating a significant amount of example code from this book into your product's documentation does require permission.

We appreciate, but generally do not require, attribution. An attribution usually includes the title, author, publisher, and ISBN. For example: "*C# Cookbook* by Joe Mayo (O'Reilly). Copyright 2022 Mayo Software, LLC, 978-1-492-09369-5."

If you feel your use of code examples falls outside fair use or the permission given above, feel free to contact us at *permissions@oreilly.com*.

O'Reilly Online Learning

 For more than 40 years, *O'Reilly Media* has provided technology and business training, knowledge, and insight to help companies succeed.

Our unique network of experts and innovators share their knowledge and expertise through books, articles, and our online learning platform. O'Reilly's online learning platform gives you on-demand access to live training courses, in-depth learning paths, interactive coding environments, and a vast collection of text and video from O'Reilly and 200+ other publishers. For more information, visit *http://oreilly.com*.

How to Contact Us

Please address comments and questions concerning this book to the publisher:

O'Reilly Media, Inc.
1005 Gravenstein Highway North
Sebastopol, CA 95472
800-998-9938 (in the United States or Canada)
707-829-0515 (international or local)
707-829-0104 (fax)

We have a web page for this book, where we list errata, examples, and any additional information. You can access this page at *https://oreil.ly/c-sharp-cb*.

Email *bookquestions@oreilly.com* to comment or ask technical questions about this book.

For news and information about our books and courses, visit *http://oreilly.com*.

Find us on Facebook: *http://facebook.com/oreilly*

Follow us on Twitter: *http://twitter.com/oreillymedia*

Watch us on YouTube: *http://www.youtube.com/oreillymedia*

Acknowledgments

From concept to delivery, there are many people involved in creating a new book. I would like to recognize the people who helped on *C# Cookbook*.

Amanda Quinn, Senior Content Acquisitions Editor, helped form the concept for the book and provided feedback as I outlined its contents. Angela Rufino, Content Development Editor, got me started on standards and tools, provided feedback on my writing, and was incredibly helpful during the entire process. Bassam Alugili, Octavio Hernandez, and Shadman Kudchikar were tech editors, correcting errors, adding excellent insight, and sharing new ideas. Katherine Tozer, Production Editor and Vendor Coordinator, kept me up to date on new early releases and coordinated other production items. Justin Billing, Copyeditor, did a great job at improving my writing. There are many other people behind the scenes that made this book possible.

I would like to thank all of you. I am grateful for your contributions and wish you all the best.

CHAPTER 1

Constructing Types and Apps

One of the first things we do as developers is design, organize, and create new types. This chapter helps with these tasks by offering several useful recipes for setting up the project, managing object lifetime, and establishing patterns.

Establishing Architecture

When you're first setting up a project, you have to think about the overall architecture. There's a concept called *separation of concerns* wherein each part of an application has a specific purpose (e.g., the UI layer interacts with users, a business logic layer manages rules, and a data layer interacts with a data source). Each layer has a purpose or responsibilities and contains the code to perform its operations.

In addition to promoting more loosely coupled code, separation of concerns makes it easier for developers to work with that code because it's easier to find where a certain operation occurs. This makes it easier to add new features and maintain existing code. The benefits of this are higher quality applications and more productive work. It pays to get started right, which is why we have Recipe 1.5.

Related to loosely coupling code, there's inversion of control (IoC), which helps decouple code and promotes testability. Recipe 1.2 explains how this works. When we look at ensuring quality, in Chapter 3, you'll see how IoC fits in to unit testing.

Applying Patterns

A lot of the code we write is Transaction Script, where the user interacts with a UI and the code performs some type of create, read, update, or delete (CRUD) operation in the database and returns the result. Other times, we have complex interactions between objects that are difficult to organize. We need other patterns to solve these hard problems.

This chapter presents a few useful patterns in a rather informal manner. The idea is that you'll have some code to rename and adapt to your purposes and a rationale on when a given pattern would be useful. As you read through each pattern, try to think about other code you've written or other situations where that pattern would have simplified the code.

If you run into the problem of having different APIs to different systems and needing to switch between them, you'll be interested in reading Recipe 1.8. It shows how to build a single interface to solve this problem.

Managing Object Lifetime

Other important tasks we perform relate to object lifetime—that is, instantiating objects in memory, holding objects in memory for processing, and the subsequent release of that memory when the object is no longer needed. Recipes 1.3 and 1.4 show a couple of nice factory patterns that let you decouple object creation from code. This fits in with the IoC concepts mentioned previously.

One way to manage object creation is through a fluid interface, where you can include optional settings (via methods) and validate before object construction.

Another important object-lifetime consideration is disposal. Think about the drawbacks of excessive resource consumption, including memory use, file locks, and any other object that holds operating system resources. These problems often result in application crashes and are difficult to detect and fix. Performing proper resource cleanup is so important that it's the first recipe we'll cover in the book.

1.1 Managing Object End-of-Lifetime

Problem

Your application is crashing because of excessive resource usage.

Solution

Here's the object with the original problem:

```
using System;
using System.IO;

public class DeploymentProcess
{
    StreamWriter report = new StreamWriter("DeploymentReport.txt");
```

```csharp
    public bool CheckStatus()
    {
        report.WriteLine($"{DateTime.Now} Application Deployed.");

        return true;
    }
}
```

And here's how to fix the problem:

```csharp
using System;
using System.IO;

public class DeploymentProcess : IDisposable
{
    bool disposed;

    readonly StreamWriter report = new StreamWriter("DeploymentReport.txt");

    public bool CheckStatus()
    {
        report.WriteLine($"{DateTime.Now} Application Deployed.");

        return true;
    }

    protected virtual void Dispose(bool disposing)
    {
        if (!disposed)
        {
            if (disposing)
            {
                // disposal of purely managed resources goes here
            }

            report?.Close();
            disposed = true;
        }
    }

    ~DeploymentProcess()
    {
        Dispose(disposing: false);
    }

    public void Dispose()
    {
        Dispose(disposing: true);
        GC.SuppressFinalize(this);
    }
}
```

This is the Main method, using this object:

```
static void Main(string[] args)
{
    using (var deployer = new DeploymentProcess())
    {
        deployer.CheckStatus();
    }
}
```

Discussion

The problem in this code was with the `StreamWriter` `report`. Whenever you're using some type of resource, such as the `report` file reference, you need to release (or dispose) that resource. The specific problem here occurs because the app, through the `StreamWriter`, requested a file handle from the Windows OS. This app owns that file handle, and Windows expects the owning app to release the handle. If your app closes without releasing that handle, Windows prevents all applications, including subsequent running of your app, from accessing that file. In the worst case, everything crashes in a hard-to-find scenario that involves multiple people over a number of hours debugging a critical production problem. This occurs because Windows believes that file is still in use.

The solution is to implement the dispose pattern, which involves adding code that makes it easy to release resources. The solution code implements the `IDisposable` interface. `IDisposable` only specifies the `Dispose()` method, without parameters, and there's more to be done than just adding that method, including another `Dispose` method overload that keeps track of what type of disposal to do and an optional finalizer.

Complicating the implementation is a field and parameter that control disposal logic: `disposed` and `disposing`. The `disposed` field ensures that this object gets disposed only one time. Inside the `Dispose(bool)` method, there's an `if` statement, ensuring that if `disposed` is `true` (the object has been disposed), then it won't execute any disposal logic. The first time through `Dispose(bool)`, disposed will be `false` and the code in the `if` block will execute. Make sure that you also set `disposed` to `true` to ensure this code doesn't run anymore—the consequences of not doing so bring exposure to unpredictable errors like an `ObjectDisposedException`.

The `disposing` parameter tells `Dispose(bool)` how it's being called. Notice that `Dispose()` (without parameters) and the finalizer call `Dispose(bool)`. When `Dispose()` calls `Dispose(bool)`, `disposing` is `true`. This makes it easy for calling code, if written properly, to instantiate `DeploymentProcess` in a `using` statement or wrap it in the `finally` block of a `try/finally`.

The finalizer calls `Dispose(bool)` with `disposing` set to `false`, meaning that it isn't being run by calling application code. The `Dispose(bool)` method uses the `dispos`

---

ing value to determine whether it should release managed resources. Unmanaged resources are released regardless of whether `Dispose()` or the finalizer calls `Dispose(bool)`.

Let's clarify what is happening with the finalizer. The .NET CLR garbage collector (GC) executes an object's finalizer when it cleans that object from memory. The GC can make multiple passes over objects, calling finalizers being one of the last things it does. Managed objects are instantiated and managed by the .NET CLR, and you don't have control over when they're released, which could potentially result in out-of-order releases. You have to check the disposing value to prevent an `ObjectDisposed` `Exception` in case the dependent object was disposed by the GC first.

What the finalizer gives you is a way to clean up unmanaged resources. An unmanaged resource, such as the file handle that `StreamWriter` obtained, doesn't belong to the .NET CLR; it belongs to the Windows OS. There are situations where developers might need to explicitly call into a Win32/64 dynamic link library (DLL) to get a handle to an OS or third-party device. The reason you need the finalizer is that if your object doesn't get disposed properly, there's no other way to release that handle, which could crash your system for the same reason we need to release managed objects. So, the finalizer is a just-in-case mechanism to ensure the code that needs to release the unmanaged resource will execute.

A lot of applications don't have objects that use unmanaged resources. In that case, don't even add the finalizer. Having the finalizer adds overhead to the object because the GC has to do accounting to recognize objects that do have finalizers and call them in a multi-pass collection. Omitting the finalizer avoids this.

On a related note, remember to call `GC.SuppressFinalize` in the `Dispose()` method. This is another optimization telling the GC to not call the finalizer for this object, because all resources—managed and unmanaged—are released when the application calls `IDisposable.Dispose()`.

Generally, you should always call `GC.SuppressFinalize` in `Dispose()`, even if the class doesn't have a finalizer. That said, there are some nuances that you might be interested in. If a class is both `sealed` and doesn't have a finalizer, you can safely omit the call to `GC.SuppressFinalize`. However, classes that aren't `sealed` could potentially be inherited by another class that does include a finalizer. In this case, calling `GC.SuppressFinalize` protects against improper implementations.

For classes without finalizers, `GC.SuppressFinalize` has no effect. If you chose to leave out the call to `GC.SuppressFinalize` and the class has a finalizer, the CLR will call that finalizer.

The `Main` method shows how to properly use the `DeploymentProcess` object. It instantiates and wraps the object in a `using` statement. The object exists in memory until the `using` statement block ends. At that time, the program calls the `Dispose()` method.

1.2 Removing Explicit Dependencies

Problem

Your application is tightly coupled and difficult to maintain.

Solution

Define the types you need:

```csharp
public class DeploymentArtifacts
{
    public void Validate()
    {
        System.Console.WriteLine("Validating...");
    }
}

public class DeploymentRepository
{
    public void SaveStatus(string status)
    {
        System.Console.WriteLine("Saving status...");
    }
}

interface IDeploymentService
{
    void PerformValidation();
}

public class DeploymentService : IDeploymentService
{
    readonly DeploymentArtifacts artifacts;
    readonly DeploymentRepository repository;

    public DeploymentService(
        DeploymentArtifacts artifacts,
        DeploymentRepository repository)
    {
        this.artifacts = artifacts;
        this.repository = repository;
    }

    public void PerformValidation()
```

```
    {
        artifacts.Validate();
        repository.SaveStatus("status");
    }
}
```

And start the application like this:

```
using Microsoft.Extensions.DependencyInjection;
using System;

class Program
{
    readonly IDeploymentService service;

    public Program(IDeploymentService service)
    {
        this.service = service;
    }

    static void Main()
    {
        var services = new ServiceCollection();

        services.AddTransient<DeploymentArtifacts>();
        services.AddTransient<DeploymentRepository>();
        services.AddTransient<IDeploymentService, DeploymentService>();

        ServiceProvider serviceProvider =
            services.BuildServiceProvider();

        IDeploymentService deploymentService =
            serviceProvider.GetRequiredService<IDeploymentService>();

        var program = new Program(deploymentService);

        program.StartDeployment();
    }

    public void StartDeployment()
    {
        service.PerformValidation();
        Console.WriteLine("Validation complete - continuing...");
    }
}
```

Discussion

The term *tightly coupled* often means that one piece of code is overburdened with the responsibility of instantiating the types (dependencies) it uses. This requires the code to know how to construct, manage lifetime, and contain logic for dependencies. This distracts from the purpose of the code in solving the problem that it exists for. It duplicates instantiation of dependencies in different classes. This makes the code brittle because changes in dependency interfaces affect all other code that needs to instantiate that dependency. Additionally, code that instantiates its dependencies makes it difficult, if not impossible, to perform proper unit testing.

The solution is dependency injection, which is a technique to define dependency type instantiation in one place and expose a service that other types can use to obtain instances of those dependencies. There are a couple of ways to perform dependency injection: service locator and inversion of control (IoC). Which to use and when is an active debate; let's avoid venturing into theoretical territory. To keep things simple, this solution uses IoC, which is a common and straightforward approach.

The specific solution requires that you have types that rely on other dependency types, configure type constructors to accept dependencies, reference a library to help manage the IoC container, and use the container to declare how to instantiate types. The following paragraphs explain how this works. Figure 1-1 shows the relationship of objects and sequence of IoC operations for the solution.

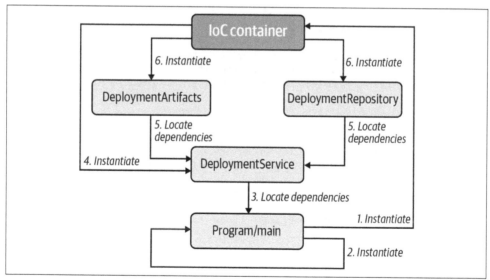

Figure 1-1. IoC for the solution

The solution is a utility to help manage a deployment process, validating whether the deployment process is configured properly. It has a `DeploymentService` class that runs the process. Notice that the `DeploymentService` constructor accepts the classes `DeploymentArtifacts` and `DeploymentRepository`. `DeploymentService` does not instantiate these classes—rather, they are injected.

To inject these classes, you can use an IoC container, which is a library that helps to automatically instantiate types and to automatically instantiate and provide instances of dependency types. The IoC container in the solution, as shown in the using declaration, is the `Microsoft.Extensions.DependencyInjection` namespace, which you can reference as the NuGet package by the same name.

While we want to inject all dependencies for every type in the application, you must still instantiate the IoC container directly, which is why the `Main` method instantiates `ServiceCollection` as services. Then use the `services` instance to add all of the dependencies, including `DeploymentService`.

The IoC container can help manage the lifetime of objects. This solution uses `AddTransient`, which means that the container should create a new instance every time its type is requested. A couple of other examples of managing object lifetime are `AddSingleton`, which instantiates an object only one time and passes that one instance to all objects, and `AddScoped`, which gives more control over the lifetime of the object. In ASP.NET, `AddScoped` is set to the current request. Over time, you'll want to think more about what the lifetime of your objects should be and investigate these options in more depth. For now, it's simple to get started with `AddTransient`.

The call to `BuildServiceProvider` converts `services`, a `ServiceCollection`, into a `ServiceProvider`. The term *IoC container* refers to this `ServiceProvider` instance—it instantiates and locates types to be injected.

You can see the container in action, calling `GetRequiredService` to return an instance implementing `IDeploymentService`. Going back to the `ServiceCollection`, notice that there's an `AddTransient` associating the `DeploymentService` class with the `IDeploymentService` interface. This means that `GetRequiredService` will return an instance of `DeploymentService`.

Finally, `Main` instantiates `Program`, with the new `DeploymentService` instance.

Going back to the constructor for `DeploymentService`, you can see that it expects to be called with instances for `DeploymentArtifacts` and `DeploymentRepository`. Because we used the IoC container to instantiate `DeploymentService`, the IoC container also knows how to instantiate its dependencies, which were also added to the `ServiceCollection`, with calls to `AddTransient`. This solution only used three types; you can build object dependency graphs much deeper than this.

Also, notice how the `DeploymentService` constructor saves the injected instances in `readonly` fields, making them available for use by `DeploymentService` members.

The beauty of IoC is that instantiation only happens in one place, and you don't have to code all of that in your constructors or in members that need a new instance of a dependency. This makes your code more loosely coupled and maintainable. It also opens the opportunity for higher quality by making the type more unit testable.

Recipe 3.1, "Writing a Unit Test"

1.3 Delegating Object Creation to a Class

Problem

You're using IoC, the type you're trying to instantiate doesn't have an interface, and you have complex construction requirements.

Solution

We want to instantiate this class:

```
using System;

public class ThirdPartyDeploymentService
{
    public void Validate()
    {
        Console.WriteLine("Validated");
    }
}
```

We'll use this class for IoC:

```
public interface IValidatorFactory
{
    ThirdPartyDeploymentService CreateDeploymentService();
}
```

And here's the IValidatorFactory implementation:

```
public class ValidatorFactory : IValidatorFactory
{
    public ThirdPartyDeploymentService CreateDeploymentService()
    {
        return new ThirdPartyDeploymentService();
    }
}
```

Then instantiate the factory like this:

```
public class Program
{
    readonly ThirdPartyDeploymentService service;

    public Program(IValidatorFactory factory)
    {
        service = factory.CreateDeploymentService();
    }
```

```
static void Main()
{
    var factory = new ValidatorFactory();
    var program = new Program(factory);
    program.PerformValidation();
}

void PerformValidation()
{
    service.Validate();
}
}
```

Discussion

As discussed in Recipe 1.2, IoC is a best practice because it decouples dependencies, making code easier to maintain, more adaptable, and easier to test. The problem is that there are exceptions and situations that cause difficulties with the best of plans. One of these problems occurs when trying to use a third-party API without an interface.

The solution shows a ThirdPartyDeploymentService class. You can see the code and what it does. In reality, even if you can read the code through reflection or disassembler, it doesn't help because you can't add your interface. Even if ThirdPartyDeploymentService were open source, you would have to weigh the decision to fork the library for your own modifications—the trade-off being that your modifications are brittle in the face of new features and maintenance to the original open source library. An example is the System.Net.HttpClient class in the .NET Framework, which doesn't have an interface. Ultimately, you'll need to evaluate the situation and make a decision that works for you, but the factory class described here can be an effective work-around.

To see how a factory class works, observe the IValidatorFactory interface. This is the interface we'll use for IoC. Next, examine how the ValidatorFactory class implements the IValidatorFactory interface. Its CreateDeploymentService instantiates and returns the ThirdPartyDeploymentService. This is what a factory does: it creates objects for us.

This is related to the proxy pattern. The ValidatorFactory controls access to a ThirdPartyDeploymentService instance. However, rather than returning an object to control access to members of ThirdPartyDeploymentService, CreateDeploymentService returns a direct ThirdPartyDeploymentService instance.

To simplify this example, the code doesn't use an IoC container—though it would be normal to use factories alongside IoC. Instead, the `Main` method instantiates `ValidatorFactory` and passes that instance to the `Program` constructor, which is the important part of this example.

Examine how the constructor takes the `IValidatorFactory` reference and calls `CreateDeploymentService`. Now we've been able to inject the dependency and maintain the loose coupling we sought.

Another benefit is that since the `ThirdPartyDeploymentService` is instantiated in the factory class, you can make any future changes to class instantiation without affecting consuming code.

See Also

Recipe 1.2, "Removing Explicit Dependencies"

1.4 Delegating Object Creation to a Method

Problem

You want a plug-in framework and need to structure object instantiation someplace other than application logic.

Solution

Here's the abstract base class with the object creation contract:

```
public abstract class DeploymentManagementBase
{
    IDeploymentPlugin deploymentService;

    protected abstract IDeploymentPlugin CreateDeploymentService();

    public bool Validate()
    {
        if (deploymentService == null)
            deploymentService = CreateDeploymentService();

        return deploymentService.Validate();
    }
}
```

These are a couple of classes that instantiate associated plug-in classes:

```
public class DeploymentManager1 : DeploymentManagementBase
{
    protected override IDeploymentPlugin CreateDeploymentService()
    {
```

```
        return new DeploymentPlugin1();
    }
}

public class DeploymentManager2 : DeploymentManagementBase
{
    protected override IDeploymentPlugin CreateDeploymentService()
    {
        return new DeploymentPlugin2();
    }
}
```

The plug-in classes implement the IDeploymentPlugin interface:

```
public interface IDeploymentPlugin
{
    bool Validate();
}
```

And here are the plug-in classes being instantiated:

```
public class DeploymentPlugin1 : IDeploymentPlugin
{
    public bool Validate()
    {
        Console.WriteLine("Validated Plugin 1");
        return true;
    }
}

public class DeploymentPlugin2 : IDeploymentPlugin
{
    public bool Validate()
    {
        Console.WriteLine("Validated Plugin 2");
        return true;
    }
}
```

Finally, here's how it all fits together:

```
class Program
{
    readonly DeploymentManagementBase[] deploymentManagers;

    public Program(DeploymentManagementBase[] deploymentManagers)
    {
        this.deploymentManagers = deploymentManagers;
    }

    static DeploymentManagementBase[] GetPlugins()
    {
        return new DeploymentManagementBase[]
        {
```

```
                new DeploymentManager1(),
                new DeploymentManager2()
        };
    }

    static void Main()
    {
        DeploymentManagementBase[] deploymentManagers = GetPlugins();

        var program = new Program(deploymentManagers);

        program.Run();
    }

    void Run()
    {
        foreach (var manager in deploymentManagers)
            manager.Validate();
    }
}
```

Discussion

Plug-in systems are all around us. Excel can consume and emit different document types, Adobe works with multiple image types, and Visual Studio Code has numerous extensions. These are all plug-in systems, and whether the only plug-ins available are via vendor or third party, they all leverage the same concept—the code must be able to adapt to handling a new abstract object type.

While the previous examples are ubiquitous in our daily lives, many developers won't be building those types of systems. That said, the plug-in model is a powerful opportunity for making our applications extensible. Application integration is a frequent use case where your application needs to consume documents from customers, other departments, or other businesses. Sure, web services and other types of APIs are popular, but needing to consume an Excel spreadsheet is normal. As soon as you do that, someone has data in a different format, like CSV, JSON, tab delimited, and more. Another side of the story is the frequent need to export data in a format that multiple users need to consume.

In this spirit, the solution demonstrates a situation where a plug-in system allows an application to add support for new deployment types. This is a typical situation where you've built the system to handle the deployment artifacts that you know about, but the system is so useful that everyone else wants to add their own deployment logic, which you never knew about when original requirements were written.

In the solution, each of the DeploymentManagers implement the abstract base class, DeploymentManagementBase. DeploymentManagementBase orchestrates the logic, and the derived DeploymentManager classes are simply factories for their associated plugins. Notice that DeploymentManagementBase uses polymorphism to let derived classes instantiate their respective plug-in classes.

 If this is getting a little complex, you might want to review Recipes 1.2 and 1.3. This is one level of abstraction above that.

The solution shows two classes that implement the IDeploymentPlugin interface. The DeploymentManagementBase class consumes the IDeploymentPlugin interface, delegating calls to its methods to the plug-in classes that implement that interface. Notice how Validate calls Validate on the IDeploymentPlugin instance.

The Program has no knowledge of the plug-in classes. It operates on instances of DeploymentManagementBase, as demonstrated where Main calls GetPlugins and receives an array of DeploymentManagementBase instances. Program doesn't care about the plug-ins. For demo simplicity, GetPlugins is a method in Program but could be another class with a mechanism for selecting which plug-ins to use. Notice in the Run method how it iterates through DeploymentManagementBase instances.

 Making DeploymentManagementBase implement an interface might make IoC more consistent if you're using interfaces everywhere else. That said, an abstract base class can often work for most IoC containers, mocking, and unit testing tools.

To recap, the DeploymentManagementBase encapsulates all functionality and delegates work to plug-in classes. The code that makes the plug-in are the deployment managers, plug-in interface, and plug-in classes. The consuming code only works with a collection of DeploymentManagementBase and is blissfully unaware of the specific plug-in implementations.

Here's where the power comes in. Whenever you or any third party you allow wants to extend the system for a new type of deployment, they do this:

1. Create a new DeploymentPlugin class that implements your IDeploymentPlugin interface.

2. Create a new DeploymentManagement class that derives from DeploymentManagementBase.

3. Implement the DeploymentManagement.CreateDeploymentService method to instantiate and return the new DeploymentPlugin.

Finally, the GetPlugins method, or some other logic of your choosing, would add that new code to its collections of plug-ins to operate on.

See Also

Recipe 1.2, "Removing Explicit Dependencies"

Recipe 1.3, "Delegating Object Creation to a Class"

1.5 Designing Application Layers

Problem

You're setting up a new application and are unsure of how to structure the project.

Solution

Here's a data access layer class:

```
public class GreetingRepository
{
    public string GetNewGreeting() => "Welcome!";

    public string GetVisitGreeting() => "Welcome back!";
}
```

Here's a business logic layer class:

```
public class Greeting
{
    GreetingRepository greetRep = new GreetingRepository();

    public string GetGreeting(bool isNew) =>
        isNew ? greetRep.GetNewGreeting() : greetRep.GetVisitGreeting();
}
```

These two classes are part of the UI layer:

```
public class SignIn
{
    Greeting greeting = new Greeting();

    public void Greet()
    {
        Console.Write("Is this your first visit? (true/false): ");
        string newResponse = Console.ReadLine();

        bool.TryParse(newResponse, out bool isNew);

        string greetResponse = greeting.GetGreeting(isNew);
```

```
        Console.WriteLine($"\n*\n* {greetResponse} \n*\n");
    }
}

public class Menu
{
    public void Show()
    {
        Console.WriteLine(
            "*------*\n" +
            "* Menu *\n" +
            "*------*\n" +
            "\n" +
            "1. ...\n" +
            "2. ...\n" +
            "3. ...\n" +
            "\n" +
            "Choose: ");
    }
}
```

This is the application entry point (part of the UI layer):

```
class Program
{
    SignIn signIn = new SignIn();
    Menu menu = new Menu();

    static void Main()
    {
        new Program().Start();
    }

    void Start()
    {
        signIn.Greet();
        menu.Show();
    }
}
```

Discussion

There are endless ways to set up and plan the structure of new projects, with some approaches better than others. Rather than viewing this discussion as a definitive conclusion, think of it as a few options with trade-offs that help you think about your own approach.

The antipattern here is Big Ball of Mud (BBoM) architecture. BBoM is where a developer opens a single project and starts adding all the code at the same layer in the application. While this approach might help knock out a quick prototype, it has severe complications in the long run. Over time most apps need new features and maintenance to fix bugs. What happens is that the code begins to run together and there's often much duplication, commonly referred to as *spaghetti code*. Seriously, no one wants to maintain code like this, and you should avoid it.

 When under time pressure, it's easy to think that creating a quick prototype might be an acceptable use of time. However, resist this urge. The cost of maintenance on a BBoM prototype project is high. The time required to work with spaghetti code to add a new feature or fix a bug quickly wipes out any perceived up-front gains from a sloppy prototype. Because of duplication, fixing a bug in one place leaves the same bug in other parts of the application. This means not only that a developer has to fix the bug multiple times but that the entire life cycle of QA, deployment, customer discovery, help desk service, and management wastes time on what would be multiple unnecessary cycles. The content in this section helps you avoid this antipattern.

The primary concept to grasp here is separation of concerns. You'll often hear this simplified as a layered architecture where you have UI, business logic, and data layers, with each section named for the type of code placed in that layer. This section uses the layered approach with the goal of showing how to achieve separation of concerns and associated benefits.

 Sometimes the idea of a layered architecture makes people think they must route application communication through the layers or that certain operations are restricted to their layer. This isn't quite true or practical. For example, business logic can be found in different layers, such as rules for validating user input in the UI layer as well as logic for how to process a certain request. Another example of exceptions to communication patterns is when a user needs to select a set of operations on a form—there isn't any business logic involved and the UI layer can request the list of items from the data layer directly. What we want is separation of concerns to enhance the maintainability of the code; any dogmatic/idealistic restrictions that don't make sense run counter to that goal.

The solution starts with a data access layer, `GreetingRepository`. This simulates the repository pattern, which is an abstraction so that calling code doesn't need to think about how to retrieve the data. Ideally, creating a separate data project promises an additional benefit of reusing that data access layer in another project that needs access to the same data. Sometimes you get reuse and other times you don't, though you always get the benefits of reducing duplication and knowing where the data access logic resides.

The business logic layer has a `Greeting` class. Notice how it uses the `isNew` parameter to determine which method of `GreetingRepository` to call. Anytime you find yourself needing to write logic for how to handle a user request, consider putting that code in another class that is considered part of the business logic layer. If you already have code like this, refactor it out into a separate object named for the type of logic it needs to handle.

Finally, there's the UI layer, which is composed of the `SignIn` and `Menu` classes. These classes handle the interaction with the user, yet they delegate any logic to the business logic layer. `Program` might be considered part of the UI layer, though it's only orchestrating interaction/navigation between other UI layer classes and doesn't perform UI operations itself.

 The way I wrote the solution was so you would see the definition of a class before it was used. However, when actually doing the design, you might start with the UI layer and then work down through business logic and data access.

There are a couple of dimensions to separation of concerns in this code. `Greeting Repository` is only concerned with data, and `Greeting` data in particular. For example, if the app needed data to show in a `Menu`, you would need another class called `MenuRepository` that did CRUD operations on `Menu` data. `Greeting` only handles business logic for `Greeting` data. If a `Menu` had its own business logic, you might consider a separate business logic layer class for that, but only if it made sense. As you can see in the UI layer, `SignIn` only handles interaction with the user for signing into the app, and `Menu` only handles interaction with the user for displaying and choosing what they want to do. The beauty is that now you or anyone else can easily go into the application and find the code concerning the subject you need to address.

Figures 1-2, 1-3, and 1-4 show how you might structure each layer into a Visual Studio solution. Figure 1-2 is for a very simple app, like a utility that is unlikely to have many features. In this case, it's OK to keep the layers in the same project because there isn't a lot of code and anything extra doesn't have tangible benefit.

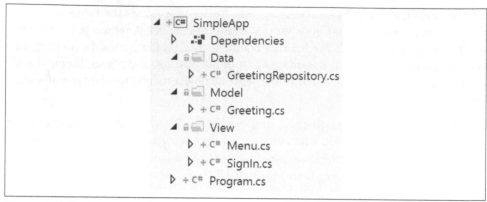

Figure 1-2. Project layout for a simple app

Figure 1-3 shows how you might structure a project that's a little larger and will grow over time, which I'll loosely call midsize for the sake of discussion. Notice that it has a separate data access layer. The purpose of that is potential reuse. Some projects offer different UIs for different customers. For example, there might be a chatbot or mobile app that accesses the data for users but a web app for administrators. Having the data access layer as a separate project makes this possible. Notice how `SystemApp.Console` has an assembly reference to `SystemApp.Data`.

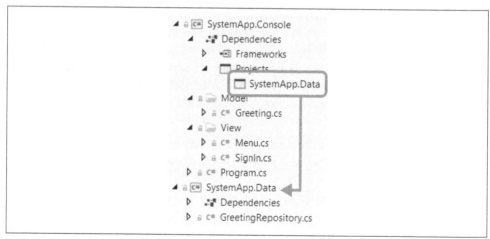

Figure 1-3. Project layout to separate UI and data layers

For larger enterprise apps, you'll want to break the layers apart, as shown in Figure 1-4. The problem to solve here is that you want a cleaner break between sections of code to encourage loose coupling. Large applications often become complex and hard to manage unless you control the architecture in a way that encourages best practices.

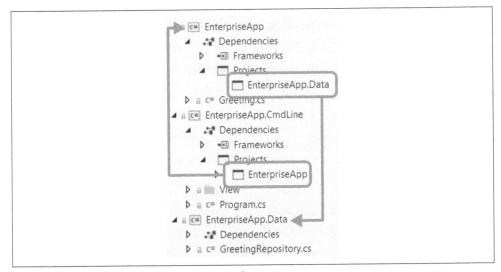

Figure 1-4. Project layout for separation of concerns

For the enterprise scenario, this example is small. However, imagine the complexity of a growing application. As you add new business logic, you'll begin finding code that gets reused. Also, you'll naturally have some code that can stand on its own, like a service layer for accessing an external API. The opportunity here is to have a reusable library that might be useful in other applications. Therefore, you'll want to refactor anything reusable into its own project. On a growing project, you can rarely anticipate every aspect or feature that an app will support, and watching for these changes and refactoring will help to keep your code, project, and architecture healthier.

1.6 Returning Multiple Values from a Method

Problem

You need to return multiple values from a method, and using classic approaches such as out parameters or returning a custom type doesn't feel intuitive.

Solution

ValidationStatus has a deconstructor:

```
public class ValidationStatus
{
    public bool Deployment { get; set; }
    public bool SmokeTest { get; set; }
    public bool Artifacts { get; set; }

    public void Deconstruct(
```

```
            out bool isPreviousDeploymentComplete,
            out bool isSmokeTestComplete,
            out bool areArtifactsReady)
        {
            isPreviousDeploymentComplete = Deployment;
            isSmokeTestComplete = SmokeTest;
            areArtifactsReady = Artifacts;
        }
    }
```

The DeploymentService shows how to return a tuple:

```
    public class DeploymentService
    {
        public
        (bool deployment, bool smokeTest, bool artifacts)
        PrepareDeployment()
        {
            ValidationStatus status = Validate();

            (bool deployment, bool smokeTest, bool artifacts) = status;

            return (deployment, smokeTest, artifacts);
        }

        ValidationStatus Validate()
        {
            return new ValidationStatus
            {
                Deployment = true,
                SmokeTest = true,
                Artifacts = true
            };
        }
    }
```

And here's how to consume the returned tuple:

```
    class Program
    {
        readonly DeploymentService deployment = new DeploymentService();
        static void Main(string[] args)
        {
            new Program().Start();
        }

        void Start()
        {
            (bool deployed, bool smokeTest, bool artifacts) =
                deployment.PrepareDeployment();

            Console.WriteLine(
                $"\nDeployment Status:\n\n" +
```

```
            $"Is Previous Deployment Complete? {deployed}\n" +
            $"Is Previous Smoke Test Complete? {smokeTest}\n" +
            $"Are artifacts for this deployment ready? {artifacts}\n\n" +
            $"Can deploy: {deployed && smokeTest && artifacts}");
    }
}
```

Discussion

Historically, the typical way to return multiple values from a method was to create a custom type or add multiple out parameters. It always felt wasteful to create a custom type that would only be used one time for the purpose of returning values. The other option, to use multiple out parameters, felt clunky too. Using a tuple is more elegant. A *tuple* is a value type that lets you group data into a single object without declaring a separate type.

The tuple type described in this section was a new feature of C# 7.0. It aliases the .NET ValueTuple, which is a mutable value type whose members are fields. In contrast, the .NET Framework has a Tuple class, which is an immutable reference type whose members are properties. Both ValueTuple and Tuple named members Item1, Item2, …, ItemN; in contrast, you're free to provide more meaningful names for C# tuple members.

If using a version of .NET prior to 4.7, you must explicitly reference the System.ValueTuple NuGet package.

The solution shows a couple of different aspects of tuples, deconstruction, and how to return a tuple from a method. The ValidationStatus class has a Deconstruct method and C# uses that to produce a tuple from an instance of the class. This class wasn't strictly necessary for this example, but it does demonstrate an interesting way of converting a class to a tuple.

The DeploymentService class shows how to return a tuple. Notice that the return type of the PrepareDeployment method is a tuple. The property names in the tuple return type are optional, though meaningful variable names could make the code easier to read.

The code calls Validate, which returns an instance of ValidationStatus. The next line, assigning status to the tuple, uses the deconstructor to return a tuple instance. PrepareDeployment uses those values to return a new tuple to the caller.

The solution implementation of PrepareDeployment shows the mechanics of working with tuples, which is useful for learning, though not very elegant. In practice, it would be cleaner to return status from the method because the deconstructor will run implicitly.

The Start method, in Program, shows how to call PrepareDeployment and consume the tuple it returns.

1.7 Converting from Legacy to Strongly Typed Classes

Problem

You have a legacy type that operates on values of type object and need to modernize to a strongly typed implementation.

Solution

Here's a Deployment class that we'll be using:

```
public class Deployment
{
    string config;

    public Deployment(string config)
    {
        this.config = config;
    }

    public bool PerformHealthCheck()
    {
        Console.WriteLine(
            $"Performed health check for config {config}.");
        return true;
    }
}
```

And here's a legacy CircularQueue collection:

```
public class CircularQueue
{
    int current = 0;
    int last = 0;
    object[] items;

    public CircularQueue(int size)
    {
        items = new object[size];
    }

    public void Add(object obj)
    {
        if (last >= items.Length)
            throw new IndexOutOfRangeException();

        items[last++] = obj;
```

```
        }

        public object Next()
        {
            current %= last;
            object item = items[current];
            current++;

            return item;
        }
    }
```

This code shows how to use the legacy collection:

```
public class HealthChecksObjects
{
    public void PerformHealthChecks(int cycles)
    {
        CircularQueue checks = Configure();

        for (int i = 0; i < cycles; i++)
        {
            Deployment deployment = (Deployment)checks.Next();
            deployment.PerformHealthCheck();
        }
    }

    private CircularQueue Configure()
    {
        var queue = new CircularQueue(5);

        queue.Add(new Deployment("a"));
        queue.Add(new Deployment("b"));
        queue.Add(new Deployment("c"));

        return queue;
    }
}
```

Next, here's the legacy collection refactored as a generic collection:

```
public class CircularQueue<T>
{
    int current = 0;
    int last = 0;
    T[] items;

    public CircularQueue(int size)
    {
        items = new T[size];
    }

    public void Add(T obj)
    {
```

```
        if (last >= items.Length)
            throw new IndexOutOfRangeException();

        items[last++] = obj;
    }

    public T Next()
    {
        current %= last;
        T item = items[current];
        current++;

        return item;
    }
}
```

With code that shows how to use the new generic collection:

```
public class HealthChecksGeneric
{
    public void PerformHealthChecks(int cycles)
    {
        CircularQueue<Deployment> checks = Configure();

        for (int i = 0; i < cycles; i++)
        {
            Deployment deployment = checks.Next();
            deployment.PerformHealthCheck();
        }
    }

    private CircularQueue<Deployment> Configure()
    {
        var queue = new CircularQueue<Deployment>(5);

        queue.Add(new Deployment("a"));
        queue.Add(new Deployment("b"));
        queue.Add(new Deployment("c"));

        return queue;
    }
}
```

Here's demo code to show both collections in action:

```
class Program
{
    static void Main(string[] args)
    {
        new HealthChecksObjects().PerformHealthChecks(5);
        new HealthChecksGeneric().PerformHealthChecks(5);
    }
}
```

Discussion

The first version of C# didn't have generics. Instead, we had a `System.Collections` namespace with collections like `Dictionary`, `List`, and `Stack` that operated on instances of type `object`. If the instances in the collection were reference types, the conversion performance to/from object was negligible. However, if you wanted to manage a collection of value types, the boxing/unboxing performance penalty became more excruciating the larger the collection got or the more operations performed.

Microsoft had always intended to add generics, and they finally arrived in C# 2. However, in the meantime, there was a ton of nongeneric code written. Imagine all of the new object-based collections that developers needed to write on their own for things like sets, priority queues, and tree data structures. Add to that types like delegates, which were the primary means of method reference and async communication and operated on objects. There's a long list of nongeneric code that's been written, and chances are that you'll encounter some of it as you progress through your career.

As C# developers, we appreciate the benefits of strongly typed code, making it easier to find and fix compile-time errors, making an application more maintainable, and improving quality. For this reason, you might have a strong desire to refactor a given piece of nongeneric code so that it too is strongly typed with generics.

The process is basically this: whenever you see type `object`, convert it to generic.

The solution shows a `Deployment` object that performs a health check on a deployed artifact. Since we have multiple artifacts, we also need to hold multiple `Deployment` instances in a collection. The collection is a (partially implemented) circular queue, and there's a `HealthCheck` class that loops through the queue and periodically performs a health check with the next `Deployment` instance.

`HealthCheckObject` operates on old nongeneric code and `HealthCheckGeneric` operates on new generic code. The difference between the two is that the `HealthCheck Object` `Configure` method instantiates a nongeneric `CircularQueue`, and the `Health CheckGeneric` `Configure` method instantiates a generic `CircularQueue<T>`. Our primary task is to convert `CircularQueue` to `CircularQueue<T>`.

Since we're working with a collection, the first task is to add the type parameter to the class, `CircularQueue<T>`. Then look for anywhere the code uses the `object` type and convert that to the class type parameter, `T`:

1. Convert the `object items[]` field to `T items[]`.
2. In the constructor, instantiate a new `T[]` instead of `object[]`.
3. Change the `Add` parameter from `object` to `T`.

4. Change the `Next` return type from `object` to `T`.

5. In `Next`, change the `object item` variable to `T item`.

After changing `object` types to `T`, you have a new strongly typed generic collection.

The `Program` class demonstrates how both of these collections work.

1.8 Making Classes Adapt to Your Interface

Problem

You have a third-party library with similar functionality as your code, but it doesn't have the same interface.

Solution

This is the interface we want to work with:

```
public interface IDeploymentService
{
    void Validate();
}
```

Here are a couple of classes that implement that interface:

```
public class DeploymentService1 : IDeploymentService
{
    public void Validate()
    {
        Console.WriteLine("Deployment Service 1 Validated");
    }
}

public class DeploymentService2 : IDeploymentService
{
    public void Validate()
    {
        Console.WriteLine("Deployment Service 2 Validated");
    }
}
```

Here's a third-party class that doesn't implement `IDeploymentService`:

```
public class ThirdPartyDeploymentService
{
    public void PerformValidation()
    {
        Console.WriteLine("3rd Party Deployment Service 1 Validated");
    }
}
```

This is the adapter that implements `IDeploymentService`:

```
public class ThirdPartyDeploymentAdapter : IDeploymentService
{
    ThirdPartyDeploymentService service = new ThirdPartyDeploymentService();

    public void Validate()
    {
        service.PerformValidation();
    }
}
```

This code shows how to include the third-party service by using the adapter:

```
class Program
{
    static void Main(string[] args)
    {
        new Program().Start();
    }

    void Start()
    {
        List<IDeploymentService> services = Configure();

        foreach (var svc in services)
            svc.Validate();
    }

    List<IDeploymentService> Configure()
    {
        return new List<IDeploymentService>
        {
            new DeploymentService1(),
            new DeploymentService2(),
            new ThirdPartyDeploymentAdapter()
        };
    }
}
```

Discussion

An adapter is a class that wraps another class but exposes the functionality of the wrapped class with the interface you need.

There are various situations where the need for an adapter class comes into play. What if you have a group of objects that implement an interface and want to use a third-party class that doesn't match the interface that your code works with? What if your code is written for a third-party API, like a payment service, and you know you want to eventually switch to a different provider with a different API? What if you need to use native code via Platform Invocation Services (P/Invoke) or Component

Object Model (COM) interop and didn't want the details of that interface to bleed into your code? These scenarios are all good candidates for considering an adapter.

The solution has `DeploymentService` classes that implement `IDeploymentService`. You can see in the `Program Start` method that it only operates on instances that implement `IDeploymentService`.

Sometime later, you encounter the need to integrate `ThirdPartyDeploymentService` into the app. However, it doesn't implement `IDeploymentService`, and you don't have the code for `ThirdPartyDeploymentService`.

The `ThirdPartyDeploymentAdapter` class solves the problem. It implements the `IDeploymentService` interface and instantiates its own copy of `ThirdPartyDeploymentService`, and the `Validate` method delegates the call to `ThirdPartyDeploymentService`. Notice that the `Program Configure` method adds an instance of `ThirdPartyDeploymentAdapter` to the collection that `Start` operates on.

This was a demo to show you how to design an adapter. In practice, the `Perform Validation` method of `ThirdPartyDeploymentService` likely has different parameters and a different return type. The `ThirdPartyDeploymentAdapter Validate` method will be responsible for preparing arguments and reshaping return values to ensure they conform to the proper `IDeploymentService` interface.

1.9 Designing a Custom Exception

Problem

The .NET Framework library doesn't have an exception type that fits your requirements.

Solution

This is a custom exception:

```
[Serializable]
public class DeploymentValidationException : Exception
{
    public DeploymentValidationException() :
        this("Validation Failed!", null, ValidationFailureReason.Unknown)
    {
    }

    public DeploymentValidationException(
        string message) :
        this(message, null, ValidationFailureReason.Unknown)
    {
    }
```

```
    public DeploymentValidationException(
        string message, Exception innerException) :
        this(message, innerException, ValidationFailureReason.Unknown)
    {
    }

    public DeploymentValidationException(
        string message, ValidationFailureReason reason) :
        this(message, null, reason)
    {
    }

    public DeploymentValidationException(
        string message,
        Exception innerException,
        ValidationFailureReason reason) :
        base(message, innerException)
    {
        Reason = reason;
    }

    public ValidationFailureReason Reason { get; set; }

    public override string ToString()
    {
        return
            base.ToString() +
            $" - Reason: {Reason} ";
    }
}
```

And this is an enum type for a property on that exception:

```
public enum ValidationFailureReason
{
    Unknown,
    PreviousDeploymentFailed,
    SmokeTestFailed,
    MissingArtifacts
}
```

This code shows how to throw the custom exception:

```
public class DeploymentService
{
    public void Validate()
    {
        throw new DeploymentValidationException(
            "Smoke test failed - check with qa@example.com.",
            ValidationFailureReason.SmokeTestFailed);
    }
}
```

And this code catches the custom exception:

```csharp
class Program
{
    static void Main()
    {
        try
        {
            new DeploymentService().Validate();
        }
        catch (DeploymentValidationException ex)
        {
            Console.WriteLine(
                $"Message: {ex.Message}\n" +
                $"Reason: {ex.Reason}\n" +
                $"Full Description: \n {ex}");
        }
    }
}
```

Discussion

The beautiful thing about C# exceptions are that they're strongly typed. When your code catches them, you can write specific handling logic for just that type of exception. The .NET Framework has a few exceptions, like `ArgumentNullException`, that get some reuse (you can throw yourself) in the average code base, but often you'll need to throw an exception with the semantics and data that gives a developer a fairer chance of figuring out why a method couldn't complete its intended purpose.

The exception in the solution is `DeploymentValidationException`, which indicates a problem related to the deployment process during the validation phase. It derives from `Exception`. Depending on how extensive your custom exception framework is, you could create your own base exception for a hierarchy and classify a derived exception tree from that. The benefit is that you would have flexibility in catch blocks to catch more general or specific exceptions as necessary. That said, if you only need a couple of custom exceptions, the extra design work of an exception hierarchy might be overkill.

The first three constructors mirror the `Exception` class options for message and inner exception. You'll also want custom constructors for instantiating with your custom data.

In the past, there's been discussion of whether a custom exception should derive from Exception or ApplicationException, where Exception was for .NET-type hierarchies and ApplicationExcep tion was for custom exception hierarchies. However, the distinction blurred over time with some .NET Framework types deriving from both with no apparent consistency or reason. So, deriving from Exception seems to be fine these days.

DeploymentValidationException has a property, of the enum type Validation FailureReason. Besides having semantics unique to the reason for throwing an exception, another purpose of a custom exception is to include important information for exception handling and/or debugging.

Overriding ToString is also a good idea. Logging frameworks might just receive the Exception reference, resulting in a call to ToString. As in this example, you'll want to ensure your custom data gets included in the string output. This ensures people can read the full state of the exception, along with the stack trace.

The Program Main method demonstrates how nice it is to be able to handle the specific type, rather than another type that might not fit or the general Exception class.

1.10 Constructing Objects with Complex Configuration

Problem

You need to build a new type with complex configuration options without an unnecessary expansion of constructors.

Solution

Here's the DeploymentService class we want to build:

```
public class DeploymentService
{
    public int StartDelay { get; set; } = 2000;
    public int ErrorRetries { get; set; } = 5;
    public string ReportFormat { get; set; } = "pdf";

    public void Start()
    {
        Console.WriteLine(
            $"Deployment started with:\n" +
            $"    Start Delay:   {StartDelay}\n" +
            $"    Error Retries: {ErrorRetries}\n" +
            $"    Report Format: {ReportFormat}");
    }
}
```

This is the class that builds the `DeploymentService` instance:

```csharp
public class DeploymentBuilder
{
    DeploymentService service = new DeploymentService();

    public DeploymentBuilder SetStartDelay(int delay)
    {
        service.StartDelay = delay;
        return this;
    }

    public DeploymentBuilder SetErrorRetries(int retries)
    {
        service.ErrorRetries = retries;
        return this;
    }

    public DeploymentBuilder SetReportFormat(string format)
    {
        service.ReportFormat = format;
        return this;
    }

    public DeploymentService Build()
    {
        return service;
    }
}
```

Here's how to use the `DeploymentBuilder` class:

```csharp
class Program
{
    static void Main()
    {
        DeploymentService service =
            new DeploymentBuilder()
                .SetStartDelay(3000)
                .SetErrorRetries(3)
                .SetReportFormat("html")
                .Build();

        service.Start();
    }
}
```

Discussion

In Recipe 1.9, the `DeploymentValidationException` class has multiple constructors. Normally, this isn't a problem. The first three constructors are a typical convention for exception classes. Subsequent constructors add new parameters for initializing new fields.

However, what if the class you were designing had a lot of options and there was a strong possibility that new features would require new options? Further, developers will want to pick and choose what options to configure the class with. Imagine the exponential explosion of new constructors for every new option added to the class. In such a scenario, constructors are practically useless. The builder pattern can solve this problem.

An example of an object that implements the builder pattern is the ASP.NET `Config Settings`. Another is the `ServiceCollection` from Recipe 1.2—the code isn't entirely written in a fluid manner, but it could be because it follows the builder pattern.

The Solution has a `DeploymentService` class, which is what we want to build. Its properties have default values in case a developer doesn't configure a given value. In general terms, the class that the builder creates will also have other methods and members for its intended purpose.

The `DeploymentBuilder` class implements the builder pattern. Notice that all of the methods, except for `Build`, return the same instance (`this`) of the same type, `Deploy mentBuilder`. They also use the parameter to configure the `DeploymentService` field that was instantiated with the `DeploymentBuilder` instance. The `Build` method returns the `DeploymentService` instance.

How the configuration and instantiation occur are implementation details of the `DeploymentBuilder` that you can vary as needed. You can also accept any parameter type you need and perform the configuration. Also, you can collect configuration data and only instantiate the target class when the `Build` method runs. Another advantage is that the order in which parameters are set is irrelevant. You have all the flexibility to design the internals of the builder for what makes sense to you.

Finally, notice how the `Main` method instantiates `DeploymentBuilder`, uses its fluent interface for configuration, and calls `Build` to return the `DeploymentService` instance. This example used every method, but that wasn't required because you have the option to use some, none, or all.

See Also

Recipe 1.2, "Removing Explicit Dependencies"

Recipe 1.9, "Designing a Custom Exception"

CHAPTER 2

Coding Algorithms

We code every day, thinking about the problem we're solving and ensuring that our algorithms work correctly. This is how it should be, and modern tools and software development kits increasingly free our time to do just that. Even so, there are features of C#, .NET, and coding in general that have significant effects on efficiency, performance, and maintainability.

Performance

A few subjects in this chapter discuss application performance, such as the efficient handling of strings, caching data, or delaying the instantiation of a type until you need it. In some simple scenarios, these things might not matter. However, in complex enterprise apps that need the performance and scale, keeping an eye on these techniques can help avoid expensive problems in production.

Maintainability

How you organize code can significantly affect its maintainability. Building on the discussions in Chapter 1, you'll see a new pattern and strategy and understand how they can help simplify an algorithm and make an app more extensible. Another section discusses using recursion for naturally occurring hierarchical data. Collecting these techniques and thinking about the best way to approach an algorithm can make a significant difference in the maintainability and quality of code.

Mindset

A couple of sections of this chapter might be interesting in specific contexts, illustrating different ways to think about solving problems. You might not use regular expressions every day, but they're very useful when you need them. Another section, on converting to/from Unix time, looks into the future of .NET as a cross-platform language, knowing that we need a certain mindset to think about designing algorithms in an environment we might not have ever considered in the past.

2.1 Processing Strings Efficiently

Problem

A profiler indicates a problem in part of your code that builds a large string iteratively and you need to improve performance.

Solution

Here's an `InvoiceItem` class we'll be working with:

```
public class InvoiceItem
{
    public decimal Cost { get; set; }
    public string Description { get; set; }
}
```

This method produces sample data for the demo:

```
static List<InvoiceItem> GetInvoiceItems()
{
    var items = new List<InvoiceItem>();
    var rand = new Random();
    for (int i = 0; i < 100; i++)
        items.Add(
            new InvoiceItem
            {
                Cost = rand.Next(i),
                Description = "Invoice Item #" + (i+1)
            });

    return items;
}
```

There are two methods for working with strings. First, the inefficient method:

```
static string DoStringConcatenation(List<InvoiceItem> lineItems)
{
    string report = "";

    foreach (var item in lineItems)
```

```
        report += $"{item.Cost:C} - {item.Description}\n";

    return report;
}
```

Next is the more efficient method:

```
static string DoStringBuilderConcatenation(List<InvoiceItem> lineItems)
{
    var reportBuilder = new StringBuilder();

    foreach (var item in lineItems)
        reportBuilder.Append($"{item.Cost:C} - {item.Description}\n");

    return reportBuilder.ToString();
}
```

The `Main` method ties all of this together:

```
static void Main(string[] args)
{
    List<InvoiceItem> lineItems = GetInvoiceItems();

    DoStringConcatenation(lineItems);

    DoStringBuilderConcatenation(lineItems);
}
```

Discussion

There are different reasons why we need to gather data into a longer string. Reports, whether text based or formatted via HTML or other markup, require combining text strings. Sometimes we add items to an email or manually build PDF content as an email attachment. Other times we might need to export data in a nonstandard format for legacy systems. Too often, developers use string concatenation when `String Builder` is the superior choice.

String concatenation is intuitive and quick to code, which is why so many people do it. However, concatenating strings can also kill application performance. The problem occurs because each concatenation performs expensive memory allocations. Let's examine both the wrong way to build strings and the right way.

The logic in the `DoStringConcatenation` method extracts `Cost` and `Description` from each `InvoiceItem` and concatenates that to a growing string. Concatenating just a few strings might go unnoticed. However, imagine if this was 25, 50, or 100 lines or more. Using an example similar to this recipe's solution, Recipe 3.10 shows how string concatenation is an exponentially time-intensive operation that destroys application performance.

When concatenating within the same expression, e.g., string1 + string2, the C# compiler can optimize the code. It's the loop with concatenation that causes the huge performance hit.

The DoStringBuilderConcatenation method fixes this problem. It uses the String Builder class, which is in the System.Text namespace. It uses the builder pattern, described in Recipe 1.10, where each AppendText adds the new string to the String Builder instance, reportsBuilder. Before returning, the method calls ToString to convert the StringBuilder contents to a string.

As a rule of thumb, once you've gone past four string concatenations, you'll receive better performance by using StringBuilder.

Fortunately, the .NET ecosystem has many .NET Framework libraries and third-party libraries that help with forming strings of common format. You should use one of these libraries whenever possible because they're often optimized for performance and will save time and make the code easier to read. To give you an idea, Table 2-1 shows a few libraries to consider for common formats.

Table 2-1. Data formats and libraries

Data format	Library
JSON .NET 5	System.Text.Json
JSON ⇐ .NET 4.x	Json.NET
XML	LINQ to XML
CSV	LINQ to CSV
HTML	System.Web.UI.HtmlTextWriter
PDF	Various commercial and open source providers
Excel	Various commercial and open source providers

One more thought: custom search and filtering panels are common for giving users a simple way to query corporate data. Too frequently, developers use string concatenation to build Structured Query Language (SQL) queries. While string concatenation is easier, beyond performance, the problem with that is security. String-concatenated SQL statements open the opportunity for SQL injection attack. In this case, String Builder isn't a solution. Instead, you should use a data library that parameterizes user input to circumvent SQL injection. There's ADO.NET, LINQ providers, and other third-party data libraries that do input value parameterization for you. For dynamic queries, using a data library might be harder, but it is possible. You might want to seriously consider using LINQ, which I discuss in Chapter 4.

See Also

Recipe 1.10, "Constructing Objects with Complex Configuration"

Recipe 3.10, "Measuring Performance"

Chapter 4, "Querying with LINQ"

2.2 Simplifying Instance Cleanup

Problem

Old using statements cause unnecessary nesting and you want to clean up and simplify code.

Solution

This program has using statements for reading and writing to a text file:

```
class Program
{
    const string FileName = "Invoice.txt";

    static void Main(string[] args)
    {
        Console.WriteLine(
            "Invoice App\n" +
            "-----------\n");

        WriteDetails();

        ReadDetails();
    }

    static void WriteDetails()
    {
        using var writer = new StreamWriter(FileName);

        Console.WriteLine("Type details and press [Enter] to end.\n");

        string detail;
        do
        {
            Console.Write("Detail: ");
            detail = Console.ReadLine();
            writer.WriteLine(detail);
        }
```

```
        while (!string.IsNullOrWhiteSpace(detail));
    }

    static void ReadDetails()
    {
        Console.WriteLine("\nInvoice Details:\n");

        using var reader = new StreamReader(FileName);

        string detail;
        do
        {
            detail = reader.ReadLine();
            Console.WriteLine(detail);
        }
        while (!string.IsNullOrWhiteSpace(detail));
    }
}
```

Discussion

Before C# 8, using statement syntax required parentheses for IDisposable object instantiation and an enclosing block. During runtime, when the program reached the closing block, it would call Dispose on the instantiated object. If you needed multiple using statements to operate at the same time, developers would often nest them, resulting in extra space in addition to normal statement nesting. This pattern was enough of an annoyance to some developers that Microsoft added a feature to the language to simplify using statements.

In the solution, you can see a couple of places where the new using statement syntax occurs: instantiating the StreamWriter in WriteDetails and instantiating the Stream Reader in ReadDetails. In both cases, the using statement is on a single line. Gone are the parentheses and curly braces, and each statement terminates with a semicolon.

The scope of the new using statement is its enclosing block, calling the using object's Dispose method when execution reaches the end of the enclosing block. In the solution, the enclosing block is the method, which causes each using object's Dispose method to be called at the end of the method.

What's different about the single-line using statement is that it will work with both IDisposable objects and objects that implement a disposable pattern. In this context, a disposable pattern means that the object doesn't implement IDisposable, yet it has a parameterless Dispose method.

See Also

Recipe 1.1, "Managing Object End-of-Lifetime"

2.3 Keeping Logic Local

Problem

An algorithm has complex logic that is better refactored to another method, but the logic is really only used in one place.

Solution

The program uses the `CustomerType` and `InvoiceItem`:

```
public enum CustomerType
{
    None,
    Bronze,
    Silver,
    Gold
}

public class InvoiceItem
{
    public decimal Cost { get; set; }
    public string Description { get; set; }
}
```

This method generates and returns a demo set of invoices:

```
static List<InvoiceItem> GetInvoiceItems()
{
    var items = new List<InvoiceItem>();
    var rand = new Random();
    for (int i = 0; i < 100; i++)
        items.Add(
            new InvoiceItem
            {
                Cost = rand.Next(i),
                Description = "Invoice Item #" + (i + 1)
            });

    return items;
}
```

Finally, the `Main` method shows how to use a local function:

```
static void Main()
{
    List<InvoiceItem> lineItems = GetInvoiceItems();
```

```csharp
decimal total = 0;

foreach (var item in lineItems)
    total += item.Cost;

total = ApplyDiscount(total, CustomerType.Gold);

Console.WriteLine($"Total Invoice Balance: {total:C}");

decimal ApplyDiscount(decimal total, CustomerType customerType)
{
    switch (customerType)
    {
        case CustomerType.Bronze:
            return total - total * .10m;
        case CustomerType.Silver:
            return total - total * .05m;
        case CustomerType.Gold:
            return total - total * .02m;
        case CustomerType.None:
        default:
            return total;
    }
}
}
}
```

Discussion

Local methods are useful whenever code is only relevant to a single method and you want to isolate that code. Reasons for isolating code are to give meaning to a set of complex logic, reuse logic and simplify calling code (perhaps a loop), or allow an async method to throw an exception before awaiting the enclosing method.

The Main method in the solution has a local method, named ApplyDiscount. This example demonstrates how a local method can simplify code. If you examine the code in ApplyDiscount, it might not be immediately clear what its purpose is. However, by separating that logic into its own method, anyone can read the method name and know what the purpose of the logic is. This is a great way to make code more maintainable, by expressing intent and making that logic local where another developer won't need to hunt for a class method that might move around after future maintenance.

2.4 Operating on Multiple Classes the Same Way

Problem

An application must be extensible, for adding new plug-in capabilities, but you don't want to rewrite existing code for new classes.

Solution

This is a common interface for several classes to implement:

```
public interface IInvoice
{
    bool IsApproved();

    void PopulateLineItems();

    void CalculateBalance();

    void SetDueDate();
}
```

Here are a few classes that implement IInvoice:

```
public class BankInvoice : IInvoice
{
    public void CalculateBalance()
    {
        Console.WriteLine("Calculating balance for BankInvoice.");
    }

    public bool IsApproved()
    {
        Console.WriteLine("Checking approval for BankInvoice.");
        return true;
    }

    public void PopulateLineItems()
    {
        Console.WriteLine("Populating items for BankInvoice.");
    }

    public void SetDueDate()
    {
        Console.WriteLine("Setting due date for BankInvoice.");
    }
}

public class EnterpriseInvoice : IInvoice
{
    public void CalculateBalance()
```

```
    {
        Console.WriteLine("Calculating balance for EnterpriseInvoice.");
    }

    public bool IsApproved()
    {
        Console.WriteLine("Checking approval for EnterpriseInvoice.");
        return true;
    }

    public void PopulateLineItems()
    {
        Console.WriteLine("Populating items for EnterpriseInvoice.");
    }

    public void SetDueDate()
    {
        Console.WriteLine("Setting due date for EnterpriseInvoice.");
    }
}

public class GovernmentInvoice : IInvoice
{
    public void CalculateBalance()
    {
        Console.WriteLine("Calculating balance for GovernmentInvoice.");
    }

    public bool IsApproved()
    {
        Console.WriteLine("Checking approval for GovernmentInvoice.");
        return true;
    }

    public void PopulateLineItems()
    {
        Console.WriteLine("Populating items for GovernmentInvoice.");
    }

    public void SetDueDate()
    {
        Console.WriteLine("Setting due date for GovernmentInvoice.");
    }
}
```

This method populates a collection with objects that implement IInvoice:

```
static IEnumerable<IInvoice> GetInvoices()
{
    return new List<IInvoice>
    {
        new BankInvoice(),
        new EnterpriseInvoice(),
```

```
        new GovernmentInvoice()
    };
}
```

The `Main` method has an algorithm that operates on the `IInvoice` interface:

```csharp
static void Main(string[] args)
{
    IEnumerable<IInvoice> invoices = GetInvoices();

    foreach (var invoice in invoices)
    {
        if (invoice.IsApproved())
        {
            invoice.CalculateBalance();
            invoice.PopulateLineItems();
            invoice.SetDueDate();
        }
    }
}
```

Discussion

As a developer's career progresses, chances are they'll encounter requirements that customers want an application to be "extensible." Although the exact meaning is imprecise to even the most seasoned architects, there's a general understanding that "extensibility" should be a theme in the application's design. We generally move in this direction by identifying areas of the application that can and will change over time. Patterns can help with this, such as the factory classes of Recipe 1.3, factory methods of Recipe 1.4, and builders in Recipe 1.10. In a similar light, the strategy pattern described in this section helps organize code for extensibility.

The strategy pattern is useful when there are multiple object types to work with at the same time and you want them to be interchangeable and write code one time that operates on each object the same way. In object-oriented terms, this is interface polymorphism. The software we use every day are classic examples of where a strategy could work. Office applications have different document types and allow developers to write their own add-ins. Browsers have add-ins that developers can write. The editors and integrated development environments (IDEs) you use every day have plug-in capabilities.

The solution describes an application that operates on different types of invoices in the domains of banking, enterprise, and government. Each of these domains has its own business rules related to legal or other requirements. What makes this extensible is the fact that, in the future, we can add another class to handle invoices in another domain.

The glue to making this work is the IInvoice interface. It contains the required methods (or contract) that each implementing class must define. You can see that the BankInvoice, EnterpriseInvoice, and GovernmentInvoices each implement IInvoice.

GetInvoices simulates the situation where you would write code to populate invoices from a data source. Whenever you need to extend the framework, by adding a new IInvoice derived type, this is the only code that changes. Because all classes are IInvoice, they can all be returned via the same IEnumerable<IInvoice> collection.

Even though the GetInvoices implementation operated on List<IInvoice>, it returned an IEnumerable<IInvoice> from GetInvoices. By returning an interface here, IEnumerable<T>, callers don't make any assumptions about the underlying collection implementation. That way, a future version of GetInvoices could potentially work with another collection type that implemented IEnumerable<T> if that other collection type was better for the new implementation. The benefit is that the code can change without changing the method signature and not break calling code.

Finally, examine the Main method. It iterates on each IInvoice object, calling its methods. Main doesn't care what the specific implementation is, and so its code never needs to change to accommodate instance-specific logic. You don't need if or switch statements for special cases, which blow up into spaghetti code in maintenance. Any future changes will be on how Main works with the IInvoice interface. Any changes to business logic associated with invoices is limited to the invoice types themselves. This is easy to maintain, and it's easy to figure out where logic is and should be. Further, it's also easy to extend by adding a new plug-in class that implements IInvoice.

See Also

Recipe 1.3, "Delegating Object Creation to a Class"

Recipe 1.4, "Delegating Object Creation to a Method"

Recipe 1.10, "Constructing Objects with Complex Configuration"

2.5 Checking for Type Equality

Problem

You need to search for objects in a collection, and default equality won't work.

Solution

The Invoice class implements IEquatable<T>:

```csharp
public class Invoice : IEquatable<Invoice>
{
    public int CustomerID { get; set; }

    public DateTime Created { get; set; }

    public List<string> InvoiceItems { get; set; }

    public decimal Total { get; set; }

    public bool Equals(Invoice other)
    {
        if (ReferenceEquals(other, null))
            return false;

        if (ReferenceEquals(this, other))
            return true;

        if (GetType() != other.GetType())
            return false;

        return
            CustomerID == other.CustomerID &&
            Created.Date == other.Created.Date;
    }

    public override bool Equals(object other)
    {
        return Equals(other as Invoice);
    }

    public override int GetHashCode()
    {
        return (CustomerID + Created.Ticks).GetHashCode();
    }

    public static bool operator ==(Invoice left, Invoice right)
    {
        if (ReferenceEquals(left, null))
            return ReferenceEquals(right, null);

        return left.Equals(right);
    }

    public static bool operator !=(Invoice left, Invoice right)
    {
        return !(left == right);
```

```
        }
    }
```

This code returns a collection of Invoice classes:

```
static List<Invoice> GetAllInvoices()
{
    DateTime date = DateTime.Now;

    return new List<Invoice>
    {
        new Invoice { CustomerID = 1, Created = date },
        new Invoice { CustomerID = 2, Created = date },
        new Invoice { CustomerID = 1, Created = date },
        new Invoice { CustomerID = 3, Created = date }
    };
}
```

Here's how to use the Invoice class:

```
static void Main(string[] args)
{
    List<Invoice> allInvoices = GetAllInvoices();

    Console.WriteLine($"# of All Invoices: {allInvoices.Count}");

    var invoicesToProcess = new List<Invoice>();

    foreach (var invoice in allInvoices)
    {
        if (!invoicesToProcess.Contains(invoice))
            invoicesToProcess.Add(invoice);
    }

    Console.WriteLine($"# of Invoices to Process: {invoicesToProcess.Count}");
}
```

Discussion

The default equality semantics for reference types is reference equality and for value types is value equality. Reference equality means that when comparing objects, these objects are equal when their references refer to the same exact object instance. Value equality occurs when each member of an object is compared before two objects are considered equal. The problem with reference equality is that sometimes you have two instances of the same class, but you really want to compare their corresponding members to see if they are equal. Value equality might also pose a problem because you might only want to check part of the object to see if they're equal.

To solve the problem of inadequate default equality, the solution implements custom equality on Invoice. The Invoice class implements the IEquatable<T> interface, where T is Invoice. Although IEquatable<T> requires an Equals(T other) method, you should also implement `Equals(object other)`, `GetHashCode()`, and the `==` and `!=` operators, resulting in a consistent definition of equality for all scenarios.

There's a lot of science in picking a good hash code, which is out of scope for this book, so the solution implementation is minimal.

 C# 9.0 Records give you `IEquatable<T>` logic by default. However, Records give you value equality, and you would want to implement `IEquatable<T>` yourself if you needed to be more specific. For instance, if your object has free-form text fields that don't contribute to the identity of the object, why waste resources doing the unnecessary field comparisons? Another problem (maybe more rare) could be that some parts of a record might be different for temporal reasons, e.g., temporary timestamps, status, or globally unique identifiers (GUIDs) that will cause the objects to never be equal during processing.

The equality implementation avoids repeating code. The `!=` operator invokes (and negates) the `==` operator. The `==` operator checks references and returns `true` if both references are `null` and `false` if only one reference is `null`. Both the `==` operator and the `Equals(object other)` method call the `Equals(Invoice other)` method.

The current instance is clearly not `null`, so `Equals(Invoice other)` only checks the `other` reference and returns `false` if it's `null`. Then it checks to see if `this` and `other` have reference equality, which would obviously mean they are equal. Then, if the objects aren't the same type, they are not considered equal. Finally, return the results of the values to compare. In this example, the only things that make sense are the `CustomerID` and `Date`.

 One part of the `Equals(Invoice other)` method that you might change is the type check. You could have a different opinion, based on the requirements of your application. e.g., what if you wanted to check equality even if `other` was a derived type? Then change the logic to accept derived types also.

The `Main` method processes invoices, ensuring we don't add duplicate invoices to a list. The loop calls the collection `Contains` method, which checks the object's equality. If there isn't a matching object, `Contains` adds the new `Invoice` instance to the `invoicesToProcess` list. When running the program, there are four invoices that exist in `allInvoices`, but only three are added to `invoicesToProcess` because there's one duplicate (based on `CustomerID` and `Created`) in `allInvoices`.

2.6 Processing Data Hierarchies

Problem

An app needs to work with hierarchical data, and an iterative approach is too complex and unnatural.

Solution

This is the format of data we're starting with:

```
public class BillingCategory
{
    public int ID { get; set; }
    public string Name { get; set; }
    public int? Parent { get; set; }
}
```

This method returns a collection of hierarchically related records:

```
static List<BillingCategory> GetBillingCategories()
{
    return new List<BillingCategory>
    {
        new BillingCategory { ID = 1, Name = "First 1",  Parent = null },
        new BillingCategory { ID = 2, Name = "First 2",  Parent = null },
        new BillingCategory { ID = 4, Name = "Second 1", Parent = 1 },
        new BillingCategory { ID = 3, Name = "First 3",  Parent = null },
        new BillingCategory { ID = 5, Name = "Second 2", Parent = 2 },
        new BillingCategory { ID = 6, Name = "Second 3", Parent = 3 },
        new BillingCategory { ID = 8, Name = "Third 1",  Parent = 5 },
        new BillingCategory { ID = 8, Name = "Third 2",  Parent = 6 },
        new BillingCategory { ID = 7, Name = "Second 4", Parent = 3 },
        new BillingCategory { ID = 9, Name = "Second 5", Parent = 1 },
        new BillingCategory { ID = 8, Name = "Third 3",  Parent = 9 }
    };
}
```

This is a recursive algorithm that transforms the flat data into a hierarchical form:

```
static List<BillingCategory> BuildHierarchy(
    List<BillingCategory> categories, int? catID, int level)
{
    var found = new List<BillingCategory>();

    foreach (var cat in categories)
    {
        if (cat.Parent == catID)
        {
            cat.Name = new string('\t', level) + cat.Name;
            found.Add(cat);
            List<BillingCategory> subCategories =
```

```
                    BuildHierarchy(categories, cat.ID, level + 1);
                found.AddRange(subCategories);
            }
        }

        return found;
    }
```

The `Main` method runs the program and prints out the hierarchical data:

```
static void Main(string[] args)
{
    List<BillingCategory> categories = GetBillingCategories();

    List<BillingCategory> hierarchy =
        BuildHierarchy(categories, catID: null, level: 0);

    PrintHierarchy(hierarchy);
}

static void PrintHierarchy(List<BillingCategory> hierarchy)
{
    foreach (var cat in hierarchy)
        Console.WriteLine(cat.Name);
}
```

Discussion

It's hard to tell how many times you have or will encounter iterative algorithms with complex logic and conditions on how the loop operates. Loops like `for`, `foreach`, and `while` are familiar and often used, even when more elegant solutions are available. I'm not suggesting there's anything wrong with loops, which are integral parts of our language toolset. However, it's useful to expand our minds to other techniques that might lend themselves to more elegant and maintainable code for given situations. Sometimes a declarative approach, like a lambda on a collection's `ForEach` operator, is simple and clear. LINQ is a nice solution for working with object collections in memory, which is the subject of Chapter 4. Another alternative is recursion—the subject of this section.

The main point I'm making here is that we need to write algorithms using the techniques that are most natural for a given situation. A lot of algorithms do use loops naturally, like iterating through a collection. Other tasks beckon for recursion. A class of algorithms that work on hierarchies might be excellent candidates for recursion.

The solution demonstrates one of the areas where recursion simplifies processing and makes the code clear. It processes a list of categories based on billing. Notice that the `BillingCategory` class has both an `ID` and a `Parent`. These manage the hierarchy, where the `Parent` identifies the parent category. Any `BillingCategory` with a `null`

Parent is a top-level category. This is a single table relational database (DB) representation of hierarchical data.

The GetBillingCategories represents how the BillingCategories arrive from a DB. It's a flat structure. Notice how the Parent properties reference their parent BillingCategory IDs. Another important fact about the data is that there isn't a clean ordering between parents and children. In a real application, you'll start off with a given set of categories and add new categories later. Again, maintenance in code and data over time changes how we approach algorithm design, and this would complicate an iterative solution.

The purpose of this solution is to take the flat category representation and transform it into another list that represents the hierarchical relationship between categories. This was a simple solution, but you might imagine an object-based representation where parent categories contained a collection with child categories. The recursive algorithm that does this is the BuildHierarchy method.

The BuildHierarchy method accepts three parameters: categories, catID, and level. The categories parameter is the flat collection from the DB and every recursive call receives a reference to this same collection. A potential optimization might be to remove categories that have already been processed, though the demo avoids anything distracting from presented concepts. The catID parameter is the ID for the current BillingCategory, and the code is searching for all subcategories whose Parent matches catID—as demonstrated by the if statement inside the foreach loop. The level parameter helps manage the visual representation of each category. The first statement inside the if block uses level to determine how many tabs (\t) to prefix to the category name. Every time we make a recursive call to BuildHierarchy, we increment level so that subcategories are indented more than their parents.

The algorithm calls BuildHierarchy with the same categories collection. Also, it uses the ID of the current category, not the catID parameter. This means that it recursively calls BuildHierarchy until it reaches the bottom-most categories. It will know it's at the bottom of the hierarchy because the foreach loop completes with no new categories, because there aren't any subcategories for the current (bottom) category.

After reaching the bottom, BuildHierarchy returns and continues the foreach loop, collecting all of the categories under the catID—that is, their Parent is catID. Then it appends any matching subcategories to the found collection to the calling BuildHierarchy. This continues until the algorithm reaches the top level and all root categories are processed.

The recursive algorithm in this solution is referred to as depth-first search (DFS).

Having arrived at the top level, `BuildHierarchy` returns the entire collection to its original caller, which is `Main`. `Main` originally called `BuildHierarchy` with the entire flat `categories` collection. It set `catID` to `null`, indicating that `BuildHierarchy` should start at the root level. The `level` argument is `0`, indicating that we don't want any tab prefixes on root-level category names. Here's the output:

```
First 1
        Second 1
        Second 5
                Third 3
First 2
        Second 2
                Third 1
First 3
        Second 3
                Third 2
        Second 4
```

Looking back at the `GetBillingCategories` method, you can see how the visual representation matches the data.

2.7 Converting from/to Unix Time

Problem

A service is sending date information in seconds or ticks since the Linux epoch needs to be converted to a C#/.NET `DateTime`.

Solution

Here are some values we'll be using:

```
static readonly DateTime LinuxEpoch =
    new DateTime(1970, 1, 1, 0, 0, 0, 0);
static readonly DateTime WindowsEpoch =
    new DateTime(0001, 1, 1, 0, 0, 0, 0);
static readonly double EpochMillisecondDifference =
    new TimeSpan(
        LinuxEpoch.Ticks - WindowsEpoch.Ticks).TotalMilliseconds;
```

These methods convert from and to Linux epoch timestamps:

```
public static string ToLinuxTimestampFromDateTime(DateTime date)
{
```

```
        double dotnetMilliseconds = TimeSpan.FromTicks(date.Ticks).TotalMilliseconds;

        double linuxMilliseconds = dotnetMilliseconds - EpochMillisecondDifference;

        double timestamp = Math.Round(
            linuxMilliseconds, 0, MidpointRounding.AwayFromZero);

        return timestamp.ToString();
    }

    public static DateTime ToDateTimeFromLinuxTimestamp(string timestamp)
    {
        ulong.TryParse(timestamp, out ulong epochMilliseconds);
        return LinuxEpoch + +TimeSpan.FromMilliseconds(epochMilliseconds);
    }
```

The `Main` method demonstrates how to use those methods:

```
static void Main()
{
    Console.WriteLine(
        $"WindowsEpoch == DateTime.MinValue: " +
        $"{WindowsEpoch == DateTime.MinValue}");

    DateTime testDate = new DateTime(2021, 01, 01);

    Console.WriteLine($"testDate: {testDate}");

    string linuxTimestamp = ToLinuxTimestampFromDateTime(testDate);

    TimeSpan dotnetTimeSpan =
        TimeSpan.FromMilliseconds(long.Parse(linuxTimestamp));
    DateTime problemDate =
        new DateTime(dotnetTimeSpan.Ticks);

    Console.WriteLine(
        $"Accidentally based on .NET Epoch: {problemDate}");

    DateTime goodDate = ToDateTimeFromLinuxTimestamp(linuxTimestamp);

    Console.WriteLine(
        $"Properly based on Linux Epoch: {goodDate}");
}
```

Discussion

Sometimes developers represent date/time data as milliseconds or ticks in a database. Ticks are measured as 100 nanoseconds. Both milliseconds and ticks represent time starting at a predefined epoch, which is some point in time that is the minimum date for a computing platform. For .NET, the epoch is 01/01/0001 00:00:00, corresponding to the `WindowsEpoch` field in the solution. This is the same as `DateTime.MinValue`, but defining it this way makes the example more explicit. For MacOS, the epoch is 1 January 1904, and for Linux, the epoch is 1 January 1970, as shown by the `Linux Epoch` field in the solution.

 There are various opinions on whether representing `DateTime` values as milliseconds or ticks is a proper design. However, I leave that debate to other people and venues. My habit is to use the `DateTime` format of the database I'm using. I also translate the `DateTime` to UTC because many apps need to exist beyond the local time zone and you need consistent translatable representation.

Increasingly, developers are more likely to encounter situations where they need to build cross-platform solutions or integrate with a third-party system with milliseconds or ticks based on a different epoch. For instance, the Twitter API began using milliseconds based on the Linux epoch in their 2020 version 2.0 release. The solution example is inspired by code that works with milliseconds from Twitter API responses. The release of .NET Core gave us cross-platform capabilities for C# developers for console and ASP.NET MVC Core applications. .NET 5 continues the cross-platform story and the roadmap for .NET 6 includes the first rich GUI interface, codenamed Maui. If you've been accustomed to working solely in the Microsoft and .NET platforms, this should indicate that things continue to change along the type of thinking required for future development.

The `ToLinuxTimestampFromDateTime` takes a .NET `DateTime` and converts it to a Linux timestamp. The Linux timestamp is the number of milliseconds from the Linux epoch. Since we're working in milliseconds, the `TimeSpan` converts the `DateTime` ticks to milliseconds. To perform the conversion, we subtract the number of milliseconds between the .NET time and the equivalent Linux time, which we precalculated in `EpochMillisecondDifference` by subtracting the .NET (Windows) epoch from the Linux epoch. After the conversion, we need to round the value to eliminate excess precision. The default to `Math.Round` uses what's called Bankers' Rounding, which is often not what we need, so the overload with `MidpointRounding.AwayFromZero` does the rounding we expect. The solution returns the final value as a string, and you can change that for what makes sense for your implementation.

The `ToDateTimeFromLinuxTimestamp` method is remarkably simpler. After converting to a `ulong`, it creates a new timestamp from the milliseconds and adds that to the LinuxEpoch. Here's the output from the `Main` method:

```
WindowsEpoch == DateTime.MinValue: True
testDate: 1/1/2021 12:00:00 AM
Accidentally based on .NET Epoch: 1/2/0052 12:00:00 AM
Properly based on Linux Epoch: 1/1/2021 12:00:00 AM
```

As you can see, `DateTime.MinValue` is the same as the Windows epoch. Using 1/1/2021 as a good date (at least we hope so), `Main` starts by properly converting that date to a Linux timestamp. Then it shows the wrong way to process that date. Finally, it calls `ToDateTimeFromLinuxTimestamp`, performing the proper translation.

2.8 Caching Frequently Requested Data

Problem

Network latency is causing an app to run slowly because static, frequently used data is being fetched too often.

Solution

Here's the type of data that will be cached:

```
public class InvoiceCategory
{
    public int ID { get; set; }

    public string Name { get; set; }
}
```

This is the interface for the repository that retrieves the data:

```
public interface IInvoiceRepository
{
    List<InvoiceCategory> GetInvoiceCategories();
}
```

This is the repository that retrieves and caches the data:

```
public class InvoiceRepository : IInvoiceRepository
{
    static List<InvoiceCategory> invoiceCategories;

    public List<InvoiceCategory> GetInvoiceCategories()
    {
        if (invoiceCategories == null)
            invoiceCategories = GetInvoiceCategoriesFromDB();

        return invoiceCategories;
    }

    List<InvoiceCategory> GetInvoiceCategoriesFromDB()
    {
        return new List<InvoiceCategory>
        {
            new InvoiceCategory { ID = 1, Name = "Government" },
            new InvoiceCategory { ID = 2, Name = "Financial" },
            new InvoiceCategory { ID = 3, Name = "Enterprise" },
```

```
            };
        }
    }
```

Here's the program that uses that repository:

```
class Program
{
    readonly IInvoiceRepository invoiceRep;

    public Program(IInvoiceRepository invoiceRep)
    {
        this.invoiceRep = invoiceRep;
    }

    void Run()
        List<InvoiceCategory> categories =
            invoiceRep.GetInvoiceCategories();

        foreach (var category in categories)
            Console.WriteLine(
                $"ID: {category.ID}, Name: {category.Name}");
    }

    static void Main()
    {
        new Program(new InvoiceRepository()).Run();
    }
}
```

Discussion

Depending on the technology you're using, there could be plenty of options for caching data through mechanisms like CDN, HTTP, and data source solutions. Each has a place and purpose, and this section doesn't try to cover all of those options. Rather, it just has a quick and simple technique for caching data that could be helpful in many scenarios.

You might have experienced a scenario where there's a set of data used in a lot of different places. The nature of the data is typically lookup lists or business rule data. In the course of everyday work, we build queries that include this data either in direct select queries or in the form of database table joins. We forget about it until someone starts complaining about application performance. Analysis might reveal that there are a lot of queries that request that same data over and over again. If it's practical, you can cache that data in memory to avoid network latency exacerbated by excessive queries to the same set of data.

This isn't a blanket solution because you have to think about whether it's practical in your situation. For example, it's impractical to hold too much data in memory, which will cause other scalability problems. Ideally, it's a finite and relatively small set of data, like invoice categories. That data shouldn't change too often because if you need real-time access to dynamic data, this won't work. If the underlying data source changes, the cache is likely to be holding the old stale data.

The solution shows an `InvoiceCategory` class that we're going to cache. It's for a lookup list, just two values per object, a finite and relatively small set of values, and something that doesn't change much. You can imagine that every query for invoices as well as admin or search screens with lookup lists would require this data. It might speed up invoice queries by removing the extra join and returning less data over the wire where you can join the cached data after the DB query.

The solution has an `InventoryRepository` that implements the `IInvoiceRepository` interface. This wasn't strictly necessary for this example, though it does support demonstrating another example of IoC, as discussed in Recipe 1.2.

The `InvoiceRepository` class has an `invoiceCategories` field for holding a collection of `InvoiceCategory`. The `GetInvoiceCategories` method would normally make a DB query and return the results. However, this example only does the DB query if `invoiceCategories` is null, and caches the result in `invoiceCategories`. This way, subsequent requests get the cached version and don't require a DB query.

 The `invoiceCategories` field is static because you only want a single cache. In stateless web scenarios, as in ASP.NET, the Internet Information Services (IIS) process recycles unpredictably, and developers are advised not to rely on static variables. This situation is different because if the recycle clears out `invoiceCategories`, leaving it null, the next query will repopulate it.

The `Main` method uses IoC to instantiate `InvoiceRepository` and performs a query for the `InvoiceCategory` collection.

See Also

Recipe 1.2, "Removing Explicit Dependencies"

2.9 Delaying Type Instantiation

Problem

A class has heavy instantiation requirements, and you can save on resource usage by delaying the instantiation to only when necessary.

Solution

Here's the data we'll work with:

```csharp
public class InvoiceCategory
{
    public int ID { get; set; }

    public string Name { get; set; }
}
```

This is the repository interface:

```csharp
public interface IInvoiceRepository
{
    void AddInvoiceCategory(string category);
}
```

This is the repository that we delay instantiation of:

```csharp
public class InvoiceRepository : IInvoiceRepository
{
    public InvoiceRepository()
    {
        Console.WriteLine("InvoiceRepository Instantiated.");
    }

    public void AddInvoiceCategory(string category)
    {
        Console.WriteLine($"for category: {category}");
    }
}
```

This program shows a few ways to perform lazy initialization of the repository:

```csharp
class Program
{
    public static ServiceProvider Container;

    readonly Lazy<InvoiceRepository> InvoiceRep =
        new Lazy<InvoiceRepository>();

    readonly Lazy<IInvoiceRepository> InvoiceRepFactory =
        new Lazy<IInvoiceRepository>(CreateInvoiceRepositoryInstance);

    readonly Lazy<IInvoiceRepository> InvoiceRepIoC =
        new Lazy<IInvoiceRepository>(CreateInvoiceRepositoryFromIoC);

    static IInvoiceRepository CreateInvoiceRepositoryInstance()
    {
        return new InvoiceRepository();
    }

    static IInvoiceRepository CreateInvoiceRepositoryFromIoC()
```

```
    {
        return Container.GetRequiredService<IInvoiceRepository>();
    }

    static void Main()
    {
        Container =
            new ServiceCollection()
                .AddTransient<IInvoiceRepository, InvoiceRepository>()
                .BuildServiceProvider();

        new Program().Run();
    }

    void Run()
    {
        IInvoiceRepository viaLazyDefault = InvoiceRep.Value;
        viaLazyDefault.AddInvoiceCategory("Via Lazy Default \n");

        IInvoiceRepository viaLazyFactory = InvoiceRepFactory.Value;
        viaLazyFactory.AddInvoiceCategory("Via Lazy Factory \n");

        IInvoiceRepository viaLazyIoC = InvoiceRepIoC.Value;
        viaLazyIoC.AddInvoiceCategory("Via Lazy IoC \n");
    }
}
```

Discussion

Sometimes you have objects with heavy startup overhead. They might need some initial calculations or have to wait on data that takes a while to get because of network latency or dependencies on poorly performing external systems. This can have serious negative consequences, especially on application startup. Imagine an app that is losing potential customers during trial because it starts too slow, or even enterprise users whose work is impacted by wait times. Although you may or may not be able to fix the root cause of the performance bottleneck, another option might be to delay instantiation of that object until you need it. For example, what if you really don't need that object immediately and can show a start screen right away?

The solution demonstrates how to use Lazy<T> to delay object instantiation. The object in question is the InvoiceRepository, and we're assuming it has a problem in its constructor logic that causes a delay in instantiation.

Program has three fields whose type is Lazy<InvoiceRepository>, showing three different ways to instantiate. The first field, InvoiceRep, instantiates a Lazy<Invoice Repository> with no parameters. It assumes that InvoiceRepository has a default constructor (parameterless) and will be called to create a new instance when the code accesses the Value property.

The `InvoiceRepFactory` field instance references the `CreateInvoiceRepository` `Instance` method. When code accesses this field, it calls the `CreateInvoiceReposi` `toryInstance` to construct the object. Since it's a method, you have a lot of flexibility in building the object.

In addition to the other two options, the `InvoiceRepIoC` field shows how you can use lazy instantiation with IoC. Notice that the `Main` method builds an IoC container, as described in Recipe 1.2. The `CreateInvoiceRepositoryFromIoC` method uses that IoC container to request an instance of `InvoiceRepository`.

Finally, the `Run` method shows how to access the fields through the `Lazy<T>.Value` property.

See Also

Recipe 1.2, "Removing Explicit Dependencies"

2.10 Parsing Data Files

Problem

The application needs to extract data from a custom external format, and string type operations lead to complex and less efficient code.

Solution

Here's the data types we'll be working with:

```
public class InvoiceItem
{
    public decimal Cost { get; set; }
    public string Description { get; set; }
}

public class Invoice
{
    public string Customer { get; set; }
    public DateTime Created { get; set; }
    public List<InvoiceItem> Items { get; set; }
}
```

This method returns the raw string data that we want to extract and convert to invoices:

```
static string GetInvoiceTransferFile()
{
    return
        "Creator 1::8/05/20::Item 1\t35.05\t" +
        "Item 2\t25.18\tItem 3\t13.13::Customer 1::Note 1\n" +
```

```
        "Creator 2::8/10/20::Item 1\t45.05" +
        "::Customer 2::Note 2\n" +
        "Creator 1::8/15/20::Item 1\t55.05\t" +
        "Item 2\t65.18::Customer 3::Note 3\n";
}
```

These are utility methods for building and saving invoices:

```
static Invoice GetInvoice(
    string matchCustomer, ..., string matchItems)
{
    List<InvoiceItem> lineItems = GetLineItems(matchItems);

    DateTime.TryParse(matchCreated, out DateTime created);

    var invoice =
        new Invoice
        {
            Customer = matchCustomer,
            Created = created,
            Items = lineItems
        };
    return invoice;
}

static List<InvoiceItem> GetLineItems(string matchItems)
{
    var lineItems = new List<InvoiceItem>();

    string[] itemStrings = matchItems.Split('\t');

    for (int i = 0; i < itemStrings.Length; i += 2)
    {
        decimal.TryParse(itemStrings[i + 1], out decimal cost);
        lineItems.Add(
            new InvoiceItem
            {
                Description = itemStrings[i],
                Cost = cost
            });
    }

    return lineItems;
}

static void SaveInvoices(List<Invoice> invoices)
{
    Console.WriteLine($"{invoices.Count} invoices saved.");
}
```

This method uses regular expressions to extract values from raw string data:

```
static List<Invoice> ParseInvoices(string invoiceFile)
{
```

```
    var invoices = new List<Invoice>();

    Regex invoiceRegEx = new Regex(
        @"^.+?::(?<created>.+?)::(?<items>.+?)::(?<customer>.+?)::.+");

    foreach (var invoiceString in invoiceFile.Split('\n'))
    {
        Match match = invoiceRegEx.Match(invoiceString);

        if (match.Success)
        {
            string matchCustomer = match.Groups["customer"].Value;
            string matchCreated = match.Groups["created"].Value;
            string matchItems = match.Groups["items"].Value;

            Invoice invoice =
                GetInvoice(matchCustomer, matchCreated, matchItems);
            invoices.Add(invoice);
        }
    }

    return invoices;
}
```

The Main method runs the demo:

```
static void Main(string[] args)
{
    string invoiceFile = GetInvoiceTransferFile();

    List<Invoice> invoices = ParseInvoices(invoiceFile);

    SaveInvoices(invoices);
}
```

Discussion

Sometimes, we'll encounter textual data that doesn't fit standard data formats. It might come from existing document files, log files, or external and legacy systems. Often, we need to ingest that data and process it for storage in a DB. This section explains how to do that with regular expressions.

The solution shows the data format we want to generate is an Invoice with a collection of InvoiceItem. The GetInvoiceTransferFile method shows the format of the data. The demo suggests that the data might come from a legacy system that already produced that format, and it's easier to write C# code to ingest that than to add code in that system for a better-supported format. The specific data we're interested in extracting are the created date, invoice items, and customer name. Notice that newlines (\n) separate records, double colons (::) separate invoice fields, and tabs (\t) separate invoice item fields.

The `GetInvoice` and `GetLineItems` methods construct the objects from extracted data and serve to separate object construction from the regular expression extraction logic.

The `ParseInvoices` method uses regular expressions to extract values from the input string. The `RegEx` constructor parameter contains the regular expression string used to extract values.

While an entire discussion of regular expressions is out of scope, here's what this string does:

- `^` says to start at the beginning of the string.
- `.+?::` matches all characters, up to the next invoice field separator (`::`). That said, it ignores the contents that were matched.
- `(?<created>.+?)::`, `(?<items>.+?)::`, and `(?<customer>.+?)::` are similar to `.+?::` but go a step further by extracting values into groups based on the given name. For example, `(?<created>.+?)::` means that it will extract all matched data and put the data in a group named "created."
- `.+` matches all remaining characters.

The `foreach` loop relies on the `\n` separator in the string to work with each invoice. The `Match` method executes the regular expression match, extracting values. If the match was successful, the code extracts values from groups, calls `GetInvoice`, and adds the new invoice to the `invoices` collection.

You might have noticed that we're using `GetLineItems` to extract data from the `match Items` parameter, from the regular expression `items` field. We could have used a more sophisticated regular expression to take care of that too. However, this was intentional for contrast in demonstrating how regular expression processing is a more elegant solution in this situation.

 As an enhancement, you might log any situations where `match.Suc cess` is `false` if you're concerned about losing data and/or want to know if there's a bug in the regular expression or original data formatting.

Finally, the application returns the new line items to the calling code, `Main`, so it can save them.

CHAPTER 3

Ensuring Quality

All the best practices, fancy algorithms, and patterns in the world mean nothing if the code doesn't work properly. We all want to build the best app possible and minimize bugs. The themes of this chapter revolve around maintainability, error prevention, and writing correct code.

When working on a team, other developers must work with the code you write. They add new features and fix bugs. If you write code that's easy to read, it will be more maintainable—that is, other developers will be able to read and understand it. Even if you're the sole developer, coming back to code you've written in the past can be a new experience. Increased maintainability leads to fewer new bugs being introduced and quicker task turnaround. Fewer bugs mean fewer software life-cycle costs and more time for other value-added features. It is this spirit of maintainability that motivates the content in this chapter.

Similar to maintainability, error prevention is an important quality concept. Users can and will use apps in a way that finds the one bug that we never thought would happen. Recipes 3.1 and 3.4 give essential tools to help. Proper exception handling is an important skill and you'll learn that too.

Another feature of quality is to ensure the code is correct, and unit testing is an essential practice. Although unit testing has been with us for a long time, it isn't a solved problem. A lot of developers still don't write unit tests. However, it's such an important topic that the first section in this chapter shows you how to write a unit test.

3.1 Writing a Unit Test

Problem

Quality-assurance professionals are continually finding problems during integration, testing, and you want to reduce the number of bugs that are checked in.

Solution

Here's the code to test:

```
public enum CustomerType
{
    Bronze,
    Silver,
    Gold
}

public class Order
{
    public decimal CalculateDiscount(
        CustomerType custType, decimal amount)
    {
        decimal discount;

        switch (custType)
        {
            case CustomerType.Silver:
                discount = amount * 1.05m;
                break;
            case CustomerType.Gold:
                discount = amount * 1.10m;
                break;
            case CustomerType.Bronze:
            default:
                discount = amount;
                break;
        }

        return discount;
    }
}
```

A separate test project has unit tests:

```
public class OrderTests
{
    [Fact]
    public void
    CalculateDiscount_WithBronzeCustomer_GivesNoDiscount()
    {
```

```
        const decimal ExpectedDiscount = 5.00m;

        decimal actualDiscount =
            new Order().CalculateDiscount(CustomerType.Bronze, 5.00m);

        Assert.Equal(ExpectedDiscount, actualDiscount);
    }

    [Fact]
    public void
    CalculateDiscount_WithSilverCustomer_GivesFivePercentDiscount()
    {
        const decimal ExpectedDiscount = 5.25m;

        decimal actualDiscount =
            new Order().CalculateDiscount(CustomerType.Silver, 5.00m);

        Assert.Equal(ExpectedDiscount, actualDiscount);
    }

    [Fact]
    public void
    CalculateDiscount_WithGoldCustomer_GivesTenPercentDiscount()
    {
        const decimal ExpectedDiscount = 5.50m;

        decimal actualDiscount =
            new Order().CalculateDiscount(CustomerType.Gold, 5.00m);

        Assert.Equal(ExpectedDiscount, actualDiscount);
    }
}
```

Discussion

The code to test is the system under test (SUT), and the code that tests it is called a *unit test*. Unit tests are typically in a separate project, referencing the SUT, avoiding bloating the deliverable assembly by not shipping test code with production code. The size of the unit to test is often a type like a class, record, or struct. The solution has an Order class (SUT) with a CalculateDiscount method. The unit tests ensure CalculateDiscount operates correctly.

There are several well-known unit test frameworks, and you can try a few and use the one you like best. These examples use XUnit. Most of the unit test frameworks integrate with Visual Studio and other IDEs.

Unit test frameworks help identify unit test code with attributes. Some have an attribute for the test class, but XUnit doesn't. With XUnit, you only need to add a [Fact] attribute to the unit test and it will work with the IDE or other tooling you're using. The XUnit authors wanted to reduce excessive attribute usage and make it easier for F# (and other .NET languages) to use the framework.

 That unit testing frameworks use attributes to identify tests is interesting. They do this using a .NET feature called *reflection*. Recipe 5.1 shows how you can use reflection to work with attributes in your code so you can build your own tools.

The naming convention of the unit tests indicates their purpose, making it easy to read. The `OrderTests` class indicates that its unit tests operate on the `Order` class. Unit test method names have the following pattern:

```
<MethodToTest>_<Condition>_<ExpectedOutcome>
```

The first unit test, `CalculateDiscount_WithBronzeCustomer_GivesNoDiscount`, follows this pattern where:

- `CalculateDiscount` is the method to test.
- `WithBronzeCustomer` specifies what is unique about the input for this particular test.
- `GivesNoDiscount` is the result to verify.

The organization of the unit tests uses a format called Arrange, Act, and Assert (AAA). The following discussion covers each of these parts of the test format.

The arrange section creates all the necessary types for the test to occur. In these unit tests, the arrange creates a `const ExpectedDiscount`. In more complex scenarios, the arrange part will instantiate input parameters that establish the appropriate conditions for the test. In this example, the conditions were so simple that they are written as constant parameters in the act part.

The act part is a method call that takes parameters, if any, that create the conditions to be tested. In these examples, the act part instantiates an `Order` instance and calls `CalculateDiscount` with the appropriate parameter values, assigning the response to `actualDiscount`.

The `Assert` class belongs to the XUnit testing framework. Appropriately named, `Assert` statements are used in the assert part of the test. Notice the naming convention I used for `actualDiscount` and `ExpectedDiscount`. The `Assert` class has several methods, with `Equal` being very popular because it allows you to compare what you expected to what you actually received during the act part.

The benefits you get from unit tests potentially include better code design, verification that the code does what was intended, protection against regressions, deployment validation, and documentation. The key word here is *potential* because different people and/or teams choose the benefit they want from unit tests.

The better code design comes from writing tests before writing the code. You might have heard this technique discussed in agile or behavior-driven development (BDD) environments. In making the developer think about expected behavior ahead of time, a clearer design might evolve. On the other hand, you might want to write unit tests after the code is written. Developers write code and unit tests both ways and opinions differ on what is preferable. Ultimately, having the tests, regardless of how you arrived there, is more likely to improve code quality better than not having tests.

The second point of verifying that the code does what is intended is the biggest benefit. For simple methods that serve more as code documentation, it isn't a big deal. However, for complex algorithms or something critical like ensuring customers receive the right discount, unit tests save the day.

Another important benefit is protecting against regressions. When, not if, the code changes, you or another developer could introduce bugs where the original intent of the code was accidentally changed. By running the unit tests after changing code, you can find and fix bugs at the source and not later by quality-assurance professionals or (even worse) customers.

With modern DevOps, we have the ability to automate builds through continuous deployment. You can add unit test runs to a DevOps pipeline, which catches errors before they're merged with the rest of the code. The more unit tests you have, the more this technique reduces the possibility of any developers breaking the build.

Finally, you have another level of documentation. That's why the naming conventions for unit tests are important. If another developer, unfamiliar with an application, needs to understand the code, the unit tests can explain what the correct behavior of that code should be.

This discussion was to get you started with unit tests, if you aren't already using them. You can learn more by searching for XUnit and other unit testing frameworks to see how they work. If you haven't done so yet, please review Recipe 1.2, which describes techniques that make code more testable.

See Also

Recipe 1.2, "Removing Explicit Dependencies"

Recipe 5.1, "Reading Attributes with Reflection"

3.2 Versioning Interfaces Safely

Problem

You need to update an interface in one of your libraries without breaking deployed code.

Solution

Interface before update:

```
public interface IOrder
{
    string PrintOrder();
}
```

Interface after update:

```
public interface IOrder
{
    string PrintOrder();

    decimal GetRewards() => 0.00m;
}
```

CompanyOrder before update:

```
public class CompanyOrder : IOrder
{
    public string PrintOrder()
    {
        return "Company Order Details";
    }
}
```

CompanyOrder after update:

```
public class CompanyOrder : IOrder
{
    decimal total = 25.00m;

    public string PrintOrder()
    {
        return "Company Order Details";
    }

    public decimal GetRewards()
    {
        return total * 0.01m;
    }
}
```

CustomerOrder before and after update:

```
class CustomerOrder : IOrder
{
    public string PrintOrder()
    {
        return "Customer Order Details";
    }
}
```

Here's how the types are used:

```
class Program
{
    static void Main()
    {
        var orders = new List<IOrder>
        {
            new CustomerOrder(),
            new CompanyOrder()
        };

        foreach (var order in orders)
        {
            Console.WriteLine(order.PrintOrder());
            Console.WriteLine($"Rewards: {order.GetRewards()}");
        }
    }
}
```

Discussion

Prior to C# 8, we couldn't add new members to an existing interface without changing all the types that implement that interface. If those implementing types resided in the same code base, it was a recoverable change. However, for framework libraries where developers relied on an interface to work with that library, this would be a breaking change.

The solution describes how to update interfaces and the effects. The scenario is for a customer that might want to apply some reward points, earned previously, to a current order.

Looking at IOrder, you can see that the after update version adds a GetRewards method. Historically, interfaces were not allowed to have implementations. However, in the new version of IOrder, the GetRewards method has a default implementation that returns $0.00 as the rewards.

The solution also has a before and after version of the CompanyOrder class, where the after version contains an implementation of GetRewards. Now, instead of the default implementation, any code invoking GetRewards through a CompanyOrder instance will execute the CompanyOrder implementation.

In contrast, the solution shows a CustomerOrder class that also implements IOrder. The difference here is that CustomerOrder didn't change. Any code invoking GetRewards through a CompanyOrder instance will execute the default IOrder implementation.

The Program Main method shows how this works. The orders is a list of IOrder, with runtime instances of CustomerOrder and CompanyOrder. The foreach loops through orders, calling IOrder methods. As described earlier, invoking GetRewards for the CompanyOrder instance uses that class's implementation, whereas CustomerOrder uses the default IOrder implementation.

Essentially, the change means that if a developer implements IOrder in their own class, such as CustomerOrder, their code doesn't break when updating the library to the latest version.

3.3 Simplifying Parameter Validation

Problem

You're always looking for ways to simplify code, including parameter validation.

Solution

Verbose parameter validation syntax:

```
static void ProcessOrderOld(string customer, List<string> lineItems)
{
    if (customer == null)
    {
        throw new ArgumentNullException(
            nameof(customer), $"{nameof(customer)} is required.");
    }

    if (lineItems == null)
    {
        throw new ArgumentNullException(
            nameof(lineItems), $"{nameof(lineItems)} is required.");
    }

    Console.WriteLine($"Processed {customer}");
}
```

Brief parameter validation syntax:

```
static void ProcessOrderNew(string customer, List<string> lineItems)
{
```

```
    _ = customer ?? throw new ArgumentNullException(
        nameof(customer), $"{nameof(customer)} is required.");
    _ = lineItems ?? throw new ArgumentNullException(
        nameof(lineItems), $"{nameof(lineItems)} is required.");

    Console.WriteLine($"Processed {customer}");
}
```

Discussion

The first code of a public method is often concerned with parameter validation, which can sometimes be verbose. This section shows how to save a few lines of code so they don't obscure the code pertaining to the original purpose of the method.

The solution has two parameter validation techniques: verbose and brief. The verbose method is typical, where the code ensures that a parameter isn't null and throws otherwise. The parentheses aren't required in this single-line throw statement, but some developers/teams prefer for them to be there anyway if their coding standards require the parentheses because of a style issue or to avoid future maintenance mistakes for statements that should be in the if block.

The brief method is an alternative that can save a few lines of code. It relies on newer features of C#: the variable discard, _; and coalescing operator, ??.

The simplified parameter validation with coalescing operator and discard fits on a single line. However, for formatting in the book, it's necessary to use two lines.

On the line validating customer, the code starts with an assignment to the discard, because we need an expression. The coalescing operator is a guard that detects when the expression is null. When the expression is null, the next statement executes, throwing an exception.

This example was for parameter evaluation. However, there are other scenarios where the code encounters a variable that was set to null and needs to throw for an invalid condition or a situation that never should have occurred. This technique lets you handle that quickly in a single line of code.

See Also

Recipe 3.4, "Protecting Code from NullReferenceException"

3.4 Protecting Code from NullReferenceException

Problem

You're building a reusable library and need to communicate nullable reference semantics.

Solution

This is old-style code that doesn't handle null references:

```
public class OrderLibraryNonNull
{
    // nullable property
    public string DealOfTheDay { get; set; }

    // method with null parameter
    public void AddItem(string item)
    {
        Console.Write(item.ToString());
    }

    // method with null return value
    public List<string> GetItems()
    {
        return null;
    }

    // method with null type parameter
    public void AddItems(List<string> items)
    {
        foreach (var item in items)
            Console.WriteLine(item.ToString());
    }
}
```

The following project file turns on the new nullable reference feature:

```
<Project Sdk="Microsoft.NET.Sdk">
    <PropertyGroup>
        <OutputType>Exe</OutputType>
        <TargetFramework>netcoreapp3.1</TargetFramework>
        <RootNamespace>Section_03_04</RootNamespace>
        <Nullable>enable</Nullable>
    </PropertyGroup>
</Project>
```

Here's the updated library code that communicates nullable references:

```
public class OrderLibraryWithNull
{
    // nullable property
    public string? DealOfTheDay { get; set; }

    // method with null parameter
    public void AddItem(string? item)
    {
        _ = item ?? throw new ArgumentNullException(
            nameof(item), $"{nameof(item)} must not be null");

        Console.Write(item.ToString());
    }

    // method with null return value
    public List<string>? GetItems()
    {
        return null;
    }

    // method with null type parameter
    public void AddItems(List<string?> items)
    {
        foreach (var item in items)
            Console.WriteLine(item?.ToString() ?? "None");
    }
}
```

This is an example of old-style consuming code that ignores nullable references:

```
static void HandleWithNullNoHandling()
{
    var orders = new OrderLibraryWithNull();

    string deal = orders.DealOfTheDay;
    Console.WriteLine(deal.ToUpper());

    orders.AddItem(null);
    orders.AddItems(new List<string> { "one", null });

    foreach (var item in orders.GetItems().ToArray())
        Console.WriteLine(item.Trim());
}
```

Figure 3-1 shows the warning wall the user sees from consuming code that ignores nullable references.

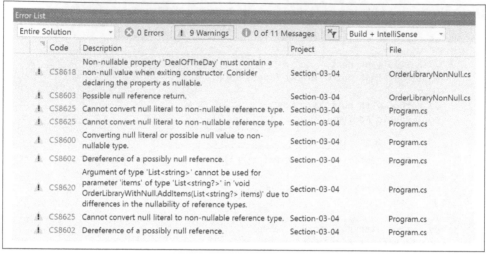

Figure 3-1. Nullable reference warnings in Visual Studio

Finally, here's how the consuming code can properly react to the reusable library with the proper checks and validation for nullable references:

```
static void HandleWithNullAndHandling()
{
    var orders = new OrderLibraryWithNull();

    string? deal = orders.DealOfTheDay;
    Console.WriteLine(deal?.ToUpper() ?? "Deals");

    orders.AddItem(null);
    orders.AddItems(new List<string?> { "one", null });

    List<string>? items = orders.GetItems();

    if (items != null)
        foreach (var item in items.ToArray())
            Console.WriteLine(item.Trim());
}
```

Discussion

If you've been programming C# for any length of time, it's likely that you've encountered NullReferenceExceptions. A NullReferenceException occurs when referencing a member of a variable that is still null, essentially trying to use an object that doesn't yet exist. Nullable references, first introduced in C# 8, help write higher-quality code by reducing the number of NullReferenceException exceptions being thrown. The whole concept revolves around giving the developer compile-time notice of situations where variables are null and could potentially result in a thrown

`NullReferenceException`. This scenario is based on the need to write a reusable library, perhaps a separate class library or NuGet package, for other developers. Your goal is to let them know where a potential null reference occurs in the library so they can write code to protect against a `NullReferenceException`.

To demonstrate, the solution shows library code that doesn't communicate null references. Essentially, this is old-style code, representing what developers would have written before C# 8. You'll also see how to configure a project to support C# 8 nullable references. Then you'll view how to change that library code so it communicates null references to a developer who might consume it. Finally, you'll see two examples of consuming code: one that doesn't handle null references and another that shows how to protect against null references.

In the first solution example, the `OrderLibraryNonNull` class has members with parameters or return types that are reference types, such as `string` and `List<string>`, both of which could potentially be set to null. In both a nullable and non-nullable context, this code won't generate any warnings. Even in a nullable context, the reference types aren't marked as nullable and dangerously communicate to users that they'll never receive a `NullReferenceException`. However, because there could be potential `NullReferenceExceptions`, we don't want to write our code like this anymore.

The XML listing, in the solution, is the project file with a `/Project/PropertyGroup/Nullable` element. Setting this to `true` puts the project in a nullable context. Putting a separate class library into a nullable context might provide warnings for the class library developer, but the consumer of that code won't ever see those warnings.

The next solution code snippet for `OrderLibraryWithNull` fixes this problem. Compare it with `OrderLibraryNonNull` to tell the differences. When evaluating null references, go member by member through a type to think about how parameters and return values affect a consumer of your library in regards to null references. There are a lot of different null scenarios, but this example captures three common ones: property type, method parameter type, and generic parameter type, explained in the following paragraphs.

 There are times when a method genuinely doesn't ever return a null reference. Then it makes sense to not use the nullable operator to communicate to the consumer that they don't need to check for null.

The `DealOfTheDay` shows the property type null reference scenario. Its `getter` property returns a `string`, which could potentially be a `null` value. Fix those with the nullable operator, `?` and return `string?`.

`AddItems` is similar, except it takes a `string` parameter, demonstrating the method parameter scenario. Since `string` could be `null`, changing it to `string?` lets the compiler know too. Notice how I used the simplified parameter checking described in Recipe 3.3.

Sometimes, you'll encounter nullable generic parameter types. The `GetItems` method returns a `List<string>`, and `List<T>` is a reference type. Therefore, changing that to `List<string>?` fixes the problem.

Finally, here's one that's a little tricky. The items parameter in `AddItems` is a `List<string>`. It's easy enough to do a parameter check to test for a `null` parameter, but leaving the nullable operator off is also a good approach to let the user know that they shouldn't pass a `null` value.

That said, what if one of the values in the `List<string>` were `null`? In this case, it's a `List<string>`, but what about scenarios where the users were allowed to pass in a `Dictionary<string, string>`, where the value could be `null`? Then annotate the type parameter, as the example does with `List<string?>`, to say it's OK for a value to be `null`. Since you know that the parameter can be `null`, it's important to check before referencing its members—to avoid a `NullReferenceException`.

Now you have library code that's useful for a consumer. However, it will only be useful if the consumer puts their project into a nullable context too, as shown in the project file.

The `HandleWithNullNoHandling` method shows how a developer might have written code before C# 8. However, once they put the project into a nullable context, they will receive several warnings, as illustrated in the warning wall showing the Visual Studio Error List window. Comparing that with the `HandleWithNullAndHandling` method, the contrast is strong.

The whole process cascades, so start at the top of the method and work your way down:

1. Because the `DealOfTheDay` getter can return `null`, set deal type to `string?`.

2. Since `deal` can be `null`, use the null reference operator and a coalescing operator to ensure `Console.WriteLine` has something sensible to write.

3. The type passed to `AddItems` needs to be `List<string?>` to make the statement that you're aware that an item can be `null`.

4. Instead of inlining `orders.GetItems` in the `foreach` loop, refactor it out into a new variable. This lets you check for `null` to avoid consuming a `null` iterator.

See Also

Recipe 3.3, "Simplifying Parameter Validation"

3.5 Avoiding Magic Strings

Problem

A const string resides in multiple places in the app and you need a way to change it without breaking other code.

Solution

Here's an Order object:

```
public class Order
{
    public string DeliveryInstructions { get; set; }

    public List<string> Items { get; set; }
}
```

Here are some constants:

```
public class Delivery
{
    public const string NextDay = "Next Day";
    public const string Standard = "Standard";
    public const string LowFare = "Low Fare";

    public const int StandardDays = 7;
}
```

This is the program that uses Order and constants to calculate the number of days for delivery:

```
static void Main(string[] args)
{
    var orders = new List<Order>
    {
        new Order { DeliveryInstructions = Delivery.LowFare },
        new Order { DeliveryInstructions = Delivery.NextDay },
        new Order { DeliveryInstructions = Delivery.Standard },
    };

    foreach (var order in orders)
    {
        int days;

        switch (order.DeliveryInstructions)
        {
```

```
            case Delivery.LowFare:
                days = 15;
                break;
            case Delivery.NextDay:
                days = 1;
                break;
            case Delivery.Standard:
            default:
                days = Delivery.StandardDays;
                break;
        }

        Console.WriteLine(order.DeliveryInstructions);
        Console.WriteLine($"Expected Delivery Day(s): {days}");
    }
}
```

Discussion

After developing software for a while, most developers have seen their share of magic values, which are literal values, such as strings and numbers, written directly into an expression. From the perspective of the original developer, they might not be a huge problem. However, from the perspective of a maintenance developer, those literal values don't immediately make sense. It's as if they magically appeared out of nowhere, or it feels like magic that the code even works because the meaning of the literal value isn't obvious.

The goal is to write code that gives a future maintainer a chance to understand. Otherwise, project costs increase because of the time wasted trying to figure out what some seemingly random number is. The solution is often to replace the literal value with a variable whose name expresses the semantics of the value or why it's there. A commonly held belief is that readable code has a more maintainable lifetime than comments.

Going further, a local constant helps a method with readability, but constants are often reusable. The solution example demonstrates how some reusable constants can be placed in their own class for reuse by other parts of the code.

In addition to items, the Order class has a DeliveryInstructions property. Here, we make the assumption that there is a finite set of delivery instructions.

The Delivery class has const string values for NextDay, Standard, and LowFare, characterizing how an order should be delivered. Also, notice that this class has a StandardDays value, set to 7. Which program would you rather read—the one that uses 7 or the one that uses a constant named StandardDays? This makes the code easier to read, as shown in the Program class.

You might first consider that the const string values in the Delivery class might be better candidates for an enum. However, notice that they have spaces. Also, they'll be written with the order. While there are techniques for using enums as string, this was simple.

In some scenarios, you need a specific string value for lookup. It's a matter of opinion and what you think the right tool for the right job is. If you find a scenario where enums are more convenient, then use that route.

The Program class uses Orders and Delivery to calculate the number of days for delivery, based on the order's DeliveryInstructions. There are three orders in a list, each with a different setting for DeliveryInstructions. The foreach loop iterates over those orders with a switch statement that sets the number of delivery days, depending on DeliveryInstructions.

Notice that both order list construction and the switch statement use constants from Delivery. Had that not been done, there would have been strings everywhere. Now, it's easy to code with IntelliSense support, there is no duplication because the string is in one place, and the opportunity for mistyping is minimized. Further, if the strings need to change, that happens in one place. Additionally, you get IDE refactoring support to change the name everywhere that constant appears in the application.

3.6 Customizing Class String Representation

Problem

The class representation in the debugger, string parameters, and log files is illegible and you want to customize its appearance.

Solution

Here's a class with a custom ToString method:

```
public class Order
{
    public int ID { get; set; }

    public string CustomerName { get; set; }

    public DateTime Created { get; set; }

    public decimal Amount { get; set; }
```

```csharp
    public override string ToString()
    {
        var stringBuilder = new StringBuilder();

        stringBuilder.Append(nameof(Order));
        stringBuilder.Append(" {\n");

        if (PrintMembers(stringBuilder))
            stringBuilder.Append(" ");

        stringBuilder.Append("\n}");

        return stringBuilder.ToString();
    }

    protected virtual bool PrintMembers(StringBuilder builder)
    {
        builder.Append("  " + nameof(ID));
        builder.Append(" = ");
        builder.Append(ID);
        builder.Append(", \n");
        builder.Append("  " + nameof(CustomerName));
        builder.Append(" = ");
        builder.Append(CustomerName);
        builder.Append(", \n");
        builder.Append("  " + nameof(Created));
        builder.Append(" = ");
        builder.Append(Created.ToString("d"));
        builder.Append(", \n");
        builder.Append("  " + nameof(Amount));
        builder.Append(" = ");
        builder.Append(Amount);

        return true;
    }
}
```

Here's an example of how that's used:

```csharp
class Program
{
    static void Main(string[] args)
    {
        var order = new Order
        {
            ID = 7,
            CustomerName = "Acme",
            Created = DateTime.Now,
            Amount = 2_718_281.83m
        };

        Console.WriteLine(order);
```

```
      }
   }
```

And here's the output:

```
Order {
   ID = 7,
   CustomerName = Acme,
   Created = 1/23/2021,
   Amount = 2718281.83
}
```

Discussion

Some types are complex, and viewing an instance in the debugger is cumbersome because you need to dig multiple levels to examine values. Modern IDEs make this easier, but sometimes it's nicer to have a more readable representation of the class.

That's where overriding the ToString method comes in. ToString is a method of the Object type, which all types derive from. The default implementation is the fully qualified name of the type, which is Section_03_06.Order for the Order class in the solution. Since it's a virtual method, you can override it.

In fact, the Order class overrides ToString with its own representation. As covered in Recipe 2.1, the implementation uses StringBuilder. The format is using the name of the object with properties inside of curly braces, as shown in the output.

The demo code in Main generates this output via the Console.WriteLine. This works because Console.WriteLine calls an object's ToString method if a parameter isn't already a string.

See Also

Recipe 2.1, "Processing Strings Efficiently"

3.7 Rethrowing Exceptions

Problem

An app is throwing exceptions, yet the messages are missing information, and you need to ensure all relevant data is available during processing.

Solution

This object throws an exception:

```
public class Orders
{
```

```
        public void Process()
        {
            throw new IndexOutOfRangeException(
                "Expected 10 orders, but found only 9.");
        }
    }
```

Here are different ways to handle the exception:

```
    public class OrderOrchestrator
    {
        public static void HandleOrdersWrong()
        {
            try
            {
                new Orders().Process();
            }
            catch (IndexOutOfRangeException ex)
            {
                throw new InvalidOperationException(ex.Message);
            }
        }

        public static void HandleOrdersBetter1()
        {
            try
            {
                new Orders().Process();
            }
            catch (IndexOutOfRangeException ex)
            {
                throw new InvalidOperationException("Error Processing Orders", ex);
            }
        }

        public static void HandleOrdersBetter2()
        {
            try
            {
                new Orders().Process();
            }
            catch (IndexOutOfRangeException)
            {
                throw;
            }
        }

        public static void DontHandleOrders()
        {
            new Orders().Process();
        }
    }
```

This program tests each exception-handling method:

```
class Program
{
    static void Main(string[] args)
    {
        AppDomain.CurrentDomain.UnhandledException +=
            (object sender, UnhandledExceptionEventArgs e) =>
            System.Console.WriteLine("\n\nUnhandled Exception:\n" + e);

        try
        {
            OrderOrchestrator.HandleOrdersWrong();
        }
        catch (InvalidOperationException ex)
        {
            Console.WriteLine("Handle Orders Wrong:\n" + ex);
        }

        try
        {
            OrderOrchestrator.HandleOrdersBetter1();
        }
        catch (InvalidOperationException ex)
        {
            Console.WriteLine("\n\nHandle Orders Better #1:\n" + ex);
        }

        try
        {
            OrderOrchestrator.HandleOrdersBetter2();
        }
        catch (IndexOutOfRangeException ex)
        {
            Console.WriteLine("\n\nHandle Orders Better #2:\n" + ex);
        }

        OrderOrchestrator.DontHandleOrders();
    }
}
```

Here's the output:

```
Handle Orders Wrong:
System.InvalidOperationException: Expected 10 orders, but found only 9.
    at Section_03_07.OrderOrchestrator.HandleOrdersWrong() in
    /CSharp9Cookbook/Chapter03/Section-03-07/OrderOrchestrator.cs:line 15
    at Section_03_07.Program.Main(String[] args) in
    /CSharp9Cookbook/Chapter03/Section-03-07/Program.cs:line 11


Handle Orders Better #1:
System.InvalidOperationException: Error Processing Orders
```

```
---> System.IndexOutOfRangeException: Expected 10 orders, but found only 9.
   at Section_03_07.Orders.Process() in
   /CSharp9Cookbook/Chapter03/Section-03-07/Orders.cs:line 9
   at Section_03_07.OrderOrchestrator.HandleOrdersBetter1() in
   /CSharp9Cookbook/Chapter03/Section-03-07/OrderOrchestrator.cs:line 23
   --- End of inner exception stack trace ---
   at Section_03_07.OrderOrchestrator.HandleOrdersBetter1() in
   /CSharp9Cookbook/Chapter03/Section-03-07/OrderOrchestrator.cs:line 27
   at Section_03_07.Program.Main(String[] args) in
   /CSharp9Cookbook/Chapter03/Section-03-07/Program.cs:line 20


Handle Orders Better #2:
System.IndexOutOfRangeException: Expected 10 orders, but found only 9.
   at Section_03_07.Orders.Process() in
   /CSharp9Cookbook/Chapter03/Section-03-07/Orders.cs:line 9
   at Section_03_07.OrderOrchestrator.HandleOrdersBetter2() in
   /CSharp9Cookbook/Chapter03/Section-03-07/OrderOrchestrator.cs:line 35
   at Section_03_07.Program.Main(String[] args) in
   /CSharp9Cookbook/Chapter03/Section-03-07/Program.cs:line 29

Unhandled Exception:
System.UnhandledExceptionEventArgs
Unhandled exception. System.IndexOutOfRangeException:
   Expected 10 orders, but found only 9.
   at Section_03_07.Orders.Process() in
   /CSharp9Cookbook/Chapter03/Section-03-07/Orders.cs:line 9
   at Section_03_07.OrderOrchestrator.DontHandleOrders() in
   /CSharp9Cookbook/Chapter03/Section-03-07/OrderOrchestrator.cs:line 45
   at Section_03_07.Program.Main(String[] args) in
   /CSharp9Cookbook/Chapter03/Section-03-07/Program.cs:line 40
```

Discussion

There are various ways to handle exceptions, with some being better than others. From a troubleshooting perspective, we generally want a log of exceptions with enough meaningful information to help solve the problem. That is the point of this section in determining what the better solution should be.

The Orders class Process method throws an IndexOutOfRangeException, and the OrderOrchestrator class handles that exception in a few different ways: one which you should avoid and two that are better, depending on what makes sense for your scenario.

The HandleOrdersWrong method takes the Message property of the original exception and throws a new InvalidOperationException with that message as its input. The scenario models a situation where the handling analyzes the situation and tries to throw an exception that makes more sense or provides more information than what the original exception offered. However, this causes another problem where we lose stack trace information that's critical to fixing the problem. This example has a relatively shallow hierarchy, but in practice the exception could have been thrown via multiple levels down and arrived via various paths. You can see this problem in the output where the stack trace shows that the exception originated in the OrderOrchestrator.HandleOrdersWrong method, rather than its true source in Orders.Process.

 Another thing you should never do is rethrow the original exception, like this:

```
try
{
    OrderOrchestrator.HandleOrdersWrong();
}
catch (InvalidOperationException ex)
{
    throw ex;
}
```

The problem with this is that rethrowing the original exception loses the stack trace. Without the original stack trace, developers trying to debug the program won't know where the exception originated. Further, the original exception might have been different from the one you received, potentially containing more detailed information that no one would see.

The HandleOrdersBetter1 method improves on this scenario by adding an additional argument, ex, to the innerException parameter. This provides the best of both worlds because you can now throw an exception with additional data, as well as preserving the entire stack trace. You can see that the path of the exception originated in Orders.Process in the output (delimited by --- End of inner exception stack trace ---).

HandleOrdersBetter2 just throws the original exception. The assumption here is that the logic wasn't able to do something intelligent with the exception or log and rethrow. As shown in the output, the stack trace also originates at Orders.Process.

There are a lot of strategies for handling exceptions and this covers one aspect. In this case, considering the preservation of original stack trace for later debugging, you should rethrow. As always, think about your scenario and what makes sense to you.

Occasionally, you might encounter a situation where code throws an exception and there isn't a handling strategy. The OrderOrchestrator.DontHandleOrders doesn't do any handling, and the Main method doesn't protect with a try/catch. In this case, you can still intercept the exception by adding an event handler to AppDomain.CurrentDomain.UnhandledException, as shown at the end of the Main method. You want to assign the event handler before running any code, otherwise you'll never handle the exception.

See Also

Recipe 1.9, "Designing a Custom Exception"

3.8 Managing Process Status

Problem

The user started a process, but after an exception, the user interface status wasn't updated.

Solution

This method throws an exception:

```
static void ProcessOrders()
{
    throw new ArgumentException();
}
```

This is the code you should not write:

```
static void Main()
{
    Console.WriteLine("Processing Orders Started");

    ProcessOrders();

    Console.WriteLine("Processing Orders Complete");
}
```

Here's the code you should write instead:

```
static void Main()
{
    try
    {
        Console.WriteLine("Processing Orders Started");

        ProcessOrders();
    }
    catch (ArgumentException ae)
    {
        Console.WriteLine('\n' + ae.ToString() + '\n');
    }
    finally
    {
        Console.WriteLine("Processing Orders Complete");
```

```
        }
    }
```

Discussion

The problem statement mentions there was an exception that occurred, which is true. However, from a user perspective, they won't receive a message or status explaining that a problem occurred and their job didn't finish. That's because in the first `Main` method, if an exception throws during `ProcessOrder`, the "Processing Orders Complete" message won't appear to the user.

This is a good use case for a `try/finally` block, which the second `Main` method uses. Put all the code that should run in a `try` block and a final status in the `finally` block. If an exception throws, you can catch it, log, and let the user know that their job was unsuccessful.

Although this was an example in a console application, this is a good technique for UI code too. When starting a process, you might have a wait notification like an hourglass or progress indicator. Turning the notification off is a task that the `finally` block can help with also.

See Also

Recipe 3.9, "Building Resilient Network Connections"

Recipe 3.10, "Measuring Performance"

3.9 Building Resilient Network Connections

Problem

The app communicates with an unreliable backend service and you want to prevent it from failing.

Solution

This method throws an exception:

```
static async Task GetOrdersAsync()
{
    throw await Task.FromResult(
        new HttpRequestException(
            "Timeout", null, HttpStatusCode.RequestTimeout));
}
```

Here's a technique to handle network errors:

```csharp
public static async Task Main()
{
    const int DelayMilliseconds = 500;
    const int RetryCount = 3;

    bool success = false;
    int tryCount = 0;

    try
    {
        do
        {
            try
            {
                Console.WriteLine("Getting Orders");
                await GetOrdersAsync();

                success = true;
            }
            catch (HttpRequestException hre)
                when (hre.StatusCode == HttpStatusCode.RequestTimeout)
            {
                tryCount++;

                int millisecondsToDelay = DelayMilliseconds * tryCount;
                Console.WriteLine(
                    $"Exception during processing-" +
                    $"delaying for {millisecondsToDelay} milliseconds");

                await Task.Delay(millisecondsToDelay);
            }

        } while (tryCount < RetryCount);
    }
    finally
    {
        if (success)
            Console.WriteLine("Operation Succeeded");
        else
            Console.WriteLine("Operation Failed");
    }
}
```

And here's the output:

```
Getting Orders
Exception during processing - delaying for 500 milliseconds
Getting Orders
Exception during processing - delaying for 1000 milliseconds
Getting Orders
```

```
Exception during processing - delaying for 1500 milliseconds
Operation Failed
```

Discussion

Anytime you're doing out-of-process work, there's a possibility of errors or timeouts. Often you don't have control of the application you're interacting with, and it pays to write defensive code. In particular, code that does networking is prone to errors unrelated to the quality of code at either end of the connection due to latency, timeouts, or hardware issues.

This solution simulates a network connection issue through `GetOrdersAsync`. It throws an `HttpRequestException` with a `RequestTimeout` status. This is typical, and the `Main` method shows how to mitigate these types of problems. The goal is to retry the connection a certain number of times with delay between tries.

First, notice that `success` initializes to `false`, and the `finally` of the `try/finally` lets the user know the result of the operation, based on `success`. Following the nesting of `try/do/try`, the last line of the `try` block sets `success` to `true` because all of the logic is complete—if an exception occurred earlier, the program would not have reached that line.

The `do/while` loop iterates `RetryCount` times. We initialize `tryCount` to 0 and increment it in the `catch` block. That's because if there's an error, we know we'll retry, and we want to ensure we don't exceed a specified number of retries. `RetryCount` is a `const`, initialized to 3. You can adjust `RetryCount` to as many times as it makes sense to you. If the operation is time sensitive, you might want to limit retries and send a notification of a critical error. Another scenario might be that you know the other end of the connection will eventually come back online and can set `RetryCount` to a very high number.

Whenever there is an exception, you often don't want to immediately make the request again. One of the reasons the timeout occurred might be that the other endpoint might not scale well, and overloading it with more requests can overwhelm the server. Also, some third-party APIs rate-limit clients, and immediate back-to-back requests eat up the rate-limit count. Some API providers might even block your app for excessive connection requests.

The `DelayMilliseconds` helps your retry policy, initialized to 500 milliseconds. You might adjust this if you find that retries are still too fast. If a single delay time works, then you can use that. However, a lot of situations call for a linear or exponential back-off strategy. You can see that the solution uses a linear back-off, multiplying `DelayMilliseconds` by `tryCount`. Since `tryCount` initializes to 0, we increment it first.

You might want to log retries as warning, rather than error. Administrators, QA, or anyone looking at the logs (or reports) might be unnecessarily alarmed. They see what looks like errors, whereas your application is reacting and repairing appropriately to typical network behavior.

Alternatively, you might need to use an exponential back-off strategy, such as taking DelayMilliseconds to the tryCount power—Math.Pow(DelayMilliseconds, try Count). You might experiment, e.g., log errors and review periodically, to see what works best for your situation.

3.10 Measuring Performance

Problem

You know of a few ways to write an algorithm and need to test which algorithm performs the best.

Solution

Here's the object type we'll operate on:

```
public class OrderItem
{
    public decimal Cost { get; set; }
    public string Description { get; set; }
}
```

This is the code that creates a list of OrderItem:

```
static List<OrderItem> GetOrderItems()
{
    const int ItemCount = 10000;

    var items = new List<OrderItem>();
    var rand = new Random();

    for (int i = 0; i < ItemCount; i++)
        items.Add(
            new OrderItem
            {
                Cost = rand.Next(i),
                Description = "Order Item #" + (i + 1)
            });

    return items;
}
```

Here's an inefficient string concatenation method:

```
static string DoStringConcatenation(List<OrderItem> lineItems)
{
    var stopwatch = new Stopwatch();

    try
    {
        stopwatch.Start();

        string report = "";

        foreach (var item in lineItems)
            report += $"{item.Cost:C} - {item.Description}\n";

        Console.WriteLine(
            $"Time for String Concatenation: " +
            $"{stopwatch.ElapsedMilliseconds}");

        return report;
    }
    finally
    {
        stopwatch.Stop();
    }
}
```

Here's the faster `StringBuilder` method:

```
static string DoStringBuilderConcatenation(List<OrderItem> lineItems)
{
    var stopwatch = new Stopwatch();
    try
    {
        stopwatch.Start();

        var reportBuilder = new StringBuilder();

        foreach (var item in lineItems)
            reportBuilder.Append($"{item.Cost:C} - {item.Description}\n");

        Console.WriteLine(
            $"Time for String Builder Concatenation: " +
            $"{stopwatch.ElapsedMilliseconds}");

        return reportBuilder.ToString();
    }
    finally
    {
        stopwatch.Stop();
    }
}
```

This code drives the demo:

```
static void Main()
{
    List<OrderItem> lineItems = GetOrderItems();

    DoStringConcatenation(lineItems);

    DoStringBuilderConcatenation(lineItems);
}
```

And here's the output:

```
Time for String Concatenation: 1137
Time for String Builder Concatenation: 2
```

Discussion

Recipe 2.1 discussed the benefits of `StringBuilder` over string concatenation, which stressed performance as the primary driver. However, it didn't explain how to measure the performance of the code. This section builds on that and shows how to measure algorithmic performance through code.

 As our computers become increasingly faster by the year (or less), the results of the `StringBuilder` method will move closer to 0. To experience the real magnitude of time difference between the two methods, add another 0 to `ItemCount` in `GetOrderItems`.

In both the `StringConcatenation` and `StringBuilderConcatenation` methods, you will find an instance of `StopWatch`, which is in the `System.Diagnostics` namespace.

Calling `Start` starts the timer and `Stop` stops the timer. Notice that the algorithms use `try/finally` as described in Recipe 3.8 to ensure the timer stops.

`Console.WriteLine` uses `stopwatch.ElapsedMilliseconds` at the end of each algorithm to show how much time the algorithm used.

As shown in the output, the running time difference between `StringBuilder` and string concatenation is dramatic.

See Also

Recipe 2.1, "Processing Strings Efficiently"

Recipe 3.8, "Managing Process Status"

CHAPTER 4

Querying with LINQ

LINQ has been around since C# 3. It gives developers a means to query data sources, using syntax with accents of SQL. Because LINQ is part of the language, you experience features like syntax highlighting and IntelliSense in IDEs.

LINQ is popularly known as a tool for querying databases, with the goal of reducing what is called *impedance mismatch*, which is the difference between database representation of data and C# objects. Really, we can build LINQ providers for any data technology. In fact, the author wrote an open source provider for the Twitter API named LINQ to Twitter (*https://oreil.ly/1YEZ8*).

The examples in this chapter take a different approach. Instead of an external data source, they use a provider that specifically focuses on in-memory data sources referred to as LINQ to Objects. While any in-memory data manipulation can be performed with C# loops and imperative logic, using LINQ instead can often simplify the code because of its declarative nature—specifying what to do rather than how to do it. Each section has a unique representation of one or more entities (objects to be queried) and an InMemoryContext that sets up the in-memory data to be queried.

A couple of recipes in this chapter are simple, such as transforming object shape and simplifying queries. However, there are important points to be made that also clarify and simplify your code.

Pulling together code from different data sources can result in confusing code. The sections on joins, left joins, and grouping describe how you can simplify these scenarios. There's also a related section for operating on sets.

A huge security problem with search forms and queries appears when developers build their queries with concatenated strings. While that might sound like a quick and easy solution, the cost is often too high. This chapter has a couple of sections that show how LINQ deferred execution lets you build queries dynamically. Another section explains an important technique for search queries and how they give you the ability to use expression trees for dynamic clause generation.

4.1 Transforming Object Shape

Problem

You want data in a custom shape that differs from the original data source.

Solution

Here's the entity to reshape:

```
public class SalesPerson
{
    public int ID { get; set; }

    public string Name { get; set; }

    public string Address { get; set; }

    public string City { get; set; }

    public string PostalCode { get; set; }

    public string Region { get; set; }

    public string ProductType { get; set; }
}
```

This is the data source:

```
public class InMemoryContext
{
    List<SalesPerson> salesPeople =
        new List<SalesPerson>
        {
            new SalesPerson
            {
                ID = 1,
                Address = "123 1st Street",
                City = "First City",
                Name = "First Person",
                PostalCode = "45678",
                Region = "Region #1"
            },
            new SalesPerson
            {
                ID = 2,
                Address = "234 2nd Street",
                City = "Second City",
```

```
                Name = "Second Person",
                PostalCode = "56789",
                Region = "Region #2"
            },
            new SalesPerson
            {
                ID = 3,
                Address = "345 3rd Street",
                City = "Third City",
                Name = "Third Person",
                PostalCode = "67890",
                Region = "Region #3"
            },
        };

    public List<SalesPerson> SalesPeople => salesPeople;
}
```

This code performs the projection that reshapes the data:

```
class Program
{
    static void Main()
    {
        var context = new InMemoryContext();

        var salesPersonLookup =
            (from person in context.SalesPeople
             select (person.ID, person.Name))
            .ToList();

        Console.WriteLine("Sales People\n");

        salesPersonLookup.ForEach(person =>
            Console.WriteLine($"{person.ID}. {person.Name}"));
    }
}
```

Discussion

Transforming object shape is referred to as a *projection* in LINQ. A few common reasons you might want to do this is to create lookup lists, create a view or view model object, or translate data transfer objects (DTOs) to something your app works with better.

When doing database queries using LINQ to Entities (a different provider for databases), or consuming DTOs, data often arrives in a format representing the original data source. However, if you want to work with domain data or bind to UIs, the pure data representation doesn't have the right shape. Moreover, data representation often has attributes and semantics of the object-relational model (ORM) or data access library. Some developers try to bind these data objects to their UI because they don't want to create a new object type. While that's understandable, because no one wants to do more work than is necessary, problems occur because UI code often requires a different shape of the data and requires its own validation and attributes. So, the problem here is that you're using one object for two different purposes. Ideally, an object should have a single responsibility, and mixing it up like this often results in confusing code that's not as easy to maintain.

Another scenario that the solution demonstrates is the case where you only want a lookup list, with an ID and displayable value. This is useful when populating UI elements such as checkbox lists, radio button groups, combo boxes, or dropdowns. Querying entire entities is wasteful and slow (in the case of an out-of-process or cross-network database connection) when you only need the ID and something to display to the user.

The Main method of the solution demonstrates this. It queries the SalesPeople property of InMemoryContext, which is a list of SalesPerson, and the select clause re-shapes the result into a tuple of ID and Name.

 The select clause in the solution uses a tuple. However, you could project (only the requested fields) into an anonymous type, a Sales Person type, or a new custom type.

Although this was an in-memory operation, the benefit of this technique comes when querying a database with a library like LINQ to Entities. In that case, LINQ to Entities translates the LINQ query into a database query that only requests the fields specified in the select clause.

4.2 Joining Data

Problem

You need to pull data from different sources into one record.

Solution

Here are the entities to join:

```
public class Product
{
    public int ID { get; set; }

    public string Name { get; set; }

    public string Type { get; set; }
```

```csharp
        public decimal Price { get; set; }

        public string Region { get; set; }
    }

    public class SalesPerson
    {
        public int ID { get; set; }

        public string Name { get; set; }

        public string Address { get; set; }

        public string City { get; set; }

        public string PostalCode { get; set; }

        public string Region { get; set; }

        public string ProductType { get; set; }
    }
```

This is the data source:

```csharp
    public class InMemoryContext
    {
        List<SalesPerson> salesPeople =
            new List<SalesPerson>
            {
                new SalesPerson
                {
                    ID = 1,
                    Address = "123 1st Street",
                    City = "First City",
                    Name = "First Person",
                    PostalCode = "45678",
                    Region = "Region #1",
                    ProductType = "Type 2"
                },
                new SalesPerson
                {
                    ID = 2,
                    Address = "234 2nd Street",
                    City = "Second City",
                    Name = "Second Person",
                    PostalCode = "56789",
                    Region = "Region #2",
                    ProductType = "Type 3"
                },
                new SalesPerson
                {
                    ID = 3,
```

```csharp
                    Address = "345 3rd Street",
                    City = "Third City",
                    Name = "Third Person",
                    PostalCode = "67890",
                    Region = "Region #3",
                    ProductType = "Type 1"
                },
                new SalesPerson
                {
                    ID = 4,
                    Address = "678 9th Street",
                    City = "Fourth City",
                    Name = "Fourth Person",
                    PostalCode = "90123",
                    Region = "Region #1",
                    ProductType = "Type 2"
                },
            };

    List<Product> products =
        new List<Product>
        {
            new Product
            {
                ID = 1,
                Name = "Product 1",
                Price = 123.45m,
                Type = "Type 2",
                Region = "Region #1",
            },
            new Product
            {
                ID = 2,
                Name = "Product 2",
                Price = 456.78m,
                Type = "Type 2",
                Region = "Region #2",
            },
            new Product
            {
                ID = 3,
                Name = "Product 3",
                Price = 789.10m,
                Type = "Type 3",
                Region = "Region #1",
            },
            new Product
            {
                ID = 4,
                Name = "Product 4",
                Price = 234.56m,
                Type = "Type 2",
```

```
                Region = "Region #1",
            },
        };

    public List<SalesPerson> SalesPeople => salesPeople;

    public List<Product> Products => products;
}
```

This is the code that joins the entities:

```
class Program
{
    static void Main()
    {
        var context = new InMemoryContext();

        var salesProducts =
            (from person in context.SalesPeople
            join product in context.Products on
            (person.Region, person.ProductType)
            equals
            (product.Region, product.Type)
            select new
            {
                Person = person.Name,
                Product = product.Name,
                product.Region,
                product.Type
            })
            .ToList();

        Console.WriteLine("Sales People\n");

        salesProducts.ForEach(salesProd =>
            Console.WriteLine(
                $"Person: {salesProd.Person}\n" +
                $"Product: {salesProd.Product}\n" +
                $"Region: {salesProd.Region}\n" +
                $"Type: {salesProd.Type}\n"));
    }
}
```

Discussion

LINQ joins are useful when data comes from more than one source. A company
might have merged and you need to pull in data from each of their databases, you
might be using a microservice architecture where the data comes from different services, or some of the data was created in-memory and you need to correlate it with
database records.

Often, you can't use an ID because if the data comes from different sources, they'll never match anyway. The best you can hope for is that some of the fields line up. That said, if you have a single field that matches, that's great. The `Main` method of the solution uses a composite key of `Region` and `ProductType`, relying on the value equality inherent in tuples.

> The `select` clause uses an anonymous type for a custom projection. Another example of shaping object data is discussed in Recipe 4.1.

Even though this example uses a tuple for the composite key, you could use an anonymous type for the same results. The tuple uses slightly less syntax.

See Also

Recipe 4.1, "Transforming Object Shape"

4.3 Performing Left Joins

Problem

You need a join on two data sources, but one of those data sources doesn't have a matching record.

Solution

Here are the entities to perform a left join with:

```
public class Product
{
    public int ID { get; set; }

    public string Name { get; set; }

    public string Type { get; set; }

    public decimal Price { get; set; }

    public string Region { get; set; }
}

public class SalesPerson
{
    public int ID { get; set; }
```

```
        public string Name { get; set; }

        public string Address { get; set; }

        public string City { get; set; }

        public string PostalCode { get; set; }

        public string Region { get; set; }

        public string ProductType { get; set; }
    }
```

This is the data source:

```
public class InMemoryContext
{
    List<SalesPerson> salesPeople =
        new List<SalesPerson>
        {
            new SalesPerson
            {
                ID = 1,
                Address = "123 1st Street",
                City = "First City",
                Name = "First Person",
                PostalCode = "45678",
                Region = "Region #1",
                ProductType = "Type 2"
            },
            new SalesPerson
            {
                ID = 2,
                Address = "234 2nd Street",
                City = "Second City",
                Name = "Second Person",
                PostalCode = "56789",
                Region = "Region #2",
                ProductType = "Type 3"
            },
            new SalesPerson
            {
                ID = 3,
                Address = "345 3rd Street",
                City = "Third City",
                Name = "Third Person",
                PostalCode = "67890",
                Region = "Region #3",
                ProductType = "Type 1"
            },
            new SalesPerson
            {
                ID = 3,
```

```
                Address = "678 9th Street",
                City = "Fourth City",
                Name = "Fourth Person",
                PostalCode = "90123",
                Region = "Region #1",
                ProductType = "Type 2"
            },
        };

    List<Product> products =
        new List<Product>
        {
            new Product
            {
                ID = 1,
                Name = "Product 1",
                Price = 123.45m,
                Type = "Type 2",
                Region = "Region #1",
            },
            new Product
            {
                ID = 2,
                Name = "Product 2",
                Price = 456.78m,
                Type = "Type 2",
                Region = "Region #2",
            },
            new Product
            {
                ID = 3,
                Name = "Product 3",
                Price = 789.10m,
                Type = "Type 3",
                Region = "Region #1",
            },
            new Product
            {
                ID = 4,
                Name = "Product 4",
                Price = 234.56m,
                Type = "Type 2",
                Region = "Region #1",
            },
        };

    public List<SalesPerson> SalesPeople => salesPeople;

    public List<Product> Products => products;
}
```

The following code performs the left join operation:

```
class Program
{
    static void Main()
    {
        var context = new InMemoryContext();

        var salesProducts =
            (from product in context.Products
             join person in context.SalesPeople on
             (product.Region, product.Type)
             equals
             (person.Region, person.ProductType)
             into prodPersonTemp
             from prodPerson in prodPersonTemp.DefaultIfEmpty()
             select new
             {
                 Person = prodPerson?.Name ?? "(none)",
                 Product = product.Name,
                 product.Region,
                 product.Type
             })
            .ToList();

        Console.WriteLine("Sales People\n");

        salesProducts.ForEach(salesProd =>
            Console.WriteLine(
                $"Person: {salesProd.Person}\n" +
                $"Product: {salesProd.Product}\n" +
                $"Region: {salesProd.Region}\n" +
                $"Type: {salesProd.Type}\n"));
    }
}
```

And here's the output:

```
Sales People

Person: First Person
Product: Product 1
Region: Region #1
Type: Type 2

Person: Fourth Person
Product: Product 1
Region: Region #1
Type: Type 2

Person: (none)
Product: Product 2
Region: Region #2
```

```
Type: Type 2

Person: (none)
Product: Product 3
Region: Region #1
Type: Type 3

Person: First Person
Product: Product 4
Region: Region #1
Type: Type 2

Person: Fourth Person
Product: Product 4
Region: Region #1
Type: Type 2
```

Discussion

This solution is similar to the `join`, discussed in Recipe 4.3. The difference is in the LINQ query in the `Main` method. Notice the `into prodPersonTemp` clause. This is a temporary holder for the joined data. The second `from` clause (below `into`) queries `prodPersonTemp.DefaultIfEmpty()`.

The `DefaultIfEmpty()` causes the left join, where the `prodPerson` range variable receives all of the product objects and only the matching person objects.

The first `from` clause specifies the left side of the query, `Products`. The `join` clause specifies the right side of the query, `SalesPeople`, which might not have matching values.

Notice how the `select` clause checks `prodPerson?.Name` for `null` and replaces it with `(none)`. This ensures the output indicates that there wasn't a match, rather than relying on later code to check for null.

Demonstrating left join results in the solution output. Notice that output for Product 1 and Product 4 have a Person entry. However, there wasn't a matching Person, showing as `(none)`, for Products 2 and 3.

4.4 Grouping Data

Problem

You need to aggregate data into custom groups.

Solution

Here's the entity to group:

```csharp
public class SalesPerson
{
    public int ID { get; set; }

    public string Name { get; set; }

    public string Address { get; set; }

    public string City { get; set; }

    public string PostalCode { get; set; }

    public string Region { get; set; }

    public string ProductType { get; set; }
}
```

This is the data source:

```csharp
public class InMemoryContext
{
    List<SalesPerson> salesPeople =
        new List<SalesPerson>
        {
            new SalesPerson
            {
                ID = 1,
                Address = "123 1st Street",
                City = "First City",
                Name = "First Person",
                PostalCode = "45678",
                Region = "Region #1"
            },
            new SalesPerson
            {
                ID = 2,
                Address = "234 2nd Street",
                City = "Second City",
                Name = "Second Person",
                PostalCode = "56789",
                Region = "Region #2"
            },
            new SalesPerson
            {
                ID = 3,
                Address = "345 3rd Street",
                City = "Third City",
                Name = "Third Person",
                PostalCode = "67890",
                Region = "Region #3"
            },
            new SalesPerson
            {
```

```
                ID = 4,
                Address = "678 9th Street",
                City = "Second City",
                Name = "Fourth Person",
                PostalCode = "56788",
                Region = "Region #2"
            },
        };

    public List<SalesPerson> SalesPeople => salesPeople;
}
```

The following code groups the data:

```
class Program
{
    static void Main()
    {
        var context = new InMemoryContext();

        var salesPeopleByRegion =
            (from person in context.SalesPeople
             group person by person.Region
             into personGroup
             select personGroup)
            .ToList();

        Console.WriteLine("Sales People by Region");

        foreach (var region in salesPeopleByRegion)
        {
            Console.WriteLine($"\nRegion: {region.Key}");

            foreach (var person in region)
                Console.WriteLine($"  {person.Name}");
        }
    }
}
```

Discussion

Grouping is useful when you need a hierarchy of data. It creates a parent/children relationship between data where the parent is the main category and the children are objects (representing data records) in that category.

In the solution, each SalesPerson has a Region property, whose values are repeated in the InMemoryContext data source. This helps show how multiple SalesPerson entities can be grouped into a single region.

In the Main method query, there's a group by clause, specifying the range variable, person, to group and the key, Region, to group by. The personGroup holds the result.

In this example, the select clause uses the entire personGroup, rather than doing a custom projection.

Inside of salesPeopleByRegion is a set of top-level objects, representing each group. Each of those groups has a collection of objects belonging to that group, like this:

```
Key (Region):
    Items (IEnumerable<SalesPerson>)
```

 LINQ providers targeting databases, such as LINQ to Entities for SQL Server, return IQueryable<T>, for nonmaterialized queries. Materialization occurs when you use an operator, such as Count() or ToList(), that actually executes the query and returns an int or List<T>, respectively. In contrast, the nonmaterialized type returned by LINQ to Objects is IEnumerable<T>.

The foreach loop demonstrates this group structure and how it could be used. At the top level, each object has a Key property. Because the original query was by Region, that key will have the name of the Region.

The nested foreach loop iterates on the group, reading each SalesPerson instance in that group. You can see where it prints out the Name of each SalesPerson instance in that group.

4.5 Building Incremental Queries

Problem

You need to customize a query based on a user's search criteria but don't want to concatenate strings.

Solution

This is the type to query:

```
public class SalesPerson
{
    public int ID { get; set; }

    public string Name { get; set; }

    public string Address { get; set; }

    public string City { get; set; }

    public string PostalCode { get; set; }
```

```
        public string Region { get; set; }

        public string ProductType { get; set; }
    }
```

Here's the data source:

```
public class InMemoryContext
{
    List<SalesPerson> salesPeople =
        new List<SalesPerson>
        {
            new SalesPerson
            {
                ID = 1,
                Address = "123 1st Street",
                City = "First City",
                Name = "First Person",
                PostalCode = "45678",
                Region = "Region #1",
                ProductType = "Type 2"
            },
            new SalesPerson
            {
                ID = 2,
                Address = "234 2nd Street",
                City = "Second City",
                Name = "Second Person",
                PostalCode = "56789",
                Region = "Region #2",
                ProductType = "Type 3"
            },
            new SalesPerson
            {
                ID = 3,
                Address = "345 3rd Street",
                City = "Third City",
                Name = "Third Person",
                PostalCode = "67890",
                Region = "Region #3",
                ProductType = "Type 1"
            },
            new SalesPerson
            {
                ID = 4,
                Address = "678 9th Street",
                City = "Fourth City",
                Name = "Fourth Person",
                PostalCode = "90123",
                Region = "Region #1",
                ProductType = "Type 2"
            },
        };
```

```
        public List<SalesPerson> SalesPeople => salesPeople;
    }
```

This code builds a dynamic query:

```
class Program
{
    static void Main()
    {
        SalesPerson searchCriteria = GetCriteriaFromUser();

        List<SalesPerson> salesPeople = QuerySalesPeople(searchCriteria);

        PrintResults(salesPeople);
    }

    static SalesPerson GetCriteriaFromUser()
    {
        var person = new SalesPerson();

        Console.WriteLine("Sales Person Search");
        Console.WriteLine("(press Enter to skip an entry)\n");

        Console.Write($"{nameof(SalesPerson.Address)}: ");
        person.Address = Console.ReadLine();

        Console.Write($"{nameof(SalesPerson.City)}: ");
        person.City = Console.ReadLine();

        Console.Write($"{nameof(SalesPerson.Name)}: ");
        person.Name = Console.ReadLine();

        Console.Write($"{nameof(SalesPerson.PostalCode)}: ");
        person.PostalCode = Console.ReadLine();

        Console.Write($"{nameof(SalesPerson.ProductType)}: ");
        person.ProductType = Console.ReadLine();

        Console.Write($"{nameof(SalesPerson.Region)}: ");
        person.Region = Console.ReadLine();

        return person;
    }

    static List<SalesPerson> QuerySalesPeople(SalesPerson criteria)
    {
        var ctx = new InMemoryContext();

        IEnumerable<SalesPerson> salesPeopleQuery =
            from people in ctx.SalesPeople
            select people;
```

```
        if (!string.IsNullOrWhiteSpace(criteria.Address))
            salesPeopleQuery = salesPeopleQuery.Where(
                person => person.Address == criteria.Address);

        if (!string.IsNullOrWhiteSpace(criteria.City))
            salesPeopleQuery = salesPeopleQuery.Where(
                person => person.City == criteria.City);

        if (!string.IsNullOrWhiteSpace(criteria.Name))
            salesPeopleQuery = salesPeopleQuery.Where(
                person => person.Name == criteria.Name);

        if (!string.IsNullOrWhiteSpace(criteria.PostalCode))
            salesPeopleQuery = salesPeopleQuery.Where(
                person => person.PostalCode == criteria.PostalCode);

        if (!string.IsNullOrWhiteSpace(criteria.ProductType))
            salesPeopleQuery = salesPeopleQuery.Where(
                person => person.ProductType == criteria.ProductType);

        if (!string.IsNullOrWhiteSpace(criteria.Region))
            salesPeopleQuery = salesPeopleQuery.Where(
                person => person.Region == criteria.Region);

        List<SalesPerson> salesPeople = salesPeopleQuery.ToList();

        return salesPeople;
    }

    static void PrintResults(List<SalesPerson> salesPeople)
    {
        Console.WriteLine("\nSales People\n");

        salesPeople.ForEach(person =>
            Console.WriteLine($"{person.ID}. {person.Name}"));
    }
}
```

Discussion

One of the worst things a developer can do from a security perspective is to build a concatenated string from user input to send as a SQL statement to a database. The problem is that string concatenation allows the user's input to be interpreted as part of the query. In most cases, people just want to perform a search. However, there are malicious users who intentionally probe systems for this type of vulnerability. They don't have to be professional hackers as there are plenty of novices (often referred to as *script kiddies*) who want to practice and have fun. In the worst case, hackers can access private or proprietary information or even take over a machine. Once into one machine on a network, the hacker is on the inside and can monkey bar into other computers and take over your network. This particular problem is called a *SQL injection attack* and this section explains how to avoid it.

 From a security point of view, no computer is theoretically 100% secure because there's always a level of effort, either physical or virtual, where a computer can be broken into. In practice, security efforts can grow to a point that they become prohibitively expensive to build, purchase, and maintain. Your goal is to perform a threat assessment of a system (outside the scope of this book) that's strong enough to deter potential hackers. In most cases, having not been able to perform the typical attacks, like SQL injection, a hacker will assess their own costs of attacking your system and move on to a different system that is less time consuming or expensive. This section offers a low-cost option to solve a high-cost security disaster.

The scenario for this section imagines a situation where the user can perform a search. They fill in the data and the application dynamically builds a query, based on the criteria the user entered.

In the solution, the `Program` class has a method named `GetCriteriaFromUser`. The purpose of this method is to ask for a matching value for each field inside of `Sales Person`. This becomes the criteria for building a dynamic query. Any fields left blank aren't included in the final query.

The `QuerySalesPeople` method starts with a LINQ query for `ctx.SalesPeople`. However, notice that this isn't in parentheses or calling the `ToList` operator, like previous sections. Calling `ToList` would have materialized the query, causing it to execute. However, we aren't doing that here—the code is just building a query. That's why the `salesPersonQuery` has the `IEnumerable<SalesPerson>` type, indicating that it's a LINQ to Objects result, rather than a `List<SalesPerson>` we would have gotten back via a call to `ToList`.

 This recipe takes advantage of a feature of LINQ, known as *deferred query execution*, which allows you to build the query that won't execute until you tell it to. In addition to facilitating dynamic query construction, deferred execution is also efficient because there's only a single query sent to the database, rather than each time the algorithm calls a specific LINQ operator.

With the `salesPersonQuery` reference, the code checks each `SalesPerson` field for a value. If the user did enter a value for that field, the code uses a `Where` operator to check for equality with what the user entered.

You've seen LINQ queries with language syntax in previous sections. However, this section takes advantage of another way to use LINQ via a fluent interface, called *method syntax*. This is much like the builder pattern you learned about in Recipe 1.10.

So far, the only thing that has happened is that we've dynamically built a LINQ query and, because of deferred execution, the query hasn't run yet. Finally, the code calls `ToList` on `salesPersonQuery`, materializing the query. As the return type of this method indicates, this returns a `List<SalesPerson>`.

Now, the algorithm has built and executed a dynamic query, protected from SQL injection attack. This protection comes from the fact that the LINQ provider always parameterizes user input so it will be treated as parameter data, rather than as part of the query. As a side benefit, you also have a method with strongly typed code, where you don't have to worry about inadvertent and hard-to-find typos.

See Also

Recipe 1.10, "Constructing Objects with Complex Configuration"

4.6 Querying Distinct Objects

Problem

You have a list of objects with duplicates and need to transform that into a distinct list of unique objects.

Solution

Here's an object that won't support distinct queries:

```
public class SalesPerson
{
    public int ID { get; set; }

    public string Name { get; set; }

    public string Address { get; set; }

    public string City { get; set; }

    public string PostalCode { get; set; }

    public string Region { get; set; }

    public string ProductType { get; set; }
}
```

Here's how to fix that object to support distinct queries:

```
public class SalesPersonComparer : IEqualityComparer<SalesPerson>
{
    public bool Equals(SalesPerson x, SalesPerson y)
    {
        return x.ID == y.ID;
    }

    public int GetHashCode(SalesPerson obj)
    {
        return obj.GetHashCode();
    }
}

public class SalesPerson
{
    public int ID { get; set; }

    public string Name { get; set; }

    public string Address { get; set; }

    public string City { get; set; }

    public string PostalCode { get; set; }

    public string Region { get; set; }

    public string ProductType { get; set; }
}
```

Here's the data source:

```
public class InMemoryContext
{
    List<SalesPerson> salesPeople =
        new List<SalesPerson>
        {
            new SalesPerson
            {
                ID = 1,
                Address = "123 1st Street",
                City = "First City",
                Name = "First Person",
                PostalCode = "45678",
                Region = "Region #1",
                ProductType = "Type 2"
            },
            new SalesPerson
            {
                ID = 2,
                Address = "234 2nd Street",
```

```
                City = "Second City",
                Name = "Second Person",
                PostalCode = "56789",
                Region = "Region #2",
                ProductType = "Type 3"
            },
            new SalesPerson
            {
                ID = 3,
                Address = "345 3rd Street",
                City = "Third City",
                Name = "Third Person",
                PostalCode = "67890",
                Region = "Region #3",
                ProductType = "Type 1"
            },
            new SalesPerson
            {
                ID = 4,
                Address = "678 9th Street",
                City = "Fourth City",
                Name = "Fourth Person",
                PostalCode = "90123",
                Region = "Region #1",
                ProductType = "Type 2"
            },
            new SalesPerson
            {
                ID = 4,
                Address = "678 9th Street",
                City = "Fourth City",
                Name = "Fourth Person",
                PostalCode = "90123",
                Region = "Region #1",
                ProductType = "Type 2"
            },
        };

    public List<SalesPerson> SalesPeople => salesPeople;
}
```

This code filters by distinct objects:

```
class Program
{
    static void Main(string[] args)
    {
        var salesPeopleWithoutComparer =
            (from person in new InMemoryContext().SalesPeople
             select person)
            .Distinct()
            .ToList();
```

```
        PrintResults(salesPeopleWithoutComparer, "Without Comparer");

        var salesPeopleWithComparer =
            (from person in new InMemoryContext().SalesPeople
             select person)
            .Distinct(new SalesPersonComparer())
            .ToList();

        PrintResults(salesPeopleWithComparer, "With Comparer");
    }

    static void PrintResults(List<SalesPerson> salesPeople, string title)
    {
        Console.WriteLine($"\n{title}\n");

        salesPeople.ForEach(person =>
            Console.WriteLine($"{person.ID}. {person.Name}"));
    }
}
```

Discussion

Sometimes you have a list of entities with duplicates, either because of some application processing or the type of database query that results in duplicates. Often, you need a list of unique objects. For instance, you're materializing into a Dictionary collection that doesn't allow duplicates.

The LINQ Distinct operator helps get a list of unique objects. At first glance, this is easy, as shown in the first query of the Main method that uses the Distinct() operator. Notice that it doesn't have parameters. However, an inspection of the results shows that you still have the same duplicates in the data that you started with.

The problem, and subsequent solution, might not be immediately obvious because it relies on combining a few different C# concepts. First, think about how Distinct should be able to tell the difference between objects—it has to perform a comparison. Next, consider that the type of SalesPerson is class. That's important because classes are reference types, which have reference equality. When Distinct does a reference comparison, no two object references are the same because each object has a unique reference. Finally, you need to write code to compare SalesPerson instances to see if they're equal and tell Distinct about that code.

The SalesPerson class is a basic class with properties and doesn't contain any syntax to indicate how to perform equality. In contrast, SalesPersonComparer implements IEqualityComparer<SalesPerson>. The SalesPerson class doesn't work because it has reference equality. However the SalesPersonComparer class that implements IEqualityComparer<SalesPerson> compares properly because it has an Equals method. In this case, checking ID is sufficient to determine that instances are equal, assuming that each entity comes from the same data source with unique ID fields.

SalesPersonComparer knows how to compare SalesPerson instances, but that isn't the end of the story because there isn't anything tying it to the query. If you ran the first query in Main with Distinct() (no parameter), the results will still have duplicates. The problem is that Distinct doesn't know how to compare the objects so it defaults to the instance type, class, which, as explained earlier, is a reference type.

The solution is to use the second query in Main that uses the call to Distinct(new SalesPersonComparer()) (with parameter). This uses the Distinct operator's overload with the IEqualityComparer<T> overload parameter. Since SalesPerson Comparer implements IEqualityComparer<SalesPerson>, this works.

See Also

Recipe 2.5, "Checking for Type Equality"

4.7 Simplifying Queries

Problem

A query has become too complex and you need to make it more readable.

Solution

Here's the entity to query:

```
public class SalesPerson
{
    public int ID { get; set; }

    public string Name { get; set; }

    public string Address { get; set; }

    public string City { get; set; }

    public string PostalCode { get; set; }

    public string Region { get; set; }

    public string ProductType { get; set; }

    public string TotalSales { get; set; }
}
```

This is the data source:

```
public class InMemoryContext
{
    List<SalesPerson> salesPeople =
        new List<SalesPerson>
        {
            new SalesPerson
            {
                ID = 1,
                Address = "123 1st Street",
                City = "First City",
                Name = "First Person",
                PostalCode = "45678",
                Region = "Region #1",
                ProductType = "Type 2",
                TotalSales = "654.32"
            },
            new SalesPerson
            {
                ID = 2,
                Address = "234 2nd Street",
                City = "Second City",
                Name = "Second Person",
                PostalCode = "56789",
                Region = "Region #2",
                ProductType = "Type 3",
                TotalSales = "765.43"
            },
            new SalesPerson
            {
                ID = 3,
                Address = "345 3rd Street",
                City = "Third City",
                Name = "Third Person",
                PostalCode = "67890",
                Region = "Region #3",
                ProductType = "Type 1",
                TotalSales = "876.54"
            },
            new SalesPerson
            {
                ID = 4,
                Address = "678 9th Street",
                City = "Fourth City",
                Name = "Fourth Person",
                PostalCode = "90123",
                Region = "Region #1",
                ProductType = "Type 2",
                TotalSales = "987.65"
            },
            new SalesPerson
            {
                ID = 4,
```

```
                    Address = "678 9th Street",
                    City = "Fourth City",
                    Name = "Fourth Person",
                    PostalCode = "90123",
                    Region = "Region #1",
                    ProductType = "Type 2",
                    TotalSales = "109.87"
                },
        };

        public List<SalesPerson> SalesPeople => salesPeople;
    }
```

The following shows how to simplify a query projection:

```
class Program
{
    static void Main(string[] args)
    {
        decimal TotalSales = 0;

        var salesPeopleWithAddresses =
            (from person in new InMemoryContext().SalesPeople
             let FullAddress =
             $"{person.Address}\n" +
             $"{person.City}, {person.PostalCode}"
             let salesOkay =
                 decimal.TryParse(person.TotalSales, out TotalSales)
             select new
             {
                 person.ID,
                 person.Name,
                 FullAddress,
                 TotalSales
             })
             .ToList();

        Console.WriteLine($"\nSales People and Addresses\n");

        salesPeopleWithAddresses.ForEach(person =>
            Console.WriteLine(
                $"{person.ID}. {person.Name}: {person.TotalSales:C}\n" +
                $"{person.FullAddress}\n"));
    }
}
```

Discussion

Sometimes LINQ queries get complex. If the code is still hard to read, it's also hard to maintain. One option is to go imperative and rewrite the query as a loop. Another is to use the let clause for simplification.

In the solution, the Main method has a query with a custom projection into an anony-mous type. Sometimes queries are complex because they have subqueries, or other logic, inside of the projection. For example, look at FullAddress, being built in a let clause. Without that simplification, the code would have ended up inside the projection.

Another scenario you might face is when parsing object input from string. The exam-ple uses a TryParse in a let clause, which is impossible to put in the projection. This is a little tricky because the out parameter, TotalSales, is outside of the query. We ignore the results of TryParse but can now assign TotalSales in the projection.

4.8 Operating on Sets

Problem

You want to combine two sets of objects without duplication.

Solution

Here's the entity to query:

```
public class SalesPerson : IEqualityComparer<SalesPerson>
{
    public int ID { get; set; }

    public string Name { get; set; }

    public string Address { get; set; }

    public string City { get; set; }

    public string PostalCode { get; set; }

    public string Region { get; set; }

    public string ProductType { get; set; }

    public bool Equals(SalesPerson x, SalesPerson y)
    {
        return x.ID == y.ID;
    }

    public int GetHashCode(SalesPerson obj)
    {
        return ID.GetHashCode();
    }
}
```

Here's the data source:

```
public class InMemoryContext
{
    List<SalesPerson> salesPeople =
        new List<SalesPerson>
        {
            new SalesPerson
            {
                ID = 1,
                Address = "123 1st Street",
                City = "First City",
                Name = "First Person",
                PostalCode = "45678",
                Region = "Region #1",
                ProductType = "Type 2"
            },
            new SalesPerson
            {
                ID = 2,
                Address = "234 2nd Street",
                City = "Second City",
                Name = "Second Person",
                PostalCode = "56789",
                Region = "Region #2",
                ProductType = "Type 3"
            },
            new SalesPerson
            {
                ID = 3,
                Address = "345 3rd Street",
                City = "Third City",
                Name = "Third Person",
                PostalCode = "67890",
                Region = "Region #3",
                ProductType = "Type 1"
            },
            new SalesPerson
            {
                ID = 4,
                Address = "678 9th Street",
                City = "Fourth City",
                Name = "Fourth Person",
                PostalCode = "90123",
                Region = "Region #1",
                ProductType = "Type 2"
            },
        };

    public List<SalesPerson> SalesPeople => salesPeople;
}
```

This code shows how to perform set operations:

```
class Program
{
    static InMemoryContext ctx = new InMemoryContext();

    static void Main()
    {
        System.Console.WriteLine("\nLINQ Set Operations");

        DoUnion();
        DoExcept();
        DoIntersection();

        System.Console.WriteLine("\nComplete.\n");
    }

    static void DoUnion()
    {
        var dataSource1 =
            (from person in ctx.SalesPeople
             where person.ID < 3
             select person)
            .ToList();

        var dataSource2 =
            (from person in ctx.SalesPeople
             where person.ID > 2
             select person)
            .ToList();

        List<SalesPerson> union =
            dataSource1
                .Union(dataSource2, new SalesPerson())
                .ToList();

        PrintResults(union, "Union Results");
    }

    static void DoExcept()
    {
        var dataSource1 =
            (from person in ctx.SalesPeople
             select person)
            .ToList();

        var dataSource2 =
            (from person in ctx.SalesPeople
             where person.ID == 4
             select person)
            .ToList();

        List<SalesPerson> union =
```

```
                dataSource1
                    .Except(dataSource2, new SalesPerson())
                    .ToList();

            PrintResults(union, "Except Results");
        }

        static void DoIntersection()
        {
            var dataSource1 =
                (from person in ctx.SalesPeople
                 where person.ID < 4
                 select person)
                .ToList();

            var dataSource2 =
                (from person in ctx.SalesPeople
                 where person.ID > 2
                 select person)
                .ToList();

            List<SalesPerson> union =
                dataSource1
                    .Intersect(dataSource2, new SalesPerson())
                    .ToList();

            PrintResults(union, "Intersect Results");
        }

        static void PrintResults(List<SalesPerson> salesPeople, string title)
        {
            Console.WriteLine($"\n{title}\n");

            salesPeople.ForEach(person =>
                Console.WriteLine($"{person.ID}. {person.Name}"));
        }
    }
```

Discussion

In Recipe 4.2, we discussed the concept of joining data from two separate data sources. The examples operate in that same spirit and show different manipulations,
based on sets.

The first method, DoUnion, gets two sets of data, intentionally filtering by ID to ensure
overlap. From the reference of the first data source, the code calls the Union operator
with the second data source as the parameter. This results in a set of data from both
data sources, including duplicates.

The DoExcept method is similar to DoUnion but uses the Except operator. This results in a set of all the objects in the first data source. However, any objects in the second data source, even if they were in the first, won't appear in the results.

Finally, DoIntersect is similar in structure to DoUnion and DoExcept. However, it queries objects that are only in both data sources. If any object is in one data source, but not the other, it won't appear in the result. This operation is called *difference in set theory*.

LINQ has many standard operators that, just like the set operators, are very powerful. Before performing any complex operation in a LINQ query, it's good practice to review standard operators to see if something exists that will simplify your task.

See Also

Recipe 4.2, "Joining Data"

Recipe 4.3, "Performing Left Joins"

4.9 Building a Query Filter with Expression Trees

Problem

The LINQ where clause combines via AND conditions, but you need a dynamic where that works as an OR condition.

Solution

Here's the entity to query:

```
public class SalesPerson
{
    public int ID { get; set; }

    public string Name { get; set; }

    public string Address { get; set; }

    public string City { get; set; }

    public string PostalCode { get; set; }

    public string Region { get; set; }

    public string ProductType { get; set; }
}
```

This is the data source:

```csharp
public class InMemoryContext
{
    List<SalesPerson> salesPeople =
        new List<SalesPerson>
        {
            new SalesPerson
            {
                ID = 1,
                Address = "123 1st Street",
                City = "First City",
                Name = "First Person",
                PostalCode = "45678",
                Region = "Region #1",
                ProductType = "Type 2"
            },
            new SalesPerson
            {
                ID = 2,
                Address = "234 2nd Street",
                City = "Second City",
                Name = "Second Person",
                PostalCode = "56789",
                Region = "Region #2",
                ProductType = "Type 3"
            },
            new SalesPerson
            {
                ID = 3,
                Address = "345 3rd Street",
                City = "Third City",
                Name = "Third Person",
                PostalCode = "67890",
                Region = "Region #3",
                ProductType = "Type 1"
            },
            new SalesPerson
            {
                ID = 4,
                Address = "678 9th Street",
                City = "Fourth City",
                Name = "Fourth Person",
                PostalCode = "90123",
                Region = "Region #1",
                ProductType = "Type 2"
            },
        };

    public List<SalesPerson> SalesPeople => salesPeople;
}
```

Here's an extension method for a filtered OR operation:

```
public static class CookbookExtensions
{
    public static IEnumerable<TParameter> WhereOr<TParameter>(
        this IEnumerable<TParameter> query,
        Dictionary<string, string> criteria)
    {
        const string ParamName = "person";

        ParameterExpression paramExpr =
            Expression.Parameter(typeof(TParameter), ParamName);

        Expression accumulatorExpr = null;

        foreach (var criterion in criteria)
        {
            MemberExpression paramMbr =
                LambdaExpression.PropertyOrField(
                    paramExpr, criterion.Key);

            MemberExpression leftExpr =
                Expression.Property(
                    paramExpr,
                    typeof(TParameter).GetProperty(criterion.Key));
            Expression rightExpr =
                Expression.Constant(criterion.Value, typeof(string));
            Expression equalExpr =
                Expression.Equal(leftExpr, rightExpr);

            accumulatorExpr = accumulatorExpr == null
                ? equalExpr
                : Expression.Or(accumulatorExpr, equalExpr);
        }

        Expression<Func<TParameter, bool>> allClauses =
            Expression.Lambda<Func<TParameter, bool>>(
                accumulatorExpr, paramExpr);

        Func<TParameter, bool> compiledClause = allClauses.Compile();

        return query.Where(compiledClause);
    }
}
```

Here's the code that consumes the new extension method:

```
class Program
{
    static void Main()
    {
        SalesPerson searchCriteria = GetCriteriaFromUser();
```

```csharp
        List<SalesPerson> salesPeople = QuerySalesPeople(searchCriteria);

        PrintResults(salesPeople);
    }

    static SalesPerson GetCriteriaFromUser()
    {
        var person = new SalesPerson();

        Console.WriteLine("Sales Person Search");
        Console.WriteLine("(press Enter to skip an entry)\n");

        Console.Write($"{nameof(SalesPerson.Address)}: ");
        person.Address = Console.ReadLine();

        Console.Write($"{nameof(SalesPerson.City)}: ");
        person.City = Console.ReadLine();

        Console.Write($"{nameof(SalesPerson.Name)}: ");
        person.Name = Console.ReadLine();

        Console.Write($"{nameof(SalesPerson.PostalCode)}: ");
        person.PostalCode = Console.ReadLine();

        Console.Write($"{nameof(SalesPerson.ProductType)}: ");
        person.ProductType = Console.ReadLine();

        Console.Write($"{nameof(SalesPerson.Region)}: ");
        person.Region = Console.ReadLine();

        return person;
    }

    static List<SalesPerson> QuerySalesPeople(SalesPerson criteria)
    {
        var ctx = new InMemoryContext();

        var filters = new Dictionary<string, string>();

        IEnumerable<SalesPerson> salesPeopleQuery =
            from people in ctx.SalesPeople
            select people;

        if (!string.IsNullOrWhiteSpace(criteria.Address))
            filters[nameof(criteria.Address)] = criteria.Address;

        if (!string.IsNullOrWhiteSpace(criteria.City))
            filters[nameof(criteria.City)] = criteria.City;

        if (!string.IsNullOrWhiteSpace(criteria.Name))
            filters[nameof(criteria.Name)] = criteria.Name;
```

```
        if (!string.IsNullOrWhiteSpace(criteria.PostalCode))
            filters[nameof(criteria.PostalCode)] = criteria.PostalCode;

        if (!string.IsNullOrWhiteSpace(criteria.ProductType))
            filters[nameof(criteria.ProductType)] = criteria.ProductType;

        if (!string.IsNullOrWhiteSpace(criteria.Region))
            filters[nameof(criteria.Region)] = criteria.Region;

        salesPeopleQuery =
            salesPeopleQuery.WhereOr<SalesPerson>(filters);

        List<SalesPerson> salesPeople = salesPeopleQuery.ToList();

        return salesPeople;
    }

    static void PrintResults(List<SalesPerson> salesPeople)
    {
        Console.WriteLine("\nSales People\n");

        salesPeople.ForEach(person =>
            Console.WriteLine($"{person.ID}. {person.Name}"));
    }
}
```

Discussion

Recipe 4.5 showed the power of dynamic queries in LINQ. However, that isn't the end of what you can do. With expression trees, you can leverage LINQ for any type of query. If the standard operators don't provide something you need, you can use expression trees. This section does just that, showing how to use expression trees to run a dynamic WhereOr operation.

The motivation for WhereOr comes from the fact that the standard Where operator combines in an AND comparison. In Recipe 4.5, all of those Where operators had an implicit AND relationship between them. This means that a given entity must have a value equal to each of the fields (that the user specified in the criteria) to get a match. With the WhereOr in this section, all of the fields have an OR relationship, and a match on only one of the fields is necessary for inclusion in results.

In the solution, the GetCriteriaFromUser method gets the values for each SalesPerson property. QuerySalesPeople starts a query for deferred execution, as explained in Recipe 4.5, and builds a Dictionary<string, string> of filters.

The CookbookExtensions class has the WhereOr extension method that accepts the filters. The high-level description of what WhereOr is trying to accomplish comes from the fact that it needs to return an `IEnumerable<SalesPerson>` for the caller to complete a LINQ query.

First, go to the bottom of `WhereOr` and notice that it returns the query with the `Where` operator and has a parameter named `compiledQuery`. Remember that the LINQ `Where` operator takes a C# lambda expression with a parameter and a predicate. We want a filter that returns an object if any one field of an object matches, based on the input criteria. Therefore, `compiledQuery` must evaluate to a lambda of the following form:

```
person => person.Field1 == "val1" || ... || person.FieldN == "valN"
```

That's a lambda with `OR` operators for each value in the `Dictionary<string, string> criteria` parameter. To get from the top of this algorithm to the bottom, we need to build an expression tree that evaluates to this form of lambda. Figure 4-1 illustrates what this code does.

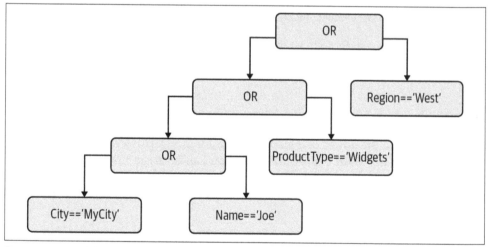

Figure 4-1. Building a `Where` expression with clauses separated by `OR` operators

Figure 4-1 shows the expression tree that the solution creates. Here, we assume that the user wants to query four values: `City`, `Name`, `ProductType`, and `Region`. Expression trees read depth-first, from left to right, where each box represents a node. Therefore, LINQ follows the tree down the left side until it finds a leaf node, which is the `City` expression. Then it moves back up the tree to find the `OR`, moves to the right and finds the `Name` expression, and builds the `OR` expression. So far, LINQ has built the following clause:

```
City == 'MyCity' || Name == 'Joe'
```

LINQ continues reading the expression tree up and to the right until it finally builds the following clause:

```
City == 'MyCity' || Name == 'Joe' || ProductType == 'Widgets' || Region == 'West'
```

Back to the solution code, the first thing `WhereOr` does is create a `ParameterExpres` `sion`. This is the `person` parameter in the lambda. It's the parameter to every comparison expression because it represents the `TParameter`, which is an instance of `Sales` `Person` in this example.

 This example is called the `ParameterExpression` person. However, if this is a generic reusable extension method, you might give it a more general name, like `parameterTerm` because `TParameter` could be any type. The choice of `person` in this example is there to clarify that the `ParameterExpression` represents a `SalesPerson` instance in this example.

The `Expression` `accumulatorExpr`, as its name suggests, gathers all of the clauses for the lambda body.

The `foreach` statement loops through the `Dictionary` collection, which returns `KeyValuePair` instances, which have `Key` and `Value` properties. As shown in the `QuerySalesPeople` method, the `Key` property is the name of the `SalesPerson` property, and the `Value` property is what the user entered.

For each clause of the lambda, the left-hand side is a reference to the property on the `SalesPerson` instance (e.g., `person.Name`). To create that, the code instantiates the `paramMbr` using the `paramExpr` (which is `person`). That becomes a parameter of `left` `Expr`. The `rightExpr` expression is a constant that holds the value to compare and its type. Then we need to complete the expression with an `Equals` expression for the left and right expressions (`leftExpr` and `rightExpr`, respectively).

Finally, we need to `OR` that expression with any others. The first time through the `foreach` loop, `accumulatorExpr` will be `null`, so we just assign the first expression. On subsequent expressions, we use an `OR` expression to append the new `Equals` expression to `accumulatorExpr`.

After iterating through each input field, we form the final `LambdaExpression` that adds the parameter that was used in the left side of each `Equals` expression. Notice that the result is an `Expression<Func<TParameter, bool>>`, which has a parameter type matching the lambda delegate type for the original query, which is `Func<Sales` `Person, bool>`.

We now have a dynamically built expression tree ready to convert into runnable code, which is a task for the `Expression.Compile` method. This gives us a compiled lambda that we can pass to the `Where` clause.

The calling code receives the `IEnumerable<SalesPerson>` from the `WhereOr` method and materializes the query with a call to `ToList`. This produces a list of `SalesPerson` objects that match at least one of the user's specified criteria.

See Also

Recipe 4.5, "Building Incremental Queries"

4.10 Querying in Parallel

Problem

You want to improve performance, and your query could benefit from multithreading.

Solution

Here's the entity to query:

```
public class SalesPerson
{
    public int ID { get; set; }

    public string Name { get; set; }

    public string Address { get; set; }

    public string City { get; set; }

    public string PostalCode { get; set; }

    public string Region { get; set; }

    public string ProductType { get; set; }
}
```

This is the data source:

```
public class InMemoryContext
{
    List<SalesPerson> salesPeople =
        new List<SalesPerson>
        {
            new SalesPerson
            {
                ID = 1,
                Address = "123 1st Street",
                City = "First City",
                Name = "First Person",
                PostalCode = "45678",
```

```
                    Region = "Region #1",
                    ProductType = "Type 2"
                },
                new SalesPerson
                {
                    ID = 2,
                    Address = "234 2nd Street",
                    City = "Second City",
                    Name = "Second Person",
                    PostalCode = "56789",
                    Region = "Region #2",
                    ProductType = "Type 3"
                },
                new SalesPerson
                {
                    ID = 3,
                    Address = "345 3rd Street",
                    City = "Third City",
                    Name = "Third Person",
                    PostalCode = "67890",
                    Region = "Region #3",
                    ProductType = "Type 1"
                },
                new SalesPerson
                {
                    ID = 4,
                    Address = "678 9th Street",
                    City = "Fourth City",
                    Name = "Fourth Person",
                    PostalCode = "90123",
                    Region = "Region #1",
                    ProductType = "Type 2"
                },
                new SalesPerson
                {
                    ID = 5,
                    Address = "678 9th Street",
                    City = "Fifth City",
                    Name = "Fifth Person",
                    PostalCode = "90123",
                    Region = "Region #1",
                    ProductType = "Type 2"
                },
            };

    public List<SalesPerson> SalesPeople => salesPeople;
}
```

This code shows how to perform a parallel query:

```
class Program
{
    static void Main()
    {
        List<SalesPerson> salesPeople = new InMemoryContext().SalesPeople;
        var result =
            (from person in salesPeople.AsParallel()
             select ProcessPerson(person))
            .ToList();
    }

    static SalesPerson ProcessPerson(SalesPerson person)
    {
        Console.WriteLine(
            $"Starting sales person " +
            $"#{person.ID}. {person.Name}");

        // complex in-memory processing
        Thread.Sleep(500);

        Console.WriteLine(
            $"Completed sales person " +
            $"#{person.ID}. {person.Name}");

        return person;
    }
}
```

Discussion

This section considers queries that can benefit from concurrency. Imagine you have a LINQ to Objects query, where the data is in memory. Perhaps work on each instance requires intensive processing, the code runs on a multithreaded/multicore CPU, and/or takes a nontrivial amount of time. Running the query in parallel might be an option.

The `Main` method performs a query, similar to any other query, except for the `AsParallel` operator on the data source. What this does is let LINQ figure out how to split up the work and operate on each range variable in parallel. Figure 4-2 illustrates what this query is doing.

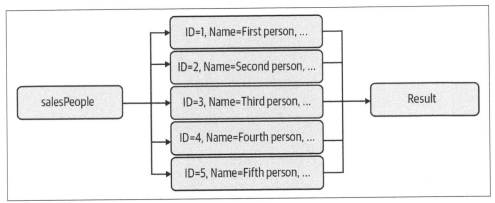

Figure 4-2. PLINQ runs members of a collection in parallel

Figure 4-2 shows the `salesPeople` collection on the left. When the query runs, it takes multiple collection objects to process in parallel, indicated by the split arrows from `salesPeople` pointing to each instance of `SalesPerson`. After processing, the query combines the responses from processing each object into a new collection, named `result`.

 This example uses a LINQ technology known as Parallel LINQ (PLINQ). Behind the scenes, PLINQ evaluates the query for various runtime optimizations such as degree of parallelism. It's even smart enough to figure out when running synchronously is faster than the overhead of starting new threads on a given machine.

This example also demonstrates another type of projection that uses a method to return an object. The assumption here is that the intensive processing occurs in `ProcessPerson`, which has a `Thread.Sleep` to simulate nontrivial processing.

In practice, you would want to do some testing to see if you're really benefiting from parallelism. Recipe 3.10 shows how to measure performance with the `System.Diagnostics.StopWatch` class. If successful, this could be an easy way to boost the performance of your application.

See Also

Recipe 3.10, "Measuring Performance"

Implementing Dynamic and Reflection

Reflection allows code to look inside of a type and examine its details and members. This is useful for libraries and tools that want to give the user maximum flexibility to submit objects to perform some automatic operation. A common example of code that does reflection are unit testing frameworks. As described in Recipe 3.1, unit tests take classes whose members have attributes to indicate which methods are tests. The unit testing framework uses reflection to find classes that are tests, locate the test methods, and execute the tests.

The example in this chapter is based on a dynamic report-building application. It uses reflection to read attributes of a class, access type members, and execute methods. The first four sections of this chapter show how to do that.

In addition to reflection, another way to work flexibly with code is a C# feature called dynamic. In C#, much of the code we write is strongly typed, and that's a huge benefit for productivity and maintainability. That said, C# has a `dynamic` keyword that allows developers to assume that objects have a certain structure. This is much like dynamic programming languages, like JavaScript and Python, where developers access objects based on documentation that specifies what members an object has. So, they just write code that uses those members. Dynamic code allows C# to do the same thing.

When performing operations requiring COM interop, dynamic is particularly useful, and there's a section explaining how that works. You'll see how dynamic can be useful in significantly reducing and simplifying the code, as compared to the verbosity and complexity of reflection. There are also types that allow us to build an inherently dynamic type. Additionally, there's a dynamic language runtime (DLR) that enables interop between C# and dynamic languages, such as Python, and you'll see two sections on interoperability between C# and Python.

5.1 Reading Attributes with Reflection

Problem

You want consumers of your library to have maximum flexibility when passing objects, but they still need to communicate important details of the object.

Solution

Here's an `Attribute` class, representing report column metadata:

```
[AttributeUsage(
    AttributeTargets.Property | AttributeTargets.Method,
    AllowMultiple = false)]
public class ColumnAttribute : Attribute
{
    public ColumnAttribute(string name)
    {
        Name = name;
    }

    public string Name { get; set; }

    public string Format { get; set; }
}
```

This class represents a record to display and uses the attribute:

```
public class InventoryItem
{
    [Column("Part #")]
    public string PartNumber { get; set; }

    [Column("Name")]
    public string Description { get; set; }

    [Column("Amount")]
    public int Count { get; set; }

    [Column("Price")]
    public decimal ItemPrice { get; set; }

    [Column("Total")]
    public decimal CalculateTotal()
    {
        return ItemPrice * Count;
    }
}
```

The `Main` method shows how to instantiate and pass the data:

```
static void Main()
{
    var inventory = new List<object>
    {
        new InventoryItem
        {
            PartNumber = "1",
            Description = "Part #1",
            Count = 3,
            ItemPrice = 5.26m
        },
        new InventoryItem
        {
            PartNumber = "2",
            Description = "Part #2",
            Count = 1,
            ItemPrice = 7.95m
        },
        new InventoryItem
        {
            PartNumber = "3",
            Description = "Part #3",
            Count = 2,
            ItemPrice = 23.13m
        },
    };

    string report = new Report().Generate(inventory);

    Console.WriteLine(report);
}
```

This Report class has methods for building a report header and generating a report:

```
public class Report
{
    // contains Generate and GetHeaders methods
}
```

This method is a member of the Report class and uses reflection to find all type members:

```
public string Generate(List<object> items)
{
    _ = items ??
        throw new ArgumentNullException(
            $"{nameof(items)} is required");

    MemberInfo[] members =
        items.First().GetType().GetMembers();

    var report = new StringBuilder("# Report\n\n");
```

```
        report.Append(GetHeaders(members));

        return report.ToString();
    }
```

This method is a member of the Report class and uses reflection to read attributes of a type:

```
const string ColumnSeparator = " | ";

StringBuilder GetHeaders(MemberInfo[] members)
{
    var columnNames = new List<string>();
    var underscores = new List<string>();

    foreach (var member in members)
    {
        var attribute =
            member.GetCustomAttribute<ColumnAttribute>();

        if (attribute != null)
        {
            string columnTitle = attribute.Name;
            string dashes = "".PadLeft(columnTitle.Length, '-');

            columnNames.Add(columnTitle);
            underscores.Add(dashes);
        }
    }

    var header = new StringBuilder();

    header.AppendJoin(ColumnSeparator, columnNames);
    header.Append("\n");

    header.AppendJoin(ColumnSeparator, underscores);
    header.Append("\n");

    return header;
}
```

And here's the output:

```
# Report

Total | Part # | Name | Amount | Price
----- | ------ | ---- | ------ | -----
```

Discussion

Attributes, which are metadata, typically exist to support tooling on code. The solution in this section takes a similar approach where the ColumnAttribute is metadata for a column of data in a report. You can see where the `AttributeUsage` specifies that you can apply `ColumnAttribute` to either properties or methods. Thinking of which features that a report column might be able to support, this attribute boils down to two typical features: `Name` and `Format`. Because a C# property name might not represent the text of a column header, `Name` lets you specify anything you want. Also, without specifying a string format, `DateTime` and `decimal` columns would take default displays, which is often not what you want. This essentially solves the problem where a consumer of a report library wants to pass any type of object they want, using `ColumnAttribute` to share important details.

`InventoryItem` shows how `ColumnAttribute` works. Notice how the positional property, `Name`, differs from the name of the properties and method. Recipe 5.2 has an example of how the `Format` property works, while this section only concentrates on how to extract and display the metadata as a Markdown formatted column.

 Architecturally, you should look at this project as two separate applications. There's a reusable report library that anyone can submit objects to. The report library consists of a `Report` class and the `ColumnAttribute` attribute. Then there's a consumer application, which is the `Main` method. For simplicity, the source code for this demo puts all the code into the same project, but in practice, these would be separate.

The `Main` method instantiates a `List<object>` that contains `InventoryItem` instances. This is data that would typically come from a database or other data source. It instantiates the `Report`, passes the data, and prints the result.

The `Generate` method belongs to the `Report` class. Notice that it accepts a `List<object>`, which is why `Main` passed a `List<object>`. Essentially, `Report` wants to be able to operate on any object type.

After validating input items, `Generate` uses reflection to discover what members exist in the objects passed. You see, we're no longer able to know because the objects aren't strongly typed, and we want maximum flexibility in what types can be passed. This is a good case for reflection. That said, we no longer have the guarantee that all instances in items are the same type, and that has to be an implied contract, rather than enforced by code. Recipe 5.3 fixes this by showing how to use generics so we have both type safety and the ability to use generics, and using interfaces might be another approach.

We're assuming all objects are the same, and `Generate` calls `First` on `items`, because it has the exact same attributes of all objects in `items`. `Generate` then calls `GetType` on the first item. The `Type` instance is the gateway for performing reflection.

After getting the `Type` instance, you can ask for anything about a type and work with particular instances. This example calls `GetMembers` to get a `MemberInfo[]`. A `Member Info` has all the information about a particular type member, like its name and type. In this example, the `MemberInfo[]` contains the properties and methods from the `InventoryItem` that `Main` passed in: `PartNumber`, `Description`, `Count`, `ItemPrice`, and `CalculateTotal`.

Because the report is a string of Markdown text and there is a lot of concatenation, the solution uses `StringBuilder`. Recipe 2.1 explains why this is a good approach.

Because we're concerned with attributes, this solution only prints the report header, and later sections in this chapter explain a lot of different ways to generate the report body, depending on your needs. The `GetHeader` method takes the `MemberInfo[]` and uses reflection to learn what those header titles should be.

In Markdown, we separate table headers with pipes, |, and add an underscore, which is why we have two arrays for `columnNames` and `underscores`. The `foreach` loop examines each `MemberInfo`, calling `GetCustomAttribute`. Notice that the type parameter for `GetCustomAttribute` is `ColumnAttribute`—members could have multiple attributes, but we only want that one. The instance returned from `GetCustom Attribute` is `ColumnAttribute`, so we have access to its properties, such as `Name`. The code populates `columnNames` with `Name` and adds an underscore that is the same length as `Name`.

Finally, `GetHeaders` concatenates values with pipes, |, and returns the resulting header. Following this back through the call chain, `Generate` appends the `GetHeaders` results and `Main` prints the header, which you can see in the solution output.

See Also

Recipe 2.1, "Processing Strings Efficiently"

Recipe 5.2, "Accessing Type Members with Reflection"

5.2 Accessing Type Members with Reflection

Problem

You need to examine an object to see what properties you can read.

Solution

This class represents a record to display:

```
public class InventoryItem
{
```

```
    [Column("Part #")]
    public string PartNumber { get; set; }

    [Column("Name")]
    public string Description { get; set; }

    [Column("Amount")]
    public int Count { get; set; }

    [Column("Price", Format = "{0:c}")]
    public decimal ItemPrice { get; set; }
}
```

Here's a class that contains metadata for each report column:

```
public class ColumnDetail
{
    public string Name { get; set; }

    public ColumnAttribute Attribute { get; set; }

    public PropertyInfo PropertyInfo { get; set; }
}
```

This method collects the data to populate column metadata:

```
Dictionary<string, ColumnDetail> GetColumnDetails(
    List<object> items)
{
    object itemInstance = items.First();
    Type itemType = itemInstance.GetType();
    PropertyInfo[] itemProperties = itemType.GetProperties();

    return
        (from prop in itemProperties
         let attribute = prop.GetCustomAttribute<ColumnAttribute>()
         where attribute != null
         select new ColumnDetail
         {
             Name = prop.Name,
             Attribute = attribute,
             PropertyInfo = prop
         })
        .ToDictionary(
            key => key.Name,
            val => val);
}
```

Here's a more streamlined way to get header data with LINQ:

```
StringBuilder GetHeaders(
    Dictionary<string, ColumnDetail> details)
{
    var header = new StringBuilder();
```

```
header.AppendJoin(
    ColumnSeparator,
    from detail in details.Values
    select detail.Attribute.Name);

header.Append("\n");

header.AppendJoin(
    ColumnSeparator,
    from detail in details.Values
    let length = detail.Attribute.Name.Length
    select "".PadLeft(length, '-'));

header.Append("\n");

return header;
}
```

This method uses reflection to pull the value out of an object property:

```
(object, Type) GetReflectedResult(
    object item, PropertyInfo property)
{
    object result = property.GetValue(item);
    Type type = property.PropertyType;

    return (result, type);
}
```

This method uses reflection to retrieve and format property data:

```
List<string> GetColumns(
    IEnumerable<ColumnDetail> details,
    object item)
{
    var columns = new List<string>();

    foreach (var detail in details)
    {
        PropertyInfo member = detail.PropertyInfo;
        string format =
            string.IsNullOrWhiteSpace(
                detail.Attribute.Format) ?
                "{0}" :
                detail.Attribute.Format;

        (object result, Type columnType) =
            GetReflectedResult(item, member);

        switch (columnType.FullName)
        {
            case "System.Decimal":
                columns.Add(
```

```
                    string.Format(format, (decimal)result));
                break;
            case "System.Int32":
                columns.Add(
                    string.Format(format, (int)result));
                break;
            case "System.String":
                columns.Add(
                    string.Format(format, (string)result));
                break;
            default:
                break;
        }
    }

    return columns;
}
```

This method combines and formats all rows of data:

```
StringBuilder GetRows(
    List<object> items,
    Dictionary<string, ColumnDetail> details)
{
    var rows = new StringBuilder();

    foreach (var item in items)
    {
        List<string> columns =
            GetColumns(details.Values, item);

        rows.AppendJoin(ColumnSeparator, columns);

        rows.Append("\n");
    }

    return rows;
}
```

Finally, this method uses all of the others to build a complete report:

```
const string ColumnSeparator = " | ";

public string Generate(List<object> items)
{
    var report = new StringBuilder("# Report\n\n");

    Dictionary<string, ColumnDetail> columnDetails =
        GetColumnDetails(items);
    report.Append(GetHeaders(columnDetails));
    report.Append(GetRows(items, columnDetails));

    return report.ToString();
}
```

And here's the output:

```
|| Total | Part # | Name | Amount | Price ||
| $15.78 | 1 | Part #1 | 3 | 5.26 |
| $7.95 | 2 | Part #2 | 1 | 7.95 |
| $46.26 | 3 | Part #3 | 2 | 23.13 |
```

Discussion

The report library in the solution receives a List<object> so that consumers can send objects of any type they want. Since the input objects aren't strongly typed, the Report class needs to perform reflection to extract data from each object. Recipe 5.1 explained how the Main method passes this data and how the solution generates the header. This section concentrates on data, and the solution doesn't repeat the exact code from Recipe 5.1.

The InventoryItem class uses ColumnAttribute attributes. Notice that ItemPrice now has the named property Format, specifying that this column should be formatted in the report as currency.

During reflection, we need to extract a set of data from the objects that helps with report layout and formatting. The ColumnDetail helps with this because when processing each column, we need to know:

- Name to ensure we're working on the right column
- Attribute for formatting column data
- PropertyInfo for getting property data

The GetColumnDetails method populates a ColumnDetail for each column. Getting the first object in the data, it gets the type and then calls GetProperties on the types for a PropertyInfo[]. Unlike Recipe 5.1, which calls GetMembers for a MemberInfo[], this only gets the properties from the type and not any other members.

 In addition to GetMembers and GetProperties, Type has other reflection methods that will only get constructors, fields, or methods. These would be useful if you need to restrict the type of member you're working with.

Because reflection returns a collection of objects (PropertyInfo[] in this solution), we can use LINQ to Objects for a more declarative approach. This is what GetColumn Details does, projecting into ColumnDetails instances and returning a Dictionary with the column name as key and ColumnDetail as value.

As you'll see later in the solution, the code iterates through the `Dic` `tionary<string, ColumnDetail>`, assuming that columns and their data are laid out in the order returned by reflection queries. However, imagine a future implementation where `ColumnAttri` `bute` had an `Order` property or the consumer could pass `include/` `exclude` column metadata that didn't guarantee that the order of the columns matches what reflection returned. In that case, having the dictionary is essential to look up `ColumnDetail` metadata based on which column you're working on. Although that's left out of this example to reduce complexity and focus on the original problem statement, it might give you ideas on how something like this could be extended.

The `GetHeaders` method does exactly the same thing as Recipe 5.1, except it's written as LINQ statements to reduce and simplify the code.

The `GetReflectedResult` returns a tuple, (`object`, `Type`). Its task is to pull out the value from the property and the type of the property from its `PropertyInfo`. Here, `item` is the actual object instance and `property` is the reflected metadata for that property. Using `property`, the code calls `GetValue` with `item` as the parameter—it reads that property from `item`. Again, we're using reflection and don't know the type for the property, so we put it in type object. `PropertyInfo` also has a `PropertyType`, which is where we get the `Type` object from.

This application uses reflection to put property data into a variable of type `object`. If the property type is a value type (e.g., `int`, `double`, `decimal`), you incur a boxing penalty, which affects application performance. If you were doing this millions of times, you might need to take a second look at your requirements and analyze whether this was a good approach for your scenario. That said, this is a report. Think about how many records you might include in a report for the purpose of displaying the data to a human. In this case, any performance issues would be negligible. It's a classic trade-off of flexibility versus performance; you just need to think about how it affects your situation.

The `GetColumns` method uses `GetReflectedResult` as it loops through each column for a given object. The collection of `ColumnDetail` is useful, providing `PropertyInfo` for the current column. The format defaults to no format if the `ColumnAttribute` for a column doesn't include the `Format` property. The `switch` statement applies the format to the object based on the `Type` returned from `GetReflectedResult`.

For simplicity, the switch statement in GetColumns only contains types in the solution, though you might imagine it including all built-in types. We might have used reflection to invoke ToString with a format specifier and type, which we'll discuss in Recipe 5.4, to reduce code. However, at some point the additional complexity doesn't add value. In this case, we're just covering a finite set of built-in types, and once that code is written, it will be unlikely to change. My thoughts on this trade-off are that sometimes being too clever results in code that's difficult to read and takes longer to write.

Finally, GetRows calls GetColumns for each row and returns to Generate. Then, having called GetHeaders and GetRows, Generate appends the results to a String Builder and returns the string to the caller with the entire report, which you can see in the solution output.

See Also

Recipe 5.1, "Reading Attributes with Reflection"

Recipe 5.4, "Invoking Methods with Reflection"

5.3 Instantiating Type Members with Reflection

Problem

You need to instantiate generic types but don't know the type or type parameters ahead of time.

Solution

The solution generates a uniquely formatted report, depending on this enum:

```
public enum ReportType
{
    Html,
    Markdown
}
```

Here's a reusable base class for generating reports:

```
public abstract class GeneratorBase<TData>
{
    public string Generate(List<TData> items)
    {
        StringBuilder report = GetTitle();

        Dictionary<string, ColumnDetail> columnDetails =
```

```
        GetColumnDetails(items);
    report.Append(GetHeaders(columnDetails));
    report.Append(GetRows(items, columnDetails));

    return report.ToString();
}

protected abstract StringBuilder GetTitle();

protected abstract StringBuilder GetHeaders(
    Dictionary<string, ColumnDetail> details);

protected abstract StringBuilder GetRows(
    List<TData> items,
    Dictionary<string, ColumnDetail> details);

Dictionary<string, ColumnDetail> GetColumnDetails(
    List<TData> items)
{
    TData itemInstance = items.First();
    Type itemType = itemInstance.GetType();
    PropertyInfo[] itemProperties = itemType.GetProperties();

    return
        (from prop in itemProperties
         let attribute = prop.GetCustomAttribute<ColumnAttribute>()
         where attribute != null
         select new ColumnDetail
         {
             Name = prop.Name,
             Attribute = attribute,
             PropertyInfo = prop
         })
        .ToDictionary(
            key => key.Name,
            val => val);
}

protected List<string> GetColumns(
    IEnumerable<ColumnDetail> details,
    TData item)
{
    var columns = new List<string>();

    foreach (var detail in details)
    {
        PropertyInfo member = detail.PropertyInfo;
        string format =
            string.IsNullOrWhiteSpace(
                detail.Attribute.Format) ?
                "{0}" :
                detail.Attribute.Format;
```

```
                (object result, Type columnType) =
                    GetReflectedResult(item, member);

                switch (columnType.Name)
                {
                    case "Decimal":
                        columns.Add(
                            string.Format(format, (decimal)result));
                        break;
                    case "Int32":
                        columns.Add(
                            string.Format(format, (int)result));
                        break;
                    case "String":
                        columns.Add(
                            string.Format(format, (string)result));
                        break;
                    default:
                        break;
                }
            }

            return columns;
        }

        (object, Type) GetReflectedResult(TData item, PropertyInfo property)
        {
            object result = property.GetValue(item);
            Type type = property.PropertyType;

            return (result, type);
        }
    }
```

This class uses that base class to generate Markdown reports:

```
    public class MarkdownGenerator<TData> : GeneratorBase<TData>
    {
        const string ColumnSeparator = " | ";

        protected override StringBuilder GetTitle()
        {
            return new StringBuilder("# Report\n\n");
        }

        protected override StringBuilder GetHeaders(
            Dictionary<string, ColumnDetail> details)
        {
            var header = new StringBuilder();

            header.AppendJoin(
                ColumnSeparator,
```

```
                from detail in details.Values
                select detail.Attribute.Name);

        header.Append("\n");

        header.AppendJoin(
            ColumnSeparator,
            from detail in details.Values
            let length = detail.Attribute.Name.Length
            select "".PadLeft(length, '-'));

        header.Append("\n");

        return header;
    }

    protected override StringBuilder GetRows(
        List<TData> items,
        Dictionary<string, ColumnDetail> details)
    {
        var rows = new StringBuilder();

        foreach (var item in items)
        {
            List<string> columns =
                GetColumns(details.Values, item);

            rows.AppendJoin(ColumnSeparator, columns);

            rows.Append("\n");
        }

        return rows;
    }
}
```

And this class uses that base class to generate HTML reports:

```
public class HtmlGenerator<TData> : GeneratorBase<TData>
{
    protected override StringBuilder GetTitle()
    {
        return new StringBuilder("<h1>Report</h1>\n");
    }

    protected override StringBuilder GetHeaders(
        Dictionary<string, ColumnDetail> details)
    {
        var header = new StringBuilder("<tr>\n");

        header.AppendJoin(
            "\n",
            from detail in details.Values
```

```
        let columnName = detail.Attribute.Name
        select $"    <th>{columnName}</th>");

    header.Append("\n</tr>\n");

    return header;
}

protected override StringBuilder GetRows(
    List<TData> items,
    Dictionary<string, ColumnDetail> details)
{
    StringBuilder rows = new StringBuilder();
    Type itemType = items.First().GetType();

    foreach (var item in items)
    {
        rows.Append("<tr>\n");

        List<string> columns =
            GetColumns(details.Values, item);

        rows.AppendJoin(
            "\n",
            from columnValue in columns
            select $"    <td>{columnValue}</td>");

        rows.Append("\n</tr>\n");
    }

    return rows;
}
}
```

This method, from the Report class, manages the report-generation process:

```
public string Generate(List<TData> items, ReportType reportType)
{
    GeneratorBase<TData> generator = CreateGenerator(reportType);

    string report = generator.Generate(items);

    return report;
}
```

Here's a method, from the Report class, that uses an enum to figure out which report format to generate:

```
GeneratorBase<TData> CreateGenerator(ReportType reportType)
{
    Type generatorType;

    switch (reportType)
```

```
    {
        case ReportType.Html:
            generatorType = typeof(HtmlGenerator<>);
            break;
        case ReportType.Markdown:
            generatorType = typeof(MarkdownGenerator<>);
            break;
        default:
            throw new ArgumentException(
                $"Unexpected ReportType: '{reportType}'");
    }

    Type dataType = typeof(TData);
    Type genericType = generatorType.MakeGenericType(dataType);

    object generator = Activator.CreateInstance(genericType);

    return (GeneratorBase<TData>)generator;
}
```

Here's another way, via convention, to figure out which report format to generate:

```
GeneratorBase<TData> CreateGenerator(ReportType reportType)
{
    Type dataType = typeof(TData);

    string generatorNamespace = "Section_05_03.";
    string generatorTypeName = $"{reportType}Generator`1";
    string typeParameterName = $"[[{dataType.FullName}]]";

    string fullyQualifiedTypeName =
        generatorNamespace +
        generatorTypeName +
        typeParameterName;

    Type generatorType = Type.GetType(fullyQualifiedTypeName);

    object generator = Activator.CreateInstance(generatorType);

    return (GeneratorBase<TData>)generator;
}
```

The Main method passes data and specifies which report format it wants:

```
static void Main()
{
    var inventory = new List<InventoryItem>
    {
        new InventoryItem
        {
            PartNumber = "1",
            Description = "Part #1",
            Count = 3,
```

```
                ItemPrice = 5.26m
        },
        new InventoryItem
        {
            PartNumber = "2",
            Description = "Part #2",
            Count = 1,
            ItemPrice = 7.95m
        },
        new InventoryItem
        {
            PartNumber = "3",
            Description = "Part #3",
            Count = 2,
            ItemPrice = 23.13m
        },
    };

    string report =
        new Report<InventoryItem>()
        .Generate(inventory, ReportType.Markdown);

    Console.WriteLine(report);
}
```

And here's the output:

```
# Report

Part # | Name | Amount | Price
------ | ---- | ------ | -----
1 | Part #1 | 3 | $5.26
2 | Part #2 | 1 | $7.95
3 | Part #3 | 2 | $23.13
```

Discussion

Recipe 5.2 created reports based on a generic object type, and this caused us to lose the type safety we are accustomed to. This section fixes that problem by using generics and showing how to use reflection to instantiate objects with a generic type parameter.

The concept of the previous sections was to generate a report in Markdown format. However, a report generator could be much more useful if it had the ability to generate reports in any format of your choosing. This example refactors the example in Recipe 5.2 to offer both a Markdown and an HTML output report.

The ReportType enum specifies the type of report output to generate: Html or Markdown. Because we can generate multiple formats, we need separate classes for each format: `HtmlGenerator` and `MarkdownGenerator`. Further, we don't want to duplicate code, so each format generation class derives from `GeneratorBase`.

Notice that `GeneratorBase` is an abstract class (you can't instantiate it), with both abstract and implemented methods. The implemented methods in `GeneratorBase` have code that is independent of output formatted and that all derived generator classes will use: `GetColumns`, `GetColumnDetails`, and `GetReflectedResult`. By definition, the derived generator classes must `override` the abstract methods, which are format specific: `GetTitle`, `GetHeaders`, `GetRows`. Looking at `HtmlGenerator` and `MarkdownGenerator`, you can see the `override` implementations for these abstract methods.

Now, let's put this all together so it makes sense. When the program starts, the first method called on the `Report` instance is `Generate`, in `GeneratorBase`. Notice how `Generate` calls the sequence: `GetTitle`, `GetColumnDetails`, `GetHeaders`, and then `GetRows`. This is essentially the same sequence as described in Recipe 5.2. You can imagine a report being generated top to bottom by writing the title, getting metadata for the rest of the report, writing the header, and then writing each of the rows of the report. To get code reuse and create an extensible framework for adding report formats in the future, we have a general abstract base class, `GeneratorBase`, and derived classes that understand the format. Using `MarkdownGenerator` as an example, here's the sequence:

1. External code calls `GeneratorBase.Generate`.

2. `Generator.Generate` calls `MarkdownGenerator.GetTitle`.

3. `Generator.Generate` calls `Generator.GetColumnDetails`.

4. `Generator.Generate` calls `MarkdownGenerator.GetHeader`.

5. `Generator.Generate` calls `MarkdownGenerator.GetRows`.

6. `MarkdownGenerator.GetRows` calls `Generator.GetColumns`.

7. `Generator.GetColumns` calls `Generator.GetReflectedResult`.

8. `MarkdownGenerator.GetRows` completes, returning to `Generator.Generate`.

9. `Generator.Generate` returns the report to calling code.

The `HtmlGenerator` works exactly the same way, and so would any future report format. In fact, Recipe 5.6 extends this example by adding a third format to support creating an Excel report.

The solution uses a pattern known as the *template pattern*. In this pattern, a base class implements common logic and delegates implementation-specific work to derived classes. This is the object-oriented principle of polymorphism at work.

The fact that we can extend this framework without needing to re-write boilerplate logic makes this a viable approach. Recipe 5.6 shows how that works.

The GenerateBase class is intentionally abstract because the only way for this to work is via an instance of a derived class. The Report.Generate method calls Genera torBase.Generate. Before doing so, it must figure out which specific GeneratorBase derived class to instantiate via CreateGenerator, of which there are two examples.

The first example of CreateGenerator examines the ReportType enum to see which type of report to generate via a switch statement. As explained in earlier sections, you need a Type object to perform reflection, which the typeof operator does. Notice that we're passing a generic type with the <> suffix, without the generic type. After that, we use the typeof operator to get the type of the type parameter passed to the Report class, TData. Now we have a type for both the generic type and its type parameter. Next, we need to bring the generic type and its parameter type together to get a fully constructed type, (e.g., HtmlGenerator<TData> for Html). Once you have a fully constructed type, you can use the Activator class to call CreateInstance, which instantiates the type. With a new instance of the GeneratorBase-derived type, CreateGener ate returns to ReportGenerate, which calls Generate on the new instance. As you learned earlier, GeneratorBase implements Generate for all derived instances.

That is one way to use reflection to instantiate a generic type, as specified by the problem statement. One thing to consider, though, is whether you want to add more formats to support in the future. You'll have to go back into the Report class and change the switch statement, which is a configuration by code change. What if you prefer to write the Report class one time and never touch it again? Further, what if you preferred a design by the principles of convention-over-configuration? A good example of convention over configuration in .NET is ASP.NET MVC. A couple of ASP.NET MVC conventions are that controllers go in a Controllers folder and views go in a Views folder. Another is that the controller name is the URL path with a Controller suffix to its name. Things just work because that's the convention. The second example of CreateGenerator uses the convention-over-configuration approach.

Notice that the second implementation of CreateGenerator builds a fully qualified type name with namespace and typename (e.g., Section_05_03.HtmlGenerator for Html). Also notice that the ReportType enum members match the class names exactly. This means that anytime in the future, you can create a new format, derived from

GeneratorBase, and add the prefix to ReportType with Generator as the suffix and it will work. No need to ever touch the Report class again, unless adding a new feature.

After getting type objects, both CreateGenerator examples call Activator.Create Instance to return a new instance to Report.Generate.

Finally, looking at the Main method, all a user of this report library needs to do is pass in the data and the ReportType they want to generate.

See Also

Recipe 5.2, "Accessing Type Members with Reflection"

Recipe 5.6, "Performing Interop with Office Apps"

5.4 Invoking Methods with Reflection

Problem

An object you've received has methods that you need to invoke.

Solution

The column metadata class has a MemberInfo property:

```csharp
public class ColumnDetail
{
    public string Name { get; set; }

    public ColumnAttribute Attribute { get; set; }

    public MemberInfo MemberInfo { get; set; }
}
```

This class, to be reflected upon, has properties and a method:

```csharp
public class InventoryItem
{
    [Column("Part #")]
    public string PartNumber { get; set; }

    [Column("Name")]
    public string Description { get; set; }

    [Column("Amount")]
    public int Count { get; set; }

    [Column("Price", Format = "{0:c}")]
    public decimal ItemPrice { get; set; }
```

```
        [Column("Total", Format = "{0:c}")]
        public decimal CalculateTotal()
        {
            return ItemPrice * Count;
        }
    }
```

This method calls `GetMembers` to work with `MemberInfo` instances:

```
Dictionary<string, ColumnDetail> GetColumnDetails(
    List<object> items)
{
    return
        (from member in
            items.First().GetType().GetMembers()
         let attribute =
            member.GetCustomAttribute<ColumnAttribute>()
         where attribute != null
         select new ColumnDetail
         {
             Name = member.Name,
             Attribute = attribute,
             MemberInfo = member
         })
        .ToDictionary(
            key => key.Name,
            val => val);
}
```

This method uses the `MemberInfo` type to determine how to retrieve a value:

```
(object, Type) GetReflectedResult(
    Type itemType, object item, MemberInfo member)
{
    object result;
    Type type;

    switch (member.MemberType)
    {
        case MemberTypes.Method:
            MethodInfo method =
                itemType.GetMethod(member.Name);
            result = method.Invoke(item, null);
            type = method.ReturnType;
            break;
        case MemberTypes.Property:
            PropertyInfo property =
                itemType.GetProperty(member.Name);
            result = property.GetValue(item);
            type = property.PropertyType;
            break;
        default:
            throw new ArgumentException(
```

```
                    "Expected property or method.");
    }

    return (result, type);
}
```

Discussion

Earlier sections in this chapter worked primarily with properties as report inputs. In this section we'll modify the example in Recipe 5.2 and add a method that we'll need to invoke via reflection.

The first change is that ColumnDetail has a MemberInfo property, which holds metadata for any type member.

The InventoryItem class has a CalculateTotal method. It multiplies the ItemPrice and Count to show the total price for that amount of items.

The change in GetColumnDetails is in the LINQ statement, where it iterates on the result of GetMembers, which is a MemberInfo[]. Unlike Recipe 5.2, we're using Member Info. This is required for this solution because we want information on both properties and methods.

Finally, GetReflectedResult has a switch statement to figure out how to get a member's value. Since the parameter is a MemberInfo, we look at the MemberType property to figure out whether we're working with a property or method. In either case, we have to call GetProperty or GetMethod to get a PropertyInfo or MethodInfo, respectively. Call the Invoke method for methods, with item as the object instance to invoke the method on. The second parameter to Invoke is null, indicating that the method, CalculateTotal in this example, doesn't have arguments. If you need to pass arguments, put an object[] in the second parameter of Invoke with the members in the order that the method expects them. As in Recipe 5.2, call GetValue on the Property Info instance, with item as the object reference to get the value of that property.

To summarize, anytime you need to call a method on an object via reflection, get its Type object, get a MethodInfo (even if you need the intermediate step of pulling from a MemberInfo), and call the Invoke method on the MethodInfo with the object instance as the argument.

See Also

Recipe 5.2, "Accessing Type Members with Reflection"

5.5 Replacing Reflection with Dynamic Code

Problem

You're using reflection but know what some of a type's members are and want to simplify code.

Solution

This class contains the list of data for a report:

```
public class Inventory
{
    public string Title { get; set; }

    public List<object> Data { get; set; }
}
```

Here's the `Main` method that populates the data:

```
static void Main()
{
    var inventory = new Inventory
    {
        Title = "Inventory Report",
        Data = new List<object>
        {
            new InventoryItem
            {
                PartNumber = "1",
                Description = "Part #1",
                Count = 3,
                ItemPrice = 5.26m
            },
            new InventoryItem
            {
                PartNumber = "2",
                Description = "Part #2",
                Count = 1,
                ItemPrice = 7.95m
            },
            new InventoryItem
            {
                PartNumber = "3",
                Description = "Part #3",
                Count = 2,
                ItemPrice = 23.13m
            },
        }
    };
```

```
        string report = new Report().Generate(inventory);

        Console.WriteLine(report);
    }
```

This method uses reflection to extract a property's values:

```
    public string Generate(object reportDetails)
    {
        Type reportType = reportDetails.GetType();
        PropertyInfo titleProp = reportType.GetProperty("Title");
        string title = (string)titleProp.GetValue(reportDetails);

        var report = new StringBuilder($"# {title}\n\n");

        PropertyInfo dataProp = reportType.GetProperty("Data");
        List<object> items =
            (List<object>)dataProp.GetValue(reportDetails);

        Dictionary<string, ColumnDetail> columnDetails =
            GetColumnDetails(items);
        report.Append(GetHeaders(columnDetails));
        report.Append(GetRows(items, columnDetails));

        return report.ToString();
    }
```

And this class extracts the same property values but uses dynamic:

```
    public string Generate(dynamic reportDetails)
    {
        string title = reportDetails.Title;

        var report = new StringBuilder(
            $"# {title}\n\n");

        List<object> items = reportDetails.Data;

        Dictionary<string, ColumnDetail> columnDetails =
            GetColumnDetails(items);
        report.Append(GetHeaders(columnDetails));
        report.Append(GetRows(items, columnDetails));

        return report.ToString();
    }
```

Discussion

The concept of this solution is again to give users of the report library maximum control over what types they want to work with. However, what if you did have some constraints? For instance, there must be some way to set the report title, and you would need to know what that property is. This solution meets the user halfway by telling them to provide an object with `Title` and `Data` properties. `Title` has the report title and `Data` has report rows. They can use any object they want as long as they provide those properties. If the input objects had other properties on the object we don't care about, it won't affect the report library.

The class we'll use is `Inventory`, with a `Title` string and `Data` collection. The `Main` method populates an `Inventory` instance and passes it to `Generate`.

We have two examples of `Generate`: one uses reflection and the other uses dynamic. After getting the type, the first example calls `GetProperty` and `GetValue` to get the value of each property. The rest of the method works just like in Recipe 5.2.

As you see, reflection can be verbose, making many method calls and converting types. This is a good case for using dynamic. We know that `Title` and `Data` exist, so why not just access them? That's what the second example does. First, notice that the `reportDetails` parameter type is `dynamic`. Then observe how the code calls `Title` and `Data`, placing them in strongly typed variables.

 The dynamic type is still type `object` but with a little extra magic performed behind the scenes by the DLR.

While you don't get IntelliSense during development because `dynamic` doesn't know what types it's working with, you do get readable code. Behind the scenes, the DLR did all the work for you. When you know the members of the types being passed to the code, `dynamic` is a better mechanism for reflection.

See Also

Recipe 5.2, "Accessing Type Members with Reflection"

5.6 Performing Interop with Office Apps

Problem

You need to populate an Excel spreadsheet with object data with the simplest code possible.

Solution

Here's an enum with extra members for Excel:

```
public enum ReportType
{
```

```
        Html,
        Markdown,
        ExcelTyped,
        ExcelDynamic
    }
```

Excel report generator without dynamic:

```
    public class ExcelTypedGenerator<TData> : GeneratorBase<TData>
    {
        ApplicationClass excelApp;
        Workbook wkBook;
        Worksheet wkSheet;

        public ExcelTypedGenerator()
        {
            excelApp = new ApplicationClass();
            excelApp.Visible = true;

            wkBook = excelApp.Workbooks.Add(Missing.Value);
            wkSheet = (Worksheet)wkBook.ActiveSheet;
        }

        protected override StringBuilder GetTitle()
        {
            wkSheet.Cells[1, 1] = "Report";

            return new StringBuilder("Added Title...\n");
        }

        protected override StringBuilder GetHeaders(
            Dictionary<string, ColumnDetail> details)
        {
            ColumnDetail[] values = details.Values.ToArray();

            for (int i = 0; i < values.Length; i++)
            {
                ColumnDetail detail = values[i];
                wkSheet.Cells[3, i+1] = detail.Attribute.Name;
            }

            return new StringBuilder("Added Header...\n");
        }

        protected override StringBuilder GetRows(
            List<TData> items,
            Dictionary<string, ColumnDetail> details)
        {
            const int DataStartRow = 4;

            int rows = items.Count;
            int cols = details.Count;
```

```
            var data = new string[rows, cols];

            for (int i = 0; i < rows; i++)
            {
                List<string> columns =
                    GetColumns(details.Values, items[i]);

                for (int j = 0; j < cols; j++)
                {
                    data[i, j] = columns[j];
                }
            }

            int FirstCol = 'A';
            int LastExcelCol = FirstCol + cols - 1;
            int LastExcelRow = DataStartRow + rows - 1;
            string EndRangeCol = ((char)LastExcelCol).ToString();
            string EndRangeRow = LastExcelRow.ToString();

            string EndRange = EndRangeCol + EndRangeRow;
            string BeginRange = "A" + DataStartRow.ToString();

            var dataRange = wkSheet.get_Range(BeginRange, EndRange);
            dataRange.Value2 = data;

            wkBook.SaveAs(
                "Report.xlsx", Missing.Value, Missing.Value,
                Missing.Value, Missing.Value, Missing.Value,
                XlSaveAsAccessMode.xlShared, Missing.Value, Missing.Value,
                Missing.Value, Missing.Value, Missing.Value);

            return new StringBuilder(
                "Added Data...\n" +
                "Excel file created at Report.xlsx");
        }
    }
```

Excel report generator with dynamic:

```
    public class ExcelDynamicGenerator<TData> : GeneratorBase<TData>
    {
        ApplicationClass excelApp;
        dynamic wkBook;
        Worksheet wkSheet;

        public ExcelDynamicGenerator()
        {
            excelApp = new ApplicationClass();
            excelApp.Visible = true;

            wkBook = excelApp.Workbooks.Add();
            wkSheet = wkBook.ActiveSheet;
        }
```

```csharp
protected override StringBuilder GetTitle()
{
    wkSheet.Cells[1, 1] = "Report";

    return new StringBuilder("Added Title...\n");
}

protected override StringBuilder GetHeaders(
    Dictionary<string, ColumnDetail> details)
{
    ColumnDetail[] values = details.Values.ToArray();

    for (int i = 0; i < values.Length; i++)
    {
        ColumnDetail detail = values[i];
        wkSheet.Cells[3, i+1] = detail.Attribute.Name;
    }

    return new StringBuilder("Added Header...\n");
}

protected override StringBuilder GetRows(
    List<TData> items,
    Dictionary<string, ColumnDetail> details)
{
    const int DataStartRow = 4;

    int rows = items.Count;
    int cols = details.Count;

    var data = new string[rows, cols];

    for (int i = 0; i < rows; i++)
    {
        List<string> columns =
            GetColumns(details.Values, items[i]);

        for (int j = 0; j < cols; j++)
        {
            data[i, j] = columns[j];
        }
    }

    int FirstCol = 'A';
    int LastExcelCol = FirstCol + cols - 1;
    int LastExcelRow = DataStartRow + rows - 1;
    string EndRangeCol = ((char)LastExcelCol).ToString();
    string EndRangeRow = LastExcelRow.ToString();

    string EndRange = EndRangeCol + EndRangeRow;
    string BeginRange = "A" + DataStartRow.ToString();
```

```
    var dataRange = wkSheet.get_Range(BeginRange, EndRange);
    dataRange.Value2 = data;

    wkBook.SaveAs(
        "Report.xlsx",
        XlSaveAsAccessMode.xlShared);

    return new StringBuilder(
        "Added Data...\n" +
        "Excel file created at Report.xlsx");
    }
}
```

Discussion

This example is based on the multiple report format generation code in Recipe 5.3, which briefly explains how to add another report type. This solution shows how to do it.

First, notice that the ReportType enum has two extra members: ExcelTyped and ExcelDynamic. Both use the convention where ExcelTyped creates a ExcelTyped Generator instance and ExcelDynamic creates an ExcelDynamicGenerator instance. The difference is that ExcelTypedGenerator uses strongly typed code to generate an Excel report, and ExcelDynamicGenerator uses dynamic code to generate an Excel report.

 You can use techniques like this to automate any Microsoft Office application. The trick is to ensure you've installed Visual Studio Tools for Office (VSTO) via the Visual Studio Installer. This will install what is called *primary interop assemblies* (PIAs). After installation, you can find these PIAs under your Visual Studio installation folder (for instance, the folder on my machine is *C:\Program Files (x86)\Microsoft Visual Studio\Shared\Visual Studio Tools for Office\PIA*) and use the version corresponding to the Microsoft Office version you have installed. Search the download options (*https://oreil.ly/vbMvL*) if you have an older version of Office that the VSTO couldn't install.

To see the differences between the two examples, go member by member. In particular, ExcelTypedGenerator has strongly typed fields, so it must use the Missing.Value placeholder anytime it doesn't use a parameter and needs to perform a conversion on return types. Notice the SaveAs method call at the end of the GetRows method, which is particularly onerous.

In contrast, compare those examples with the ExcelDynamicGenerator code. Making the wkBook field dynamic, rather than strongly typed, transforms the code. No more Missing.Value placeholders or type conversions. The code is much easier to write and easier to read.

See Also

Recipe 5.3, "Instantiating Type Members with Reflection"

5.7 Creating an Inherently Dynamic Type

Problem

You have data in a proprietary format but want to access members through an object without parsing yourself.

Solution

This class holds data to display in a report:

```
public class LogEntry
{
    [Column("Log Date", Format = "{0:yyyy-MM-dd hh:mm}")]
    public DateTime CreatedAt { get; set; }

    [Column("Severity")]
    public string Type { get; set; }

    [Column("Location")]
    public string Where { get; set; }

    [Column("Message")]
    public string Description { get; set; }
}
```

These methods get log data and return a list of DynamicObject types with that data:

```
static List<dynamic> GetData()
{
    string headers = "Date|Severity|Location|Message";

    string logData = GetLogData();

    return
        (from line in logData.Split('\n')
         select new DynamicLog(headers, line))
        .ToList<dynamic>();
}

static string GetLogData()
```

```
    {
        return
    "2022-11-12 12:34:56.7890|INFO|Section_05_07.Program|Got this far\n" +
    "2022-11-12 12:35:12.3456|ERROR|Section_05_07.Report|Index out of range\n" +
    "2022-11-12 12:55:34.5678|WARNING|Section_05_07.Report|Please check this";
    }
```

This class is a `DynamicObject` that knows how to read log files and dynamically expose properties:

```
public class DynamicLog : DynamicObject
{
    Dictionary<string, string> members =
        new Dictionary<string, string>();

    public DynamicLog(string headerString, string logString)
    {
        string[] headers = headerString.Split('|');
        string[] logData = logString.Split('|');

        for (int i = 0; i < headers.Length; i++)
            members[headers[i]] = logData[i];
    }

    public override bool TryGetMember(
        GetMemberBinder binder, out object result)
    {
        result = members[binder.Name];
        return true;
    }

    public override bool TryInvokeMember(
        InvokeMemberBinder binder, object[] args, out object result)
    {
        return base.TryInvokeMember(binder, args, out result);
    }

    public override bool TrySetMember(
        SetMemberBinder binder, object value)
    {
        members[binder.Name] = (string)value;
        return true;
    }
}
```

The `Main` method consumes the dynamic data, populates data objects, and gets a new report:

```
static void Main()
{
    List<dynamic> logData = GetData();

    var tempDateTime = DateTime.MinValue;
```

```
        List<object> inventory =
            (from log in logData
             let canParse =
                 DateTime.TryParse(
                     log.Date, out tempDateTime)
             select new LogEntry
             {
                 CreatedAt = tempDateTime,
                 Type = log.Severity,
                 Where = log.Location,
                 Description = log.Message
             })
            .ToList<object>();

        string report = new Report().Generate(inventory);

        Console.WriteLine(report);
    }
```

Discussion

The DynamicObject type is part of the .NET Framework and supports the DLR for interoperability with dynamic languages. It's a peculiar type that lets anyone call type members, and it can intercept the call and behave in any way you've programmed it to. Rather than wave hands and enumerate several ways to use DynamicObject, this solution focuses on the problem where you need an object to work on proprietary data. In this solution, the data is a log file format. Here, we'll use the DynamicObject to provide the data and the report library from Recipe 5.2 to display the log data.

The LogEntry class represents a row in the report. We can't give a DynamicObject instance to Report because there isn't a way to reflect on it and extract attributes. Any workaround is cumbersome, and it's easier to use the DynamicObject for working with the data, generate a collection of LogEntry objects, and pass them to the Report.

The GetLogData method shows what the log file looks like. GetData defines a head ers string, which is metadata for each entry of the log file. The LINQ query iterates through each line of the log, resulting in a List<dynamic>. The projection instantiates a new DynamicLog instance with the header and log entry.

The DynamicLog type derives from DynamicObject, implementing only the methods it needs. The DynamicLog implementation shows a few of these members: TryGetMem ber, TryInvokeMember, and TrySetMember. The solution doesn't use TryInvokeMem ber, but I left it in there to show that DynamicObject does more than work with properties and that there are other overloads. The Dictionary<string, string> mem bers, hold a value for each field in the log with the key coming from the header and the value coming from the identically positioned string in the log file.

The constructor populates members. It splits each field on the pipe, (|), separator and iterates through the headers until members has an entry for each column. The `TryGetMembers` method reads from the dictionary to return the value via the out `object result` parameter. Remember to return `true` when successful because returning `false` indicates that you couldn't perform the operation, and the user will receive a runtime exception. `TrySetMember` populates the dictionary with the value.

`GetMemberBinder` and `SetMemberBinder` contain metadata on the property that is being accessed. For example, the following would call `TryGetMember`:

```
string severity = log.Severity;
```

Assuming that log is an instance of `DynamicLog`, the `GetMemberBinder` `Name` property would be `Severity`. It would index into the dictionary and return whatever value is assigned to that key. Similarly, the following would call `TrySetMember`:

```
log.Severity = "ERROR";
```

In this case, `binder.Name` would be `Severity`, and it would update that key in the dictionary with the value `ERROR`.

That means now we have an object where you can set property names of your choosing and provide any log file of the same format (pipe-separated). No need for a custom class every time you want to accommodate a pipe-separated format log file.

`GetData` returns a `List<dynamic>`. Because it's a dynamic object and we already know what the property names should be (they match the header), we can project into `LogEntry` instances by only specifying the property name on the dynamic object. Additionally, you could specify what those headers should be in a configuration file or database where they can be data-driven and change every time. Maybe you even want the ability to change the delimiter on the file to accommodate handling even more file types. As you can see, that's easy to do with `DynamicObject`.

See Also

Recipe 5.2, "Accessing Type Members with Reflection"

5.8 Adding and Removing Type Members Dynamically

Problem

You want a fully dynamic object that you can add members to during runtime, as in JavaScript.

Solution

This method uses an `ExpandoObject` to collect data:

```
static List<dynamic> GetData()
{
    const int Date = 0;
    const int Severity = 1;
    const int Location = 2;
    const int Message = 3;

    var logEntries = new List<dynamic>();

    string logData = GetLogData();

    foreach (var line in logData.Split('\n'))
    {
        string[] columns = line.Split('|');

        dynamic logEntry = new ExpandoObject();

        logEntry.Date = columns[Date];
        logEntry.Severity = columns[Severity];
        logEntry.Location = columns[Location];
        logEntry.Message = columns[Message];

        logEntries.Add(logEntry);
    }

    return logEntries;
}

static string GetLogData()
{
    return
        "2022-11-12 12:34:56.7890|INFO" +
        "|Section_05_07.Program|Got this far\n" +
        "2022-11-12 12:35:12.3456|ERROR" +
        "|Section_05_07.Report|Index out of range\n" +
        "2022-11-12 12:55:34.5678|WARNING" +
        "|Section_05_07.Report|Please check this";
}
```

The `Main` method converts a `List<dynamic>` to a `List<LogEntry>` and gets the report:

```
static void Main()
{
    List<dynamic> logData = GetData();

    var tempDateTime = DateTime.MinValue;
    List<object> inventory =
        (from log in logData
```

```
            let canParse =
                DateTime.TryParse(
                    log.Date, out tempDateTime)
            select new LogEntry
            {
                CreatedAt = tempDateTime,
                Type = log.Severity,
                Where = log.Location,
                Description = log.Message
            })
            .ToList<object>();

        string report = new Report().Generate(inventory);

        Console.WriteLine(report);
    }
```

Discussion

This is similar to the `DynamicObject` example in Recipe 5.7, except it covers a simpler case where you don't need as much flexibility. What if you knew what the file format was ahead of time and that it won't change, yet you want a simple way to pull the data into a dynamic object without creating a new type every time you need to send data to the report?

In this case, you can use `ExpandoObject`, a .NET Framework type that lets you add and remove type members on the fly, the same as in JavaScript.

In the solution, the `GetData` method instantiates an `ExpandoObject`, assigning it to the `dynamic logEntry`. Then, it adds properties on the fly and populates them with the parsed log file data.

The `Main` method accepts a `List<dynamic>` from `GetData`. As long as each object has the properties it expects, everything works well.

See Also

Recipe 5.7, "Creating an Inherently Dynamic Type"

5.9 Calling Python Code from C#

Problem

You have a C# program and want to use some Python code but don't want to rewrite it.

Solution

This Python file has code that we need to use:

```python
import sys
sys.path.append(
    "/System/Library/Frameworks/Python.framework" +
    "/Versions/Current/lib/python2.7")

from random import *

class SemanticAnalysis:
    @staticmethod
    def Eval(text):
        val = random()
        return val < .5
```

This class represents social media data:

```csharp
public class Tweet
{
    [Column("Screen Name")]
    public string ScreenName { get; set; }

    [Column("Date")]
    public DateTime CreatedAt { get; set; }

    [Column("Text")]
    public string Text { get; set; }

    [Column("Semantic Analysis")]
    public string Semantics { get; set; }
}
```

The Main method gets data and generates a report:

```csharp
static void Main()
{
    List<object> tweets = GetTweets();

    string report = new Report().Generate(tweets);

    Console.WriteLine(report);
}
```

These are the required namespaces that are part of the IronPython NuGet package:

```csharp
using IronPython.Hosting;
using Microsoft.Scripting.Hosting;
```

This method sets up the Python interop:

```csharp
static List<object> GetTweets()
{
    ScriptRuntime py = Python.CreateRuntime();
```

```
dynamic semantic = py.UseFile("../../../Semantic.py");
dynamic semanticAnalysis = semantic.SemanticAnalysis();

DateTime date = DateTime.UtcNow;

var tweets = new List<object>
{
    new Tweet
    {
        ScreenName = "SomePerson",
        CreatedAt = date.AddMinutes(5),
        Text = "Comment #1",
        Semantics = GetSemanticText(semanticAnalysis, "Comment #1")
    },
    new Tweet
    {
        ScreenName = "SomePerson",
        CreatedAt = date.AddMinutes(7),
        Text = "Comment #2",
        Semantics = GetSemanticText(semanticAnalysis, "Comment #2")
    },
    new Tweet
    {
        ScreenName = "SomePerson",
        CreatedAt = date.AddMinutes(12),
        Text = "Comment #3",
        Semantics = GetSemanticText(semanticAnalysis, "Comment #3")
    },
};

return tweets;
}
```

This method calls the Python code via `dynamic` instance:

```
static string GetSemanticText(dynamic semantic, string text)
{
    bool result = semantic.Eval(text);
    return result ? "Positive" : "Negative";
}
```

Discussion

The scenario in this example is one where you're working with social media data. One of the report items is semantics, telling whether a user's tweet was positive or negative. You've got this great semantic analysis AI model, but it's built with TensorFlow in a Python module. It would be helpful to be able to reuse that code instead of rewriting it.

This is where the DLR comes in, because it lets you call Python (and other dynamic languages) from C#. Considering that it could have taken many months to build a machine learning model (or any other type of module), the advantage of reusing that code across languages can be huge.

The SemanticAnalysis class in the Python file simulates a model, returning true for a positive result or false for a negative result.

The Main method calls GetTweets to get data and uses the Report class, which is the same as in Recipe 5.2. The List<object> returned from GetTweets contains Tweet objects that can work with the report generator.

 To set this up, you'll need to reference the IronPython package, which you can find on NuGet. You also might find it useful to install Python Tools for Visual Studio via the Visual Studio Installer.

The GetTweets method needs a reference to the Python SemanticAnalysis class. Calling CreateRuntime creates a DLR reference. Then you need to specify the location of the Python file via UseFile. After that, you can instantiate the SemanticAnaly sis class. Each Tweet instance sets the Semantics property with a call to GetSemantic Text, passing the SemanticAnalysis reference and text to evaluate.

The GetSemanticText method calls Eval with text as its parameter and returns a bool result, which it then translates to a report-friendly "Positive" or "Negative" string.

In just a few lines of code, you saw how easy it is to reuse important code that was written in a dynamic language. Languages supported by the DLR include Ruby and JavaScript, among others.

See Also

Recipe 5.2, "Accessing Type Members with Reflection"

5.10 Calling C# Code from Python

Problem

You have a Python program and want to use C# code but don't want to rewrite it.

Solution

Here's the main Python application that needs to use the report generator:

```python
import clr, sys

sys.path.append(
    r"C:\Path Where You Cloned The Project" +
    "\Chapter05\Section-05-10\bin\Debug")
clr.AddReference(
    r"C:\Path Where You Cloned The Project" +
    "\Chapter05\Section-05-10\bin\Debug\PythonToCS.dll")

from PythonToCS import Report
from PythonToCS import InventoryItem
from System import Decimal

inventory = [
    InventoryItem("1", "Part #1", 3, Decimal(5.26)),
    InventoryItem("2", "Part #2", 1, Decimal(7.95)),
    InventoryItem("3", "Part #1", 2, Decimal(23.13))]

rpt = Report()

result = rpt.GenerateDynamic(inventory)

print(result)
```

This class has a constructor to make it easier to work with in Python:

```csharp
public class InventoryItem
{
    public InventoryItem(
        string partNumber, string description,
        int count, decimal itemPrice)
    {
        PartNumber = partNumber;
        Description = description;
        Count = count;
        ItemPrice = itemPrice;
    }

    [Column("Part #")]
    public string PartNumber { get; set; }

    [Column("Name")]
    public string Description { get; set; }

    [Column("Amount")]
    public int Count { get; set; }

    [Column("Price", Format = "{0:c}")]
```

```
    public decimal ItemPrice { get; set; }
}
```

Here's the C# method that the Python code calls to generate the report:

```
public string GenerateDynamic(dynamic[] items)
{
    List<object> inventory =
        (from item in items
          select new InventoryItem
          (
              item.PartNumber,
              item.Description,
              item.Count,
              item.ItemPrice
          ))
          .ToList<object>();

    return Generate(inventory);
}
```

Discussion

In Recipe 5.9, the scenario was to call Python from C#. The scenario in this problem is opposite in that I have a Python application and need to be able to generate reports. However, the report generator is written in C#. So much work has gone into the report library that it doesn't make sense to rewrite in Python. Fortunately, the DLR allows us to call that C# code with Python.

The report is the same one used in Recipe 5.2 and the C# code has the same Inventory Item class.

To set this up, you might need to install the pythonnet package (*https://oreil.ly/hY9bZ*):

```
>pip install pythonnet
```

You set up the Python code by importing clr and sys, calling sys.path.append as a reference to the path where the C# DLL resides and then calling clr.AddReference to add a reference to the C# DLL you want to use.

In Python, whenever you need to use a .NET type from either the framework or a custom assembly, use the from Namespace import type syntax, which is roughly equivalent to a C# using declaration. The namespace in the C# source code is Python ToCS and the code uses that to import a reference to Report and InventoryItem. It also uses the System namespace to get a reference to the Decimal type, which aliases the C# decimal type.

In Python, whenever you use square brackets, [], you're creating a data structure called a list. It's a collection of objects with Python semantics. In this example, we're creating a list of InventoryItem, assigning it to a variable named inventory.

Notice we're using Decimal for the last parameter, itemPrice, of the InventoryItem constructor. Python doesn't have a concept of decimal and will pass that value as a float, which causes an error because the C# InventoryItem defines that parameter as a decimal.

Next, the Python code instantiates Report, rpt, and calls GenerateDynamic, passing inventory. This calls the GenerateDynamic in Report and automatically translates inventory from a Python list into a C# dynamic[], items. Because each object in items is dynamic, we can query it using a LINQ statement, accessing the names of each object dynamically in the projection.

Finally, GenerateDynamically calls Generate, the application returns a report, and the Python code prints the report.

See Also

Recipe 5.2, "Accessing Type Members with Reflection"

Recipe 5.9, "Calling Python Code from C#"

CHAPTER 6

Programming Asynchronously

It used to be that most of the code anyone wrote was synchronous. Things like concurrency, thread pools, and parallel programming were the domain of specialized experts who sometimes still got it wrong. Historical internet forums, UseNet, and even books were full of warnings to not try multithreading unless you know what you're doing and have a strong requirement for it. However, that's changed.

In 2010, Microsoft introduced the Task Parallel Library (TPL), which made it a lot easier to write multithreaded code. This coincided with the common availability of multithread/multicore CPU architectures. One of the TPL primitives was the Task class, which represented a promise to perform some work, on a separate thread, and return the results. Interestingly, PLINQ, which is covered in Recipe 4.10, shipped in the same time frame. TPL is still an important part of the developer's toolkit for in-process CPU-intensive multithreading.

Building on the concepts of Task, from TPL, Microsoft introduced async via specialized language syntax in C# 4. While we had asynchronous programming since C# 1, through delegates, it was more complex and less efficient. In C# 5, async simplified this by introducing the async/await keywords and making the code and its order of execution very similar to synchronous code. In addition to simplification, a primary use case for C# async is out-of-process communication, as opposed to where TPL shines for in-process CPU intensive work. When going out-of-process, think about accessing the file system, making a database query, or calling a REST API. Behind the scenes, async manages the threads for these operations so they don't block and improves application performance and scalability. With async, we could reason about our logic in a simple way and still have the benefits and sophistication of asynchronous operation.

Since its introduction, Microsoft has continued to improve async, both via language features and .NET Framework libraries. This chapter covers these new features, such as async `Main` methods, the new `ValueTask` type, async iterators, and async disposal. There are also original capabilities of async that deserve special attention, such as writing safe async libraries, managing concurrent async tasks, cancellation, and progress reporting.

The theme of this chapter is checkout, where a customer has products in their shopping cart, they've started the checkout process, and the code needs to process each checkout request. We'll start with the proper way to use async with console applications.

6.1 Creating Async Console Applications

Problem

You need to use a library in a console application, but it only has an async API.

Solution

This class has async methods:

```
public class CheckoutService
{
    public async Task<string> StartAsync()
    {
        await ValidateAddressAsync();
        await ValidateCreditAsync();
        await GetShoppingCartAsync();
        await FinalizeCheckoutAsync();

        return "Checkout Complete";
    }

    async Task ValidateAddressAsync()
    {
        // perform address validation
    }

    async Task ValidateCreditAsync()
    {
        // ensure credit is good
    }

    async Task GetShoppingCartAsync()
    {
        // get contents of shopping cart
    }

    async Task FinalizeCheckoutAsync()
    {
```

```
        // complete checkout transaction
    }
}
```

Here's the old way to write an async console app:

```
class Program
{
    static void Main(string[] args)
    {
        var checkoutSvc = new CheckoutService();
        string result = string.Empty;

        Task<string> startedTask = checkoutSvc.StartAsync();
        startedTask.Wait();
        result = startedTask.Result;

        Console.WriteLine($"Result: {result}");
    }
}
```

Here's the new recommended way to write an async console app:

```
static async Task Main()
{
    var checkoutSvc = new CheckoutService();

    string result = await checkoutSvc.StartAsync();

    Console.WriteLine($"Result: {result}");
}
```

Discussion

When first introduced, async was nearly everywhere and immediately useful. Still, there were edge cases, such as Main methods and catch and finally blocks, where async couldn't be used. Fortunately, Microsoft fixed this in C# 7.1 and added more support in other parts of the .NET Framework that were lacking, for instance, async ActionResult in ASP.NET MVC. Recipe 6.3 shows how async iterators solve another async problem.

A prominent async addition, described in this section, is async Main. The problem was that, just like the CheckoutService class in the solution, many .NET Framework types and third-party libraries were written for async. However, without async Main, developers had to write problematic code. To demonstrate the problem, the solution includes two versions of a Main method: the old synchronous way and the new async approach.

With the old synchronous technique, developers were forced to use Wait() and Result, which are typical async antipatterns because of thread blocking and potential thread deadlocks and race conditions. Recipe 6.4 explains a scenario where writing code like this can cause a deadlock (and how to avoid it). These are members of the `Task` type, which async methods return. Unfortunately, this was the only choice in the first iteration of async if you wanted to write a command-line utility, text-based app, or demo app.

The second `Main` in the solution shows the new syntax, with the `async` modifier and the `Task` return type. All we have to do is `await` the call to `checkoutSvc.Start Async()` and the code works fine.

As you know, `Main` can return `void` or `int`. The solution example with `Task` is for a `void` return. You can change that to `Task<int>` for an `int` return.

Essentially, Microsoft hasn't recommended a safe way to call from synchronous code into asynchronous code. So this was a welcome addition that makes it much easier to write console apps that call async code. Also, notice that the entire call chain, from `Main` to `CheckoutService.StartAsync` and to other `CheckoutService` methods, is all async. Ideally, the entire call chain is async, but occasionally you will have an async method that only calls synchronous methods; you can learn more about that in Recipe 6.6.

See Also

Recipe 6.3, "Creating Async Iterators"

Recipe 6.4, "Writing Safe Async Libraries"

Recipe 6.6, "Calling Synchronous Code from Async Code"

6.2 Reducing Memory Allocations for Async Return Values

Problem

You want to reduce memory consumption for your async code.

Solution

Here's how to use `ValueTask` instead of `Task` in async methods:

```
public class CheckoutService
{
    public async ValueTask<string> StartAsync()
    {
```

```
        await ValidateAddressAsync();
        await ValidateCreditAsync();
        await GetShoppingCartAsync();
        await FinalizeCheckoutAsync();

        return "Checkout Complete";
    }

    async ValueTask ValidateAddressAsync()
    {
        // perform address validation
    }

    async ValueTask ValidateCreditAsync()
    {
        // ensure credit is good
    }

    async ValueTask GetShoppingCartAsync()
    {
        // get contents of shopping cart
    }

    async ValueTask FinalizeCheckoutAsync()
    {
        // complete checkout transaction
    }
}
```

And here's the app that consumes that class:

```
class Program
{
    static async Task Main()
    {
        var checkoutSvc = new CheckoutService();

        string result = await checkoutSvc.StartAsync();

        Console.WriteLine($"Result: {result}");
    }
}
```

Discussion

Since the beginning of async, we've returned types by either Task or Task<T>. That has always worked and will continue to work fine for any async code. Over time, though, people identified specific circumstances that open new performance opportunities concerning the fact that Task is a reference type and the runtime caches Tasks.

The Task class, by definition, is a reference type. That means the runtime allocates heap memory every time an async method returns a Task. As you know, value types allocate memory where they are defined, but they don't cause garbage collector overhead.

Perhaps not as obvious, another feature of Tasks is that the runtime caches them. Rather than await a method, it's possible to reference the returned Task from an async method. With that Task reference, you can perform concurrent invocations on multiple tasks. You could also invoke that task more than once. The important point here is that the runtime has cached the task, resulting in more memory usage.

As mentioned, in normal coding a Task works fine and you might not care. However, think about high-performance scenarios where a lot of Task objects get allocated and you are interested in finding ways to improve performance and scalability. The solution simulates a concept where this might matter. Imagine a business that needs to process a high volume of shopping cart checkouts each day. In that case, eliminating any overhead for object allocation, garbage collection, and memory pressure could be beneficial.

To address these concerns, Microsoft added support for ValueTask (and Value Task<T>) as async return types. As its name suggests, ValueTask is a value type. Because it's a value type, the only memory allocation it incurs is wherever the value resides, on the stack in this case. By definition of a value type, there isn't any unique heap allocation or garbage collection just for that value.

Further, the runtime does not cache ValueType, resulting in less memory allocation and cache management. This works great in high-performance/scalability scenarios. The CheckoutService in the solution demonstrates how to use ValueTask: just use it in place of Task. The assumption here is that the code will always await the method and never try to reuse the ValueTask. In the solution, that's exactly what happens.

 If you're writing a reusable library for other developers, consider whether ValueTask is appropriate. By using ValueTask, you eliminate the ability of consuming code to perform concurrent task operations or any other advanced scenarios for where a Task is more appropriate. Task gives the most flexibility in this case.

As is with most things, there's a trade-off. All of the scenarios for which the runtime Task cache were useful are no longer options for ValueTask. With ValueTask, you can't combine operations or reuse a ValueTask after the first time. Recipes 6.7 and 6.8 show a couple of scenarios where ValueTask doesn't work.

To recap, use ValueTask when performance and scalability are a concern, and you're free to use Task any other time.

See Also

Recipe 6.7, "Waiting for Parallel Tasks to Complete"

Recipe 6.8, "Handling Parallel Tasks as They Complete"

6.3 Creating Async Iterators

Problem

You're working with async code and a classical synchronous iterator won't work.

Solution

Here's the data for the checkout process:

```
public class CheckoutRequest
{
    public Guid ShoppingCartID { get; set; }

    public string Name { get; set; }

    public string Card { get; set; }

    public string Address { get; set; }
}
```

This is the checkout process for each request:

```
public class CheckoutService
{
    public async ValueTask<string> StartAsync(CheckoutRequest request)
    {
        return
            $"Checkout Complete for Shopping " +
            $"Basket: {request.ShoppingCartID}";
    }
}
```

The async iterator processes each request:

```
public class CheckoutStream
{
    public async IAsyncEnumerable<CheckoutRequest> GetRequestsAsync()
    {
        while (true)
        {
            IEnumerable<CheckoutRequest> requests =
                await GetNextBatchAsync();

            foreach (var request in requests)
                yield return request;
```

```
                    await Task.Delay(1000);
            }
        }

        async Task<IEnumerable<CheckoutRequest>> GetNextBatchAsync()
        {
            return new List<CheckoutRequest>
            {
                new CheckoutRequest
                {
                    ShoppingCartID = Guid.NewGuid(),
                    Address = "123 4th St",
                    Card = "1234 5678 9012 3456",
                    Name = "First Card Name"
                },
                new CheckoutRequest
                {
                    ShoppingCartID = Guid.NewGuid(),
                    Address = "789 1st Ave",
                    Card = "2345 6789 0123 4567",
                    Name = "Second Card Name"
                },
                new CheckoutRequest
                {
                    ShoppingCartID = Guid.NewGuid(),
                    Address = "123 4th St",
                    Card = "1234 5678 9012 3456",
                    Name = "First Card Name"
                },
            };
        }
    }
```

Finally, the application consumes the iterator to process each request:

```
    static async Task Main()
    {
        var checkoutSvc = new CheckoutService();
        var checkoutStrm = new CheckoutStream();

        await foreach (var request in checkoutStrm.GetRequestsAsync())
        {
            string result = await checkoutSvc.StartAsync(request);

            Console.WriteLine($"Result: {result}");
        }
    }
```

Discussion

While iterators are essential for .NET Framework collections like List<T> or a custom collection you've written, they can also be useful abstractions that hide complex data acquisition logic. The solution demonstrates a related scenario where an iterator might be useful—processing a stream of CheckoutRequests as if it were a collection.

An important aspect of the solution is that it's impractical to hold too many Checkout Request instances in memory. If a system continuously receives orders, it needs to scale. In the solution, we imagine a polling implementation that continuously gets the next batch of CheckoutRequests. This reduces memory pressure and the iterator provides an abstraction that hides the complex details of how the program receives orders.

In the early days of async, it would have been more complex to perform a task like this because the polling is asynchronous, making an out-of-process request. It's clearly possible to find a library that lets this happen synchronously, but that ignores the benefit of async. The solution solves this problem with a newer interface for async streams, IAsyncEnumerable.

The CheckoutStream class has an iterator named GetRequestsAsync, returning IAsyncEnumerable<CheckoutRequest>. This is the async equivalent of the IEnumerable<T> for synchronous iterators. Although the while loop continues forever in this demo and you'll need to manually stop the app, Recipe 6.9 shows how to cancel the process gracefully. This iterator gets a new batch of CheckoutRequests, yields each item in the batch, and sleeps for a second before getting the next batch. The sleep, Task.Delay, is for demo purposes so you can see the output.

 The yield keyword is syntactic sugar to help turn type members into iterators. IEnumerable<T> types, including IAsyncEnumerable <T>, have MoveNext and Current members, where MoveNext loads Current with the next value it reads. Behind the scenes, when the C# compiler sees an iterator, it generates a new class with the Move Next and Current members. When invoking yield, such as in yield return request in GetRequestsAsync, the C# compiler instantiates that new class, calls MoveNext, and returns Current.

The GetNextBatchAsync method only returns a list of CheckoutRequests. However, imagine that this is really an async call to a network endpoint, queue, or service bus that has the next set of CheckoutRequest instances ready. Recipes 1.9, 3.7, and 3.9 demonstrate some of the issues you'll care about when doing this. By moving all this complexity into the iterator, application code can consume data in a much simpler manner.

The Main method shows how to consume an async iterator. The first thing to notice is the `async` modifier on the `foreach` loop. This was a new addition to C# for async streams. As you can see, it allows `foreach` to work with an `IAsyncEnumerable<T>` iterator.

See Also

Recipe 1.9, "Designing a Custom Exception"

Recipe 3.7, "Rethrowing Exceptions"

Recipe 3.9, "Building Resilient Network Connections"

Recipe 6.9, "Cancelling Async Operations"

6.4 Writing Safe Async Libraries

Problem

Your async code is causing a deadlock with the UI thread.

Solution

This class marshals the code off of the UI thread:

```
public class CheckoutService
{
    public async Task<string> StartAsync()
    {
        await ValidateAddressAsync().ConfigureAwait(false);
        await ValidateCreditAsync().ConfigureAwait(false);
        await GetShoppingCartAsync().ConfigureAwait(false);
        await FinalizeCheckoutAsync().ConfigureAwait(false);

        return "Checkout Complete";
    }

    async Task ValidateAddressAsync()
    {
        // perform address validation
    }

    async Task ValidateCreditAsync()
    {
        // ensure credit is good
    }

    async Task GetShoppingCartAsync()
    {
        // get contents of shopping cart
```

```
        }

    async Task FinalizeCheckoutAsync()
    {
        // complete checkout transaction
    }
}
```

Here's the program that calls it:

```
static async Task Main()
{
    var checkoutSvc = new CheckoutService();

    string result = await checkoutSvc.StartAsync();

    Console.WriteLine($"Result: {result}");
}
```

Discussion

UI technology such as Windows Forms, Windows Presentation Foundation (WPF), and WinUI run on a single thread—the UI thread. This simplifies the work a developer needs to do when working with UI code. However, if you're using async or writing multithreaded logic, it's easy for things to go wrong. In particular, if another thread attempts to do anything with the UI or run in the same logic of the UI thread, you run the risk of race conditions and deadlocks. To understand how bad the problem can be, consider that your application often runs perfectly in the development, QA, and production environments. Then, without notice, the UI locks up, customers begin to complain, and you can't reproduce the problem.

 In some cases, depending on the UI you're using and the .NET version, you might get an exception like the following when accessing the UI from a non-UI thread:

```
System.InvalidOperationException:
    'The calling thread cannot access this object
    because a different thread owns it.'
```

This is good because at least you know there's a problem.

Recipe 6.1 explained how calling Wait or assigning Result on a Task could cause a deadlock. The problem here occurs because Wait and Result block the UI thread, waiting on a response. The called async code executes, returns, and tries to run on the same thread. However, as just mentioned, the UI thread is blocked, causing a deadlock.

The solution fixes this problem in the CheckoutService.StartAsync method. Notice how it calls ConfigureAwait(false)—the only difference between this code and the solution in Recipe 6.1. What this does is marshal execution off of the calling thread (the UI thread) and onto a new thread. Now, when the thread returns from the async call, it won't cause a deadlock.

ConfigureAwait(true) is the default condition when awaiting a Task. Changing this default is only needed in advanced scenarios that are out of the scope of practical everyday engineering. If you ever see it in code, it might be good to question why someone needed it.

A significant point to be made here is that the problem statement clearly says *libraries*. When writing a library, you want the code to work regardless of what code called it. Therefore, the library code must be independent and unaware of who the caller is. This is an example, as stated in Recipe 1.5, where separation of concerns is important. If the library code doesn't manipulate the UI, which it never should, you'll avoid threading problems like race conditions and deadlocks.

It's important to note that if one await is on ConfigureAwait(false), all awaits in a method should be also. The reason is that some methods execute so quickly that they execute synchronously, and ConfigureAwait(false) doesn't marshal the thread. If another await then runs asynchronously, without ConfigureAwait(false), you'll have the same threading problems as if ConfigureAwait(false) was never called.

Visual Studio analyzers set warnings on all non-UI code with async calls missing ConfigureAwait(false). It might be tedious to add these, but you still should. Even if you think the first await of a method is guaranteed to run asynchronously, logic changes over time with maintenance, and you might inadvertently cause threading problems. It's safer to leave this analyzer enabled and follow the recommendations.

Another benefit of ConfigureAwait(false) is that it slightly improves efficiency. The default, ConfigureAwait(true), incurs overhead for setting up a callback that marshals the completed thread onto the UI thread. ConfigureAwait(false) avoids this.

Going back to the point about ConfigureAwait(false) being appropriate for library code, there are times when you don't want to use it. More specifically, you don't want to call ConfigureAwait(false) in UI code, in particular event handlers. Think about an event handler and what it does. It gets called in response to some user action, like a button click, and it sets status, updates waiting indicators, disables controls that the user shouldn't interact with, makes the call, and afterward resets the UI. All of this work is happening on the UI thread, as it should. In this case, you don't want to marshal off the UI thread with `ConfigureAwait(false)` because that will cause multithreaded UI problems.

Although library code should never know about a UI, there are times when the code should communicate progress or status. Rather than accessing UI code directly, there's another way to communicate status, as discussed in the next section.

See Also

Recipe 1.5, "Designing Application Layers"

Recipe 6.5, "Updating Progress Asynchronously"

6.5 Updating Progress Asynchronously

Problem

You need to display the status from an async task without blocking the UI thread.

Solution

This class holds progress status info:

```
public class CheckoutRequestProgress
{
    public int Total { get; set; }

    public string Message { get; set; }
}
```

This method reports progress:

```
public async IAsyncEnumerable<CheckoutRequest>
    GetRequestsAsync(IProgress<CheckoutRequestProgress> progress)
{
    int total = 0;

    while (true)
    {
        List<CheckoutRequest> requests =
            await GetNextBatchAsync().ConfigureAwait(false);

        total += requests.Count;

        foreach (var request in requests)
            yield return request;

        progress.Report(
            new CheckoutRequestProgress
            {
```

```
                    Total = total,
                    Message = "New Batch of Checkout Requests"
            });

        await Task.Delay(1000).ConfigureAwait(false);
    }
}
```

Here's the program that initializes and consumes progress updates:

```
static async Task Main()
{
    var checkoutSvc = new CheckoutService();
    var checkoutStrm = new CheckoutStream();

    IProgress<CheckoutRequestProgress> progress =
        new Progress<CheckoutRequestProgress>(p =>
        {
            Console.WriteLine(
                $"\n" +
                $"Total: {p.Total}, " +
                $"{p.Message}" +
                $"\n");
        });

    await foreach (var request in
        checkoutStrm.GetRequestsAsync(progress))
    {
        string result = await checkoutSvc.StartAsync(request);

        Console.WriteLine($"Result: {result}");
    }
}
```

Discussion

As explained in Recipe 6.4, library code should never update the UI directly. If properly written, it will be running on a separate thread and be oblivious to who its caller is. That said, there are times when the business layer or library code might want to inform a caller of progress or status. The solution shows a situation where an iterator updates the UI with progress, defined in the CheckoutRequestProgress class. Essentially, the library code defines what type of progress information it offers and the calling code works with that. In this case, it's the total number of orders processed and some message indicating status.

The GetRequestAsync method accepts a parameter of IProgress<CheckoutRequest Progress>, progress. The IProgress<T> is part of the .NET Framework, as is the Progress<T> class, which implements IProgress<T>. With the progress instance, GetRequestsAsync calls Report, passing an instance of CheckoutRequestProgress with populated properties. This sends the progress to a handler in the UI.

The `Main` method sets up reporting by instantiating a `Progress<CheckoutRequest Progress>` and assigning it to `progress`, an `IProgress<CheckoutRequestProgress>`. The `Progress<T>` constructor accepts an `Action` delegate, and `Main` assigns a lambda that writes progress to the console. Every time `GetRequestsAsync` calls `Report`, this lambda executes. Going full circle, `Main` passes `progress` as an argument to the `Get RequestsAsync` call, so it can reference the same object to report on.

You might have noticed that `GetRequestAsync` is running asynchronously, and the `await` on `GetNextBatchAsync` and `Task.Delay` also call `ConfigureAwait(false)`. If that code runs on another thread, other than the UI thread, what's the possibility of a deadlock? None, because `Progress<T>` marshals the call back onto the UI thread so the code can safely interact with the UI. Remember, the library code, `GetRequests Async`, has no knowledge of the lambda argument for the `Process<T>` constructor's `Action` parameter. That means the lambda can safely access any UI code as necessary for displaying progress.

See Also

Recipe 6.4, "Writing Safe Async Libraries"

6.6 Calling Synchronous Code from Async Code

Problem

The only code inside your async method is synchronous and you want to `await` it asynchronously.

Solution

This class demonstrates how to return asynchronous results from synchronous logic:

```
public class CheckoutService
{
    public async Task<string> StartAsync()
    {
        await ValidateAddressAsync().ConfigureAwait(false);
        await ValidateCreditAsync().ConfigureAwait(false);
        await GetShoppingCartAsync().ConfigureAwait(false);
        await FinalizeCheckoutAsync().ConfigureAwait(false);

        return "Checkout Complete";
    }

    async Task<bool> ValidateAddressAsync()
    {
        bool result = true;
        return await Task.FromResult(result);
```

```
        }

        async Task<bool> ValidateCreditAsync()
        {
            bool result = true;
            return await Task.FromResult(result);
        }

        async Task<bool> GetShoppingCartAsync()
        {
            bool result = true;
            return await Task.FromResult(result);
        }

        async Task FinalizeCheckoutAsync()
        {
            await Task.CompletedTask;
        }
    }
```

This is the code that runs the app:

```
static async Task Main()
{
    var checkoutSvc = new CheckoutService();

    string result = await checkoutSvc.StartAsync();

    Console.WriteLine($"Result: {result}");
}
```

Discussion

For simplicity, previous sections of this chapter call synchronous code from asynchronous code. One of the things you might have noticed is that Visual Studio (same as other IDEs) shows green squiggly underlines when an async method doesn't await anything. You'll also receive the following warning:

```
CS1998: This async method lacks 'await' operators
and will run synchronously.
Consider using the 'await' operator to await non-blocking API calls,
or 'await Task.Run(...)' to do CPU-bound work on a background thread.
```

It's good the compiler emits this warning because it could be an error. It's possible you forgot to add the await modifier to an async method call. In that case, program execution doesn't stop at the awaited method. Both the async method and the code that calls it run. The async method that wasn't awaited might not complete if the program exits.

Another problem is that if the async method that wasn't awaited throws an exception, it won't be caught because the calling code continued to run. A similar problem happens with `async void` methods where you can't `await` them and there's no way to catch exceptions.

 A couple of places in this chapter describe compiler warnings associated with async code. In a lot of circumstances, these warnings represent error conditions. Too often, I've encountered applications with unmanageable warning walls. It's as if the developers somehow don't believe warnings are a problem or aren't paying attention. Understanding the implications of how a warning could be serious, especially accidentally forgetting to `await` an async method or failing to add `ConfigureAwait(false)`, as described in Recipe 6.4, might provide the motivation to prioritize cleaning up and maintaining warnings.

Sometimes the code inside of an async method is genuinely synchronous. It might have originally been async but changed in maintenance, or you have to implement an interface. In this case, you have a couple of approaches. One is to remove the `async/await` keywords in the call chain until you reach a higher-level method that requires async. If there are multiple callers awaiting that method or it's part of a public interface for multiple applications, you might not want to do that refactoring right away. The other approach, demonstrated in the solution, is to `await Task.FromResult<T>`.

You can see how this works in the `CheckoutService`, for `StartAsync`, where each method returns the result of awaiting `Task.FromResult<T>`. The `Task.FromResult<T>` method is generic, so you can use it on any type.

Awaiting `Task.FromResult<T>` works when the method needs to return a value. However, the `FinalizeTaskAsync` method only returns `Task`. Notice how that method simply awaits `Task.CompletedTask`.

One of the things you might be thinking is that this is extra work just to get rid of a warning. While that's true, consider the benefits. You do clear the warning and enjoy the productivity boost in keeping the warning wall trimmed. More importantly, the code explicitly states its intention, and developers doing maintenance will clearly see there isn't an error from a missing `await`—the code is correct.

See Also

Recipe 6.4, "Writing Safe Async Libraries"

6.7 Waiting for Parallel Tasks to Complete

Problem

You have multiple tasks, running in parallel, and need to wait for all of them to complete before continuing.

Solution

This code runs parallel tasks:

```
public class CheckoutService
{
    class WhenAllResult
    {
        public bool IsValidAddress { get; set; }
        public bool IsValidCredit { get; set; }
        public bool HasShoppingCart { get; set; }
    }

    public async Task<string> StartAsync()
    {
        var checkoutTasks =
            new List<Task<(string, bool)>>
            {
                ValidateAddressAsync(),
                ValidateCreditAsync(),
                GetShoppingCartAsync()
            };

        Task<(string method, bool result)[]> allTasks =
            Task.WhenAll(checkoutTasks);

        if (allTasks.IsCompletedSuccessfully)
        {
            WhenAllResult whenAllResult = GetResultsAsync(allTasks);

            await FinalizeCheckoutAsync(whenAllResult);

            return "Checkout Complete";
        }
        else
        {
            throw allTasks.Exception;
        }
    }

    WhenAllResult GetResultsAsync(
        Task<(string method, bool result)[]> allTasks)
    {
        var whenAllResult = new WhenAllResult();
```

```
        foreach (var (method, result) in allTasks.Result)
            switch (method)
            {
                case nameof(ValidateAddressAsync):
                    whenAllResult.IsValidAddress = result;
                    break;
                case nameof(ValidateCreditAsync):
                    whenAllResult.IsValidCredit = result;
                    break;
                case nameof(GetShoppingCartAsync):
                    whenAllResult.HasShoppingCart = result;
                    break;
            }

        return whenAllResult;
}

async Task<(string, bool)> ValidateAddressAsync()
{
    //throw new ArgumentException("Testing!");

    return await Task.FromResult(
        (nameof(ValidateAddressAsync), true));
}

async Task<(string, bool)> ValidateCreditAsync()
{
    return await Task.FromResult(
        (nameof(ValidateCreditAsync), true));
}

async Task<(string, bool)> GetShoppingCartAsync()
{
    return await Task.FromResult(
        (nameof(GetShoppingCartAsync), true));
}

async Task<bool> FinalizeCheckoutAsync(WhenAllResult result)
{
    Console.WriteLine(
        $"{nameof(WhenAllResult.IsValidAddress)}: " +
        $"{result.IsValidAddress}");
    Console.WriteLine(
        $"{nameof(WhenAllResult.IsValidCredit)}: " +
        $"{result.IsValidCredit}");
    Console.WriteLine(
        $"{nameof(WhenAllResult.HasShoppingCart)}: " +
        $"{result.HasShoppingCart}");

    bool success = true;
    return await Task.FromResult(success);
```

```
        }
    }
```

Here's the app that requests and handles parallel task results:

```
static async Task Main()
{
    try
    {
        var checkoutSvc = new CheckoutService();

        string result = await checkoutSvc.StartAsync();

        Console.WriteLine($"Result: {result}");
    }
    catch (AggregateException aEx)
    {
        foreach (var ex in aEx.InnerExceptions)
            Console.WriteLine($"Unable to complete: {ex}");
    }
}
```

Discussion

When performing an action, such as shopping cart checkout, you don't want the user to wait too long for the app to return. Running too many operations sequentially can make the wait longer. One of the ways to improve that user experience is to run independent operations concurrently.

In the solution, the CheckoutService has four different async services. Here we assume that three of those operations, ValidateAddress Async, ValidateCredit Async, and GetShoppingCartAsync, don't have any dependencies on each other. This makes them good candidates for running at the same time.

The StartAsync method does this by creating a List<Task>. If you recall, awaiting a method is really an await on the returned Task. Without the await, each method returns a Task, but its logic doesn't run until that task is awaited.

The Task class has a WhenAll method, whose purpose is to run all of the tasks, specified by the checkoutTasks argument, concurrently. WhenAll waits until all of the Tasks complete before returning.

Awaiting a single method with a return type is straightforward from the perspective that you assign the return value to a single variable. However, when running tasks concurrently, you need to correlate responses because WhenAll returns all tasks at the same time. Making an assumption about which tasks occur in which position of the collection could be error prone and cumbersome in maintenance. The code needs to know which response goes with which Task.

The solution does this via a tuple, where the string is the name of the method and bool is the response. The tuple and choice of contents was specific for this demo, and you would shape the task type in whatever way that makes sense for your app. This lets us know which task goes with which result. The GetResultsAsync method does this by iterating through the task array, and building the WhenAllResult, based on the method parameter of each response.

Notice that the first line of ValidateAddressAsync is a commented statement that throws an ArgumentException. Uncommenting and running the app again results in an exception during the call to WhenAll. The Main method handles that exception with a catch on AggregateException. Since all tasks are running concurrently, one or more of them could throw an exception. The AggregateException collects those exceptions. Normally, you would look in the InnerException property for exception details. However, AggregateException has another property, InnerExceptions. The difference is that the AggregateException property is plural, which is intentional. For proper debugging, you can find all exceptions in the InnerExceptions property.

See Also

Recipe 6.8, "Handling Parallel Tasks as They Complete"

6.8 Handling Parallel Tasks as They Complete

Problem

You thought calling Task.WhenAny would be an efficient use of resources for processing results as they complete, but cost and performance are terrible.

Solution

This is a sequential implementation for calling multiple tasks:

```
public async Task<string> StartBigONAsync()
{
    (_, bool addressResult) = await ValidateAddressAsync();
    (_, bool creditResult) = await ValidateCreditAsync();
    (_, bool cartResult) = await GetShoppingCartAsync();

    await FinalizeCheckoutAsync(
        new AllTasksResult
        {
            IsValidAddress = addressResult,
            IsValidCredit = creditResult,
            HasShoppingCart = cartResult
        });
```

```
        return "Checkout Complete";
    }
```

Here's a parallel implementation for calling multiple tasks:

```
public async Task<string> StartBigO1Async()
{
    var checkoutTasks =
        new List<Task<(string, bool)>>
        {
            ValidateAddressAsync(),
            ValidateCreditAsync(),
            GetShoppingCartAsync()
        };

    Task<(string method, bool result)[]> allTasks =
        Task.WhenAll(checkoutTasks);

    if (allTasks.IsCompletedSuccessfully)
    {
        AllTasksResult allResult = GetResults(allTasks);

        await FinalizeCheckoutAsync(allResult);

        return "Checkout Complete";
    }
    else
    {
        throw allTasks.Exception;
    }
}
```

The next implementation processes tasks in parallel but handles each one as it
returns:

```
public async Task<string> StartBigONSquaredAsync()
{
    var checkoutTasks =
        new List<Task<(string, bool)>>
        {
            ValidateAddressAsync(),
            ValidateCreditAsync(),
            GetShoppingCartAsync()
        };

    var allResult = new AllTasksResult();

    while (checkoutTasks.Any())
    {
        Task<(string, bool)> task = await Task.WhenAny(checkoutTasks);
        checkoutTasks.Remove(task);

        GetResult(task, allResult);
```

```
        }

        await FinalizeCheckoutAsync(allResult);

        return "Checkout Complete";
    }
```

This method shows how to get the first task that completes:

```
    async Task<(string method, bool result)> ValidateCreditAsync()
    {
        var checkoutTasks =
            new List<Task<(string, bool)>>
            {
                CheckInternalCreditAsync(),
                CheckAgency1CreditAsync(),
                CheckAgency2CreditAsync()
            };

        Task<(string, bool)> task = await Task.WhenAny(checkoutTasks);

        (_, bool result) = task.Result;

        return await Task.FromResult(
            (nameof(ValidateCreditAsync), result));
    }
```

The Main method offers a choice of which method to start with:

```
    static async Task Main()
    {
        try
        {
            var checkoutSvc = new CheckoutService();

            string result = await checkoutSvc.StartBigO1Async();
            //string result = await checkoutSvc.StartBigONAsync();
            //string result = await checkoutSvc.StartBigONSquaredAsync();

            Console.WriteLine($"Result: {result}");
        }
        catch (AggregateException aEx)
        {
            foreach (var ex in aEx.InnerExceptions)
                Console.WriteLine($"Unable to complete: {ex}");
        }
    }
```

Discussion

The problem in this section explores the role of Task.WhenAny. If you try to use Task.WhenAny for processing tasks as they return, you might be surprised because it doesn't work the way you expect.

For the most part, the concept and organization of this solution operates similar to Recipe 6.7—the difference being that this solution shows different ways to run tasks and explains what you need to know to make the proper design decisions.

The StartBigONAsync method operates like previous sections of this chapter that ran sequentially. Its performance is O(N) because it processes N tasks, one after the other.

Recipe 6.7 showed how to speed up program execution when tasks don't depend on each other. It uses Task.WhenAll, shown in StartBigO1Async. The performance boost comes from its approximately O(1) performance—instead of performing N operations, it does 1. To be more accurate, this is O(2) because FinalizeCheckout Async runs after the other three complete.

In addition to Task.WhenAll, you can use Task.WhenAny. It might be natural to think that Task.WhenAny is a good way to run multiple tasks in parallel and then be able to process each task while the others are running. However, Task.WhenAny doesn't work the way you think it does. Look at StartBigONSquaredAsync and follow the following logic:

1. The while loop iterates as long as checkoutTasks still has contents.
2. Task.WhenAny starts all of the tasks in parallel.
3. The fastest task returns.
4. Since that task returned, remove it from checkoutTasks so we don't run it again.
5. Collect the results from that task.
6. Do the loop again on the remaining tasks or stop when checkoutTasks is empty.

The first surprising mental hurdle in this algorithm is incorrectly thinking that subsequent loops operate on the same tasks, each returning as they complete. The reality is that each subsequent loop starts a brand-new set of tasks. This is how async works—you can await a task multiple times, but each await starts a new task. That means the code continuously starts new instances of remaining tasks on every loop. This looping pattern, with Task.WhenAny, doesn't result in the O(1) performance you might have expected, like with Task.WhenAll, but rather $O(N^2)$. This solution only has three tasks, but imagine how performance would increasingly suffer as the task list grows.

This chapter discusses performance with Big O notation. Especially when looking at algorithms that are O(N²), there's a threshold of when too many operations ruin performance. Recipe 3.10 shows how to measure application performance and find what that threshold is, based on your performance requirements.

To pile on, take that number of tasks and multiply it by the number of checkout operations that occur over a period of time. Not only would your application performance be bad, you might slow down servers with excessive network traffic and endpoint server processing. This might affect not only your own system, but other systems running concurrently too. Also, think about times when those network requests might be to cloud services on a consumption plan and how expensive that would get. This particular use case might be considered an antipattern, unless it's used with a small number of tasks where the impact is minimal.

On the internet, you'll find articles explaining Task.WhenAny as a technique for running tasks in parallel and processing each as they complete. While that might work for a few tasks, this section explains the hazards of using Task.WhenAny for that use case.

That said, there is a use case where Task.WhenAny is effective—first task wins. In the solution, there's a ValidateCreditAsync method showing this strategy. The scenario is that you have multiple sources to learn if a customer has good credit and a response from any one of those sources is reliable. Each service has different performance characteristics and you're only interested in the one that returns first. You can discard the rest. This keeps performance at O(1).

ValidateCreditAsync has a list of tasks to run. Task.WhenAny runs those tasks in parallel and the first task to complete comes back. The code processes that task and returns.

The side effect in this solution is that tasks other than the first that returned continue running. However, you don't have access to them because only one task is returned. For this scenario, you don't care about those tasks but should stop them to avoid using more resources than necessary. You can learn how to do that in the next section on cancelling tasks.

See Also

Recipe 3.10, "Measuring Performance"

Recipe 6.7, "Waiting for Parallel Tasks to Complete"

Recipe 6.9, "Cancelling Async Operations"

6.9 Cancelling Async Operations

Problem

You have an async process in progress and need to stop it.

Solution

This class demonstrates multiple ways to cancel tasks:

```
public class CheckoutStream
{
    CancellationToken cancelToken;

    public CheckoutStream(CancellationToken cancelToken)
    {
        this.cancelToken = cancelToken;
    }

    public async IAsyncEnumerable<CheckoutRequest> GetRequestsAsync(
        IProgress<CheckoutRequestProgress> progress)
    {
        int total = 0;

        while (true)
        {
            var requests = new List<CheckoutRequest>();

            try
            {
                requests = await GetNextBatchAsync();
            }
            catch (OperationCanceledException)
            {
                break;
            }

            total += requests.Count;

            foreach (var request in requests)
            {
                if (cancelToken.IsCancellationRequested)
                    break;

                yield return request;
            }

            progress.Report(
                new CheckoutRequestProgress
                {
                    Total = total,
```

```csharp
                    Message = "New Batch of Checkout Requests"
                });


            if (cancelToken.IsCancellationRequested)
                break;

            await Task.Delay(1000);
        }

        if (cancelToken.IsCancellationRequested)
            progress.Report(
                new CheckoutRequestProgress
                {
                    Total = total,
                    Message = "Process Cancelled!"
                });
    }

    async Task<List<CheckoutRequest>> GetNextBatchAsync()
    {
        if (cancelToken.IsCancellationRequested)
            throw new OperationCanceledException();

        var requests = new List<CheckoutRequest>
        {
            new CheckoutRequest
            {
                ShoppingCartID = Guid.NewGuid(),
                Address = "123 4th St",
                Card = "1234 5678 9012 3456",
                Name = "First Card Name"
            },
            new CheckoutRequest
            {
                ShoppingCartID = Guid.NewGuid(),
                Address = "789 1st Ave",
                Card = "2345 6789 0123 4567",
                Name = "Second Card Name"
            },
            new CheckoutRequest
            {
                ShoppingCartID = Guid.NewGuid(),
                Address = "123 4th St",
                Card = "1234 5678 9012 3456",
                Name = "First Card Name"
            },
        };

        return await Task.FromResult(requests);
    }
}
```

Here's the app that initializes cancellation and shows how to cancel:

```
static async Task Main()
{
    var cancelSource = new CancellationTokenSource();
    var checkoutStrm = new CheckoutStream(cancelSource.Token);
    var checkoutSvc = new CheckoutService();

    IProgress<CheckoutRequestProgress> progress =
        new Progress<CheckoutRequestProgress>(p =>
        {
            Console.WriteLine(
                $"\n" +
                $"Total: {p.Total}, " +
                $"{p.Message}" +
                $"\n");
        });

    int count = 1;

    await foreach (var request in
        checkoutStrm.GetRequestsAsync(progress))
    {
        string result = await checkoutSvc.StartAsync(request);

        Console.WriteLine($"Result: {result}");

        if (count++ >= 10)
            break;

        if (count >= 5)
            cancelSource.Cancel();
    }
}
```

Discussion

Recipe 6.3 has an async iterator with a while loop that never ends. That worked for a demo, but real applications often need a way to stop long-running processes. Think about a dialog that pops up with ongoing process status and offers a Cancel button, allowing you to stop the operation. Task cancellation has been around since the introduction of TPL and is instrumental in cancelling async operations too.

In the solution, the Main method shows how to initialize cancellation. The Cancel lationTokenSource, cancelSource, provides both tokens and control over cancellation. See how the parameter to the CheckoutStream constructor is a CancellationToken, set via the Token property from cancelSource.

Because cancelSource can manage cancellation for all the code in its scope, you can pass a CancellationToken as a parameter to any constructors or methods with a

`CancellationToken` parameter, allowing you to cancel any operations from a single place, `cancelSource`. The solution doesn't have a button and cancels after processing 10 `CheckoutRequests`. You can see how that works with the `count` variable that's incremented in each loop, checks the number of requests, and breaks out of the loop after 10. This program never gets to 10 because of the check on `count >= 5`, calling `cancelSource.Cancel()`.

The call to `cancelSource.Cancel` sends the message that the process should be cancelled, but you still have to write code that recognizes the need to cancel. It's proper to cancel as soon as possible, and `GetRequestsAsync` has several checks on `cancelToken.IsCancellationRequested`. The `IsCancellationRequested` property is `true` when `Cancel` is called on the `CancellationTokenSource` instance that passed the `CancelToken`.

Inside the loop, `IsCancellationRequested` breaks. Outside the loop, `IsCancellationRequested` sends an `IProgress<T>` status message to let the caller know that the operation was properly cancelled.

The `GetNextBatchAsync` method shows another way to handle cancellation, by throwing an `OperationCancelledException`. If you recall, the reason a method throws is because it is unable to complete the operation it was designed to do. In this case, `GetNextBatchAsync` did not retrieve records, so this could be a semantically correct way to respond. Even if this wasn't a design decision that you would make, consider that `GetNextBatchAsync` might `await` another method, passing its `cancelToken`. When cancelled, that awaited async method could throw `OperationCancelledException`. Therefore, when handling cancellation, it's safe to anticipate and handle `OperationCancelledException`. The solution does this by wrapping the call to `GetNextBatchAsync` in a `try/catch`, breaking the loop, and letting existing code report the cancelled status to the caller.

Whenever cancelling an operation, you might also need to clean up resources. The next section, Recipe 6.10, discusses how to do that.

See Also

Recipe 6.3, "Creating Async Iterators"

Recipe 6.10, "Disposing of Async Resources"

6.10 Disposing of Async Resources

Problem

You have an async process with resources that must be disposed.

Solution

This class shows how to properly implement the async dispose pattern:

```
public class CheckoutStream : IAsyncDisposable, IDisposable
{
    CancellationTokenSource cancelSource = new CancellationTokenSource();
    CancellationToken cancelToken;
    ILogger log = new ConsoleLogger();

    FileStream asyncDisposeObj = new FileStream(
        "MyFile.txt", FileMode.OpenOrCreate, FileAccess.Write);
    HttpClient syncDisposeObj = new HttpClient();

    public CheckoutStream()
    {
        this.cancelToken = cancelSource.Token;
    }

    public async IAsyncEnumerable<CheckoutRequest> GetRequestsAsync(
        IProgress<CheckoutRequestProgress> progress)
    {
        int total = 0;

        while (true)
        {
            var requests = new List<CheckoutRequest>();

            try
            {
                requests = await GetNextBatchAsync();
            }
            catch (OperationCanceledException)
            {
                break;
            }

            total += requests.Count;

            foreach (var request in requests)
            {
                if (cancelToken.IsCancellationRequested)
                    break;

                yield return request;
            }

            progress.Report(
                new CheckoutRequestProgress
                {
                    Total = total,
                    Message = "New Batch of Checkout Requests"
```

```
            });

        if (cancelToken.IsCancellationRequested)
            break;

        await Task.Delay(1000);
    }
}

async Task<List<CheckoutRequest>> GetNextBatchAsync()
{
    if (cancelToken.IsCancellationRequested)
        throw new OperationCanceledException();

    var requests = new List<CheckoutRequest>
    {
        new CheckoutRequest
        {
            ShoppingCartID = Guid.NewGuid(),
            Address = "123 4th St",
            Card = "1234 5678 9012 3456",
            Name = "First Card Name"
        },
        new CheckoutRequest
        {
            ShoppingCartID = Guid.NewGuid(),
            Address = "789 1st Ave",
            Card = "2345 6789 0123 4567",
            Name = "Second Card Name"
        },
        new CheckoutRequest
        {
            ShoppingCartID = Guid.NewGuid(),
            Address = "123 4th St",
            Card = "1234 5678 9012 3456",
            Name = "First Card Name"
        },
    };

    return await Task.FromResult(requests);
}

public async ValueTask DisposeAsync()
{
    await DisposeAsyncCore();

    Dispose(disposing: false);
    GC.SuppressFinalize(this);
}

public void Dispose()
```

```
    {
        Dispose(disposing: true);
        GC.SuppressFinalize(this);
    }

    protected virtual void Dispose(bool disposing)
    {
        if (disposing)
        {
            syncDisposeObj?.Dispose();
            (asyncDisposeObj as IDisposable)?.Dispose();
        }

        DisposeThisObject();
    }

    protected virtual async ValueTask DisposeAsyncCore()
    {
        if (asyncDisposeObj is not null)
        {
            await asyncDisposeObj.DisposeAsync().ConfigureAwait(false);
        }

        if (syncDisposeObj is IAsyncDisposable disposable)
        {
            await disposable.DisposeAsync().ConfigureAwait(false);
        }
        else
        {
            syncDisposeObj.Dispose();
        }

        DisposeThisObject();

        await log.WriteAsync("\n\nDisposed!");
    }

    void DisposeThisObject()
    {
        cancelSource.Cancel();

        asyncDisposeObj = null;
        syncDisposeObj = null;
    }
}
```

Here's the app that demonstrates how to use an async disposable object:

```
static async Task Main()
{
    await using var checkoutStrm = new CheckoutStream();

    var checkoutSvc = new CheckoutService();
```

```
    IProgress<CheckoutRequestProgress> progress =
        new Progress<CheckoutRequestProgress>(p =>
        {
            Console.WriteLine(
                $"\n" +
                $"Total: {p.Total}, " +
                $"{p.Message}" +
                $"\n");
        });

    int count = 1;

    await foreach (var request in
        checkoutStrm.GetRequestsAsync(progress))
    {
        string result = await checkoutSvc.StartAsync(request);

        Console.WriteLine($"Result: {result}");

        if (count++ >= 10)
            break;
    }
}
```

Discussion

Recipe 1.1 describes the dispose pattern and how it solves the problem of releasing resources when an object lifetime ends. That works well for synchronous code but not for asynchronous code. This section shows how to dispose of async resources with the async dispose pattern.

In the solution, CheckoutStream has two fields: a FileStream, asyncDisposeObj, and an HttpClient, syncDisposeObj. Normally these would have names representing their purpose in the application, but in this instance, their names represent how they're used in the solution to help follow a complex set of logic. As their names suggest, asyncDisposeObj references a resource that must be disposed of asynchronously; syncDisposeObj references a resource that must be disposed of synchronously. It's important to think about both asynchronous and synchronous disposal at the same time, because it explains why their disposal processes are now intertwined.

For asynchronous and synchronous disposal, CheckoutService implements IAsync Disposable and IDisposable, respectively. As discussed in Recipe 1.1, IDisposable specifies that classes must implement Dispose, with no parameters, and we add a virtual Dispose(bool), with a bool parameter, and an optional destructor to implement the pattern. The solution doesn't implement the optional destructor. For IAsyncDis posable, CheckoutService implements the required DisposeAsync method and a virtual DisposeAsyncCore method, neither of which have parameters.

Both disposal paths, asynchronous and synchronous, could run, so they both must be prepared to release resources. On the synchronous path, `Dispose(bool)` not only calls `Dispose` on `syncDisposeObj`, but also attempts to call `Dispose` on `asyncDisposeseObj`. Notice that `Dispose(bool)` also calls `DisposeThisObject`, which holds the same code that the asynchronous path needs to call too—it reduces duplication.

While `Dispose` and `DisposeAsync` are interface members, `Dispose(bool)` and `DisposeAsyncCore` are conventions. Also notice that they're both `virtual`. This is part of the pattern, where derived classes can implement disposal by overriding these methods and calling them, via `base.Dispose(bool)` and `base.DisposeAsyncCore`, to ensure release of resources up the entire inheritance hierarchy.

Both `Dispose` and `DisposeAsync` call `Dispose(bool)`, but `DisposeAsync` sets the `disposing` argument to `false`. If you recall, `disposing` is a flag for `Dispose(bool)` to release managed resources when set to `true`. Remember that `Dispose(bool)` is the synchronous path. Instead, `DisposeAsync` calls `DisposeAsyncCore` to release asynchronous resources.

As with `Dispose(true)`, `DisposeAsyncCore` attempts to release all managed resources. The async case is obvious. However, synchronous objects have a couple of possibilities. What if the synchronous object, now or in the future, implements `IAsyncDisposable`? Then, attempting to call `DisposeAsync` is the better choice when the code is on the asynchronous path. Otherwise, call the synchronous path, with `Dispose`.

As mentioned, both `Dispose(bool)` and `DisposeAsyncCore` call `DisposeThisObject`. In the solution scenario, the `GetRequestsAsync` iterator implements cancellation, as explained in Recipe 6.9. Depending on the situation, it might be good to cancel during the dispose process. For instance, what if the code needs to persist its latest good state or has a closure protocol with a network endpoint? It's good to think through your situation, and the dispose and async dispose patterns can help.

Finally, notice how the `Main` method awaits a using statement on the `CheckoutStream` instance. This is the same `using` statement discussed in Recipe 2.2, except that now it has an `await`. This ensures the code calls `DisposeAsync` at the end of the `Main` method.

See Also

Recipe 1.1, "Managing Object End-of-Lifetime"

Recipe 2.2, "Simplifying Instance Cleanup"

Recipe 6.9, "Cancelling Async Operations"

CHAPTER 7

Manipulating Data

Every application uses data, and we need to manipulate that data from one form to another. This chapter offers several topics on data transformation in areas such as secret management, JSON serialization, and XML serialization.

Secrets are data, such as passwords or API keys, that we don't want to expose to third parties. This chapter has three sections on managing secrets for hashing, encryption, and hidden storage.

Much of the data we work with today is in JSON format. Basic serialization/deserialization is simple in modern frameworks, and it's even simpler when you own both the data consumer and provider. When consuming third-party data, you don't have control over that data's consistency or standards. That's why the JSON sections of this chapter drill down on customizations to help you handle JSON in whatever format you need.

Finally, although JSON has a dominant place among internet data formats today, there's still plenty of XML data to work with, which is the subject of the XML sections. You'll see another flavor of LINQ, called LINQ to XML, which gives you full control over the serialization/deserialization process.

7.1 Generating Password Hashes

Problem

You need to securely store user passwords.

Solution

This method generates a random salt to protect secrets:

```csharp
static byte[] GenerateSalt()
{
    const int SaltLength = 64;

    byte[] salt = new byte[SaltLength];
    var rngRand = new RNGCryptoServiceProvider();

    rngRand.GetBytes(salt);

    return salt;
}
```

The next two methods use that salt to generate hashes:

```csharp
static byte[] GenerateMD5Hash(string password, byte[] salt)
{
    byte[] passwordBytes = Encoding.UTF8.GetBytes(password);

    byte[] saltedPassword =
        new byte[salt.Length + passwordBytes.Length];

    using var hash = new MD5CryptoServiceProvider();

    return hash.ComputeHash(saltedPassword);
}

static byte[] GenerateSha256Hash(string password, byte[] salt)
{
    byte[] passwordBytes = Encoding.UTF8.GetBytes(password);

    byte[] saltedPassword =
        new byte[salt.Length + passwordBytes.Length];

    using var hash = new SHA256CryptoServiceProvider();

    return hash.ComputeHash(saltedPassword);
}
```

And here's how to use the methods to generate hashes:

```csharp
static void Main(string[] args)
{
    Console.WriteLine("\nPassword Hash Demo\n");

    Console.Write("What is your password? ");
    string password = Console.ReadLine();

    byte[] salt = GenerateSalt();

    byte[] md5Hash = GenerateMD5Hash(password, salt);
```

```
    string md5HashString = Convert.ToBase64String(md5Hash);
    Console.WriteLine($"\nMD5:    {md5HashString}");

    byte[] sha256Hash = GenerateSha256Hash(password, salt);
    string sha256HashString = Convert.ToBase64String(sha256Hash);
    Console.WriteLine($"\nSHA256: {sha256HashString}");
}
```

Discussion

ASP.NET identity has nice support for password and group/role management, which should be on anyone's list of considerations when planning a new project. However, there are a lot of situations where ASP.NET identity won't be the best option, for instance, when you have to use a database that ASP.NET identity doesn't support or must use an existing database with its own homegrown password management.

When building a custom password management solution, best practice is to hash the password with a salt. A hash is a one-way translation of a password to a string of unintelligible characters. Every time you hash a specific password, you always get the same hash. That said, an important difference from encryption is that you can't decrypt a hash—there's no way to translate a hash back into the original password. That begs the question of how to know if the user enters the correct password. Since this is a book on C#, database development is out of scope. That said, here are the steps required to verify a password:

1. When you create the user account, hash the password and store the hash in the database with the username.

2. When the user logs in, they provide the username and password.

3. With the username, your code makes a database query and retrieves the matching hash.

4. Hash the password the user entered.

5. Compare the hashed passwords.

6. If the password hashes match, validation succeeds—otherwise validation fails.

Security is a constant game of cat and mouse. As soon as we learned to protect passwords with hashes, hackers looked for ways to break through that. Ultimately, the best we can do is to find a level of security that makes it prohibitively expensive for hackers, based on our need to protect the information compared to the hacker's desire to obtain it. How much security can you afford?

Fortunately, there's an easy way to beef up password security. A security best practice around hashed passwords is to include a salt, a random array of bytes appended to a password. We save the salt in the database, along with the username and password. This is effective in protecting against a rainbow attack, described in the note. The

GenerateSalt method in the solution produces a random 64-byte value. The salt prevents a rainbow attack and forces the hacker to drop down to a dictionary attack, which is much more compute-intensive.

 If a hacker breaks into your system or figures out how to get a copy of the table holding passwords, there are a couple of common attacks: dictionary and rainbow.

In a dictionary attack, the hacker has a dictionary of words and phrases and iterates through that list, hashing each item and comparing to the database table. For all the complexity rules and the number of people who follow them, there are always some people that use single-word passwords. Spoiler alert: for all the people who think they're clever with the symbol/number character replacements—that doesn't work; the hacker's dictionaries and algorithms already account for that.

The rainbow attack is another variation of the dictionary attack, and the difference is that the rainbow attack already hashed common words, so all they need is a simple comparison to move through the password table quicker.

Both the GenerateMD5Hash and GenerateSha256 hash methods accept a password and a salt. Both methods translate the password into a byte[ ], concatenate the password and hash, and generate a hash. The syntactic difference between the MD5 and SHA256 implementations is the MD5CryptoServiceProvider versus the SHA256 CryptoServiceProvider, respectively.

In practice, there are different reasons to use specific hash algorithms. The .NET Framework has several hash algorithms, which you can find by looking up HashAlgorithm and examining its derived classes. Many recent implementations use the SHA256 hash because it provides better protection than earlier hash algorithms. I included the MD5 algorithm to make the point that you don't always have the luxury of selecting the algorithm because the password table might have already been created using MD5. In this case, the inconvenience to users might preclude the need for them to reenter passwords to accommodate another hash algorithm.

The Main method demonstrates how to use these algorithms to generate hashes. An interesting bit here is calling Convert.ToBase64String. Anytime you're moving data from one place to another, the transport mechanism has a protocol and format based on special characters. If the characters in the hashed bytes translate into special characters during transport, the software will break. A standard way to work around this is to use a data format known as Base64, which generates characters that won't conflict with special data format or transport protocol characters.

7.2 Encrypting and Decrypting Secrets

Problem

You have API keys that need to be encrypted at rest.

Solution

This class encrypts and decrypts secrets:

```
public class Crypto
{
    public byte[] Encrypt(string plainText, byte[] key)
    {
        using Aes aes = Aes.Create();
        aes.Key = key;

        using var memStream = new MemoryStream();
        memStream.Write(aes.IV, 0, aes.IV.Length);

        using var cryptoStream = new CryptoStream(
            memStream,
            aes.CreateEncryptor(),
            CryptoStreamMode.Write);

        byte[] plainTextBytes = Encoding.UTF8.GetBytes(plainText);

        cryptoStream.Write(plainTextBytes);
        cryptoStream.FlushFinalBlock();

        memStream.Position = 0;

        return memStream.ToArray();
    }

    public string Decrypt(byte[] cypherBytes, byte[] key)
    {
        using var memStream = new MemoryStream();
        memStream.Write(cypherBytes);
        memStream.Position = 0;

        using var aes = Aes.Create();

        byte[] iv = new byte[aes.IV.Length];
        memStream.Read(iv, 0, iv.Length);

        using var cryptoStream = new CryptoStream(
            memStream,
            aes.CreateDecryptor(key, iv),
            CryptoStreamMode.Read);
```

```
        int plainTextByteLength = cypherBytes.Length - iv.Length;
        var plainTextBytes = new byte[plainTextByteLength];
        cryptoStream.Read(plainTextBytes, 0, plainTextByteLength);

        return Encoding.UTF8.GetString(plainTextBytes);
    }
}
```

Here's a method that generates a random key:

```
static byte[] GenerateKey()
{
    const int KeyLength = 32;

    byte[] key = new byte[KeyLength];
    var rngRand = new RNGCryptoServiceProvider();

    rngRand.GetBytes(key);

    return key;
}
```

Here's how to use the Crypto class and a random key to encrypt and decrypt secrets:

```
static void Main()
{
    var crypto = new Crypto();

    Console.Write("Please enter text to encrypt: ");
    string userPlainText = Console.ReadLine();

    byte[] key = GenerateKey();

    byte[] cypherBytes = crypto.Encrypt(userPlainText, key);

    string cypherText = Convert.ToBase64String(cypherBytes);

    Console.WriteLine($"Cypher Text: {cypherText}");

    string decryptedPlainText = crypto.Decrypt(cypherBytes, key);

    Console.WriteLine($"Plain Text: {decryptedPlainText}");
}
```

Discussion

We often have secrets—API keys or other sensitive information—to protect. Encryption is how we protect information at rest. Before saving, we encrypt the data, and after retrieving the encrypted data, we decrypt it for use.

In the solution, the Crypto class has methods to encrypt and decrypt data. The key parameter is a secret value used by the encryption/decryption algorithms. We'll be using a technique called *symmetric key encryption*, where we use a single key to encrypt/decrypt all the data. Clearly, you don't store the encryption key in the same place as the data because if a hacker is able to read the data, they would also need to figure out where the encryption key is. In this demo, the GenerateKey method produces a random 32-bit key, required by the crypto provider.

The crypto provider is the code that uses a special algorithm to encrypt/decrypt data. The solution example uses Advanced Encryption Standard (AES), which is a modern and secure encryption algorithm.

When saving the data, you pass the plainText string, along with the key, into the Encrypt method. Calling AES.Create returns an instance of AES. The value stored in the database is the concatenated initialization vector (IV) and encrypted text. Notice how the memStream first loads the IV from the AES instance.

The three arguments to CryptoStream are the memStream (containing the IV), an ICryptoTransform (returned by the call to AES.CreateEncryptor), and a Crypto StreamMode (indicating that we're writing to the stream). The cryptoStream instance will append encrypted bytes to the IV in memStream. We're working with byte[] representations of the data, including plainText. Calling Write on cryptoStream performs the encryption, and calling FlushFinalBlock ensures all the bytes are processed and pushed into memStream.

The Decrypt method reverses this process. In addition to the key, which is the same key used to encrypt, there's a cypherBytes parameter. If you recall from the Encrypt process, the encrypted value includes both the IV and the appended encrypted value, and these are the contents of cypherBytes. After loading memStream with cypher Bytes, the code repositions memStream to the beginning and extracts the IV into iv. This leaves the memStream positioned at iv.Length, where the encrypted value begins.

This time, cryptoStream uses the encrypted text (memStream positioned appropriately). Here, ICryptoTransform is different because we call CreateDecryptor with iv and key. Also, the CryptoStreamMode needs to be Read. Calling Read on crypto Stream performs the decryption.

The Main method shows how to use the Encrypt and Decrypt methods. Notice that it uses the same key for both. The Convert.ToBase64String ensures we can work with the data without random bytes being interpreted in unexpected ways. For instance, if you print a binary file to the console, you might hear dings because some of the bytes were interpreted as bell characters. Also, when transporting data, Base64 helps avoid bytes being interpreted as transport protocol or formatting characters, which breaks code.

7.3 Hiding Development Secrets

Problem

You need to avoid accidentally checking secrets, like passwords and API keys, into source control.

Solution

Here's the project file:

```
<Project Sdk="Microsoft.NET.Sdk">
    <PropertyGroup>
    <OutputType>Exe</OutputType>
    <TargetFramework>net5.0</TargetFramework>
    <RootNamespace>Section_07_03</RootNamespace>
    <UserSecretsId>d3d91a8b-d440-414a-821e-7f11eec48f32</UserSecretsId>
    </PropertyGroup>

    <ItemGroup>
    <PackageReference
        Include="Microsoft.Extensions.Hosting" Version="5.0.0" />
    </ItemGroup>
</Project>
```

This code shows how easy it is to add code supporting hidden secrets:

```
class Program
{
    static void Main()
    {
        var config = new ConfigurationBuilder()
            .AddUserSecrets<Program>()
            .Build();

        string key = "CSharpCookbook:ApiKey";
        Console.WriteLine($"{key}: {config[key]}");
    }
}
```

Discussion

This is so common, where developers accidentally check database connection strings from configuration files into source control. Another frequent issue is when a developer needs help in an online forum and accidentally leaves secrets in their code sample. Hopefully, it's clear that these mistakes have the potential for grave damage to an application or even a business.

One solution for this is to use the Secret Manager. While the Secret Manager is normally associated with ASP.NET because of built-in configuration support, you can use it with any type of application. The solution shows how easy it is to use the secret manager with a console application.

 This is a feature that's useful for working in a development environment. In production, you would want to use a more secure option, for instance, Key Vault if you were deploying to Azure. Holding secrets in environment variables is another way to avoid storing them in code or configuration.

Some project types, such as ASP.NET already have support for ensuring you don't accidentally put development code in production, like this:

```
if (env.IsDevelopment())
{
    config.AddUserSecrets<Program>();
}
```

You can set up an application to use Secret Manager with the dotnet CLI. The first thing is to update the project by typing this on the command line:

```
dotnet user-secrets init
```

That adds a UserSecretsID tag to the project file, as previously shown. That GUID identifies the location in your file system where the secrets are stored. In this example, that location is:

```
%APPDATA%\Microsoft\UserSecrets\d3d91a8b-d440-414a-821e-7f11eec48f32
\secrets.json
```

on Windows or:

```
~/.microsoft/usersecrets/d3d91a8b-d440-414a-821e-7f11eec48f32
/secrets.json
```

for Linux or macOS machines.

After setting up, you can start adding secrets, like this (in the same location as the project folder):

```
dotnet user-secrets set "CSharpCookbook:ApiKey" "mYaPIsECRET"
```

You can verify that the secret was saved by looking at secrets.json or the following command:

```
dotnet user-secrets list
```

The Main method shows how to read Secret Manager keys. Remember to reference the Microsoft.Extensions.Hosting NuGet package. Just call AddUserSecrets on a new ConfigurationBuilder. Calling Build on that returns an IConfigurationRoot instance that provides indexer support for reading keys.

7.4 Producing JSON

Problem

You need to customize JSON output formatting.

Solution

This code shows what a `PurchaseOrder` looks like:

```
public enum PurchaseOrderStatus
{
    Received,
    Processing,
    Fulfilled
}

public class PurchaseItem
{
    [JsonPropertyName("serialNo")]
    public string SerialNumber { get; set; }

    [JsonPropertyName("description")]
    public string Description { get; set; }

    [JsonPropertyName("qty")]
    public float Quantity { get; set; }

    [JsonPropertyName("amount")]
    public decimal Price { get; set; }
}

public class PurchaseOrder
{
    [JsonPropertyName("company")]
    public string CompanyName { get; set; }
    [JsonPropertyName("address")]
    public string Address { get; set; }
    [JsonPropertyName("phone")]
    public string Phone { get; set; }

    [JsonPropertyName("status")]
    public PurchaseOrderStatus Status { get; set; }

    [JsonPropertyName("other")]
    public Dictionary<string, string> AdditionalInfo { get; set; }

    [JsonPropertyName("details")]
    public List<PurchaseItem> Items { get; set; }
}
```

This code serializes a `PurchaseOrder`:

```
public class PurchaseOrderService
{
    public void View(PurchaseOrder po)
    {
        var jsonOptions = new JsonSerializerOptions
        {
            WriteIndented = true
        };

        string poJson = JsonSerializer.Serialize(po, jsonOptions);

        // send HTTP request

        Console.WriteLine(poJson);
    }
}
```

Here's how to populate a `PurchaseOrder`:

```
static PurchaseOrder GetPurchaseOrder()
{
    return new PurchaseOrder
    {
        CompanyName = "Acme, Inc.",
        Address = "123 4th St.",
        Phone = "555-835-7609",
        AdditionalInfo = new Dictionary<string, string>
        {
            { "terms", "Net 30" },
            { "poc", "J. Smith" }
        },
        Items = new List<PurchaseItem>
        {
            new PurchaseItem
            {
                Description = "Widget",
                Price = 13.95m,
                Quantity = 5,
                SerialNumber = "123"
            }
        }
    };
}
```

The `Main` method drives the process:

```
static void Main()
{
    PurchaseOrder po = GetPurchaseOrder();
    new PurchaseOrderService().View(po);
}
```

And here's the output:

```
{
  "company": "Acme, Inc.",
  "address": "123 4th St.",
  "phone": "555-835-7609",
  "status": 0,
  "other": {
    "terms": "Net 30",
    "poc": "J. Smith"
  },
  "details": [
    {
      "serialNo": "123",
      "description": "Widget",
      "qty": 5,
      "amount": 13.95
    }
  ]
}
```

Discussion

Just calling `JsonSerializer.Serialize`, from the `System.Text.Json` namespace, is a simple and quick way to serialize objects into JSON. If you own the producing and consuming parts of an application, this might be the way to go for simplicity and speed. However, it's often the case that you're consuming a third-party API that specifies its own JSON data format. Additionally, its naming convention won't match C# Pascal-cased property names. This section shows how to perform those serializer output customizations.

 Microsoft introduced the `System.Text.Json` namespace in .NET Core 3. Previously, a popular choice was the excellently supported `Newtonsoft.Json` library.

In the solution scenario, we want to send a JSON document to an API, but the property names don't match. That's why `PurchaseOrder` (and supporting types) decorates properties with the `JsonPropertyName` attribute. The `JsonSerializer` uses `JsonPropertyName` to specify the output property name.

The `PurchaseOrderService` has a `View` method that serializes a `PurchaseOrder`. By default, the serializer output is a single line and we want to see formatted output. The code uses a `JsonSerializerOption`, with `WriteIndented` set to true, producing the output shown in the solution.

The `Main` method drives the process, getting a new `PurchaseOrder` and then calling `View` to print out the results.

Sometimes, APIs grow organically and their naming conventions lack consistency, making this the ideal approach to customizing output. However, if you are using an API with a consistent naming convention, Recipe 7.5 explains how to build a converter to avoid decorating every property with `JsonPropertyName`.

See Also

Recipe 7.5, "Consuming JSON"

7.5 Consuming JSON

Problem

You need to read a JSON object that doesn't fit default deserialization options.

Solution

Here's what a `PurchaseOrder` looks like:

```
public enum PurchaseOrderStatus
{
    Received,
    Processing,
    Fulfilled
}

public class PurchaseItem
{
    public string SerialNumber { get; set; }

    public string Description { get; set; }

    public float Quantity { get; set; }

    public decimal Price { get; set; }
}

public class PurchaseOrder
{
    public string CompanyName { get; set; }
    public string Address { get; set; }
    public string Phone { get; set; }

    [JsonConverter(typeof(PurchaseOrderStatusConverter))]
    public PurchaseOrderStatus Status { get; set; }
```

```
        public Dictionary<string, string> AdditionalInfo { get; set; }

        public List<PurchaseItem> Items { get; set; }
    }
```

Here's a custom `JsonConverter` class:

```
    public class PurchaseOrderStatusConverter
        : JsonConverter<PurchaseOrderStatus>
    {
        public override PurchaseOrderStatus Read(
            ref Utf8JsonReader reader,
            Type typeToConvert,
            JsonSerializerOptions options)
        {
            string statusString = reader.GetString();

            if (Enum.TryParse(
                statusString,
                out PurchaseOrderStatus status))
            {
                return status;
            }
            else
            {
                throw new JsonException(
                    $"{statusString} is not a valid " +
                    $"{nameof(PurchaseOrderStatus)} value.");
            }
        }

        public override void Write(
            Utf8JsonWriter writer,
            PurchaseOrderStatus value,
            JsonSerializerOptions options)
        {
            writer.WriteStringValue(value.ToString());
        }
    }
```

This is a custom JSON naming policy:

```
    public class SnakeCaseNamingPolicy : JsonNamingPolicy
    {
        public override string ConvertName(string name)
        {
            var targetChars = new List<char>();
            char[] sourceChars = name.ToCharArray();

            char first = sourceChars[0];
            if (char.IsUpper(first))
                targetChars.Add(char.ToLower(first));
            else
```

```
                targetChars.Add(first);

            for (int i = 1; i < sourceChars.Length; i++)
            {
                char ch = sourceChars[i];

                if (char.IsUpper(ch))
                {
                    targetChars.Add('_');
                    targetChars.Add(char.ToLower(ch));
                }
                else
                {
                    targetChars.Add(ch);
                }
            }

            return new string(targetChars.ToArray());
        }
    }
```

This class simulates a request, returning JSON formatted data:

```
public class PurchaseOrderService
{
    public string Get(int poID)
    {
        // get HTTP request

        return @"{
""company_name"": ""Acme, Inc."",
""address"": ""123 4th St."",
""phone"": ""555-835-7609"",
""additional_info"": {
    ""terms"": ""Net 30"",
    ""poc"": ""J. Smith"",
},
""status"": ""Processing"",
""items"": [
    {
        ""serial_number"": ""123"",
        ""description"": ""Widget"",
        ""quantity"": 5,
        ""price"": 13.95
    }
]
}";
    }
}
```

The `Main` method shows how to use custom converters, options, and policies:

```csharp
static void Main()
{
    string poJson =
        new PurchaseOrderService()
            .Get(poID: 123);

    var jsonOptions = new JsonSerializerOptions
    {
        AllowTrailingCommas = true,
        Converters =
        {
            new PurchaseOrderStatusConverter()
        },
        PropertyNameCaseInsensitive = true,
        PropertyNamingPolicy = new SnakeCaseNamingPolicy(),
        WriteIndented = true
    };

    PurchaseOrder po =
        JsonSerializer
        .Deserialize<PurchaseOrder>(poJson, jsonOptions);

    Console.WriteLine($"{po.CompanyName}");
    Console.WriteLine($"{po.AdditionalInfo["terms"]}");
    Console.WriteLine($"{po.Items[0].Description}");

    string poJson2 = JsonSerializer.Serialize(po, jsonOptions);

    Console.WriteLine(poJson2);
}
```

And here's the output:

```
Acme, Inc.
Net 30
Widget
{
  "company_name": "Acme, Inc.",
  "address": "123 4th St.",
  "phone": "555-835-7609",
  "status": "Processing",
  "additional_info": {
    "terms": "Net 30",
    "poc": "J. Smith"
  },
  "items": [
    {
      "serial_number": "123",
      "description": "Widget",
      "quantity": 5,
      "price": 13.95
```

```
        }
    ]
}
```

Discussion

JsonSerializer has a built-in converter for producing camel case property names, via JsonInitializerOptions, like this:

```
var serializeOptions = new JsonSerializerOptions
{
    PropertyNamingPolicy = JsonNamingPolicy.CamelCase
};
```

That handles a lot of scenarios, but what if a third-party API didn't use Pascal case or camel case property names? This solution includes support for property names that are snake case, where words are divided by an underscore. For instance, SnakeCase becomes snake_case. In addition to a new naming policy, the solution also includes other customizations, including enum support.

Notice that PurchaseOrder doesn't decorate any properties with JsonPropertyName. Instead, we use a custom naming policy, defined in the SnakeCaseNamingPolicy class, which derives from JsonNamingPolicy. The algorithm in ConvertName assumes that it has received a Pascal case property name. It iterates through characters, looking for an uppercase character. When encountering an uppercase character it appends an underscore, _, lowercases the letter, and appends the lowercase of the letter into the results. Otherwise, it appends the character, which is already lowercase.

The Main method instantiates a JsonSerializerOptions, setting PropertyNaming Policy to an instance of SnakeCaseNamingPolicy. This applies the naming policy to all property names, producing snake case property names.

 As with many situations, you might encounter an exception to the rule, where a JSON property doesn't conform to snake case rules. In that situation, use a JsonPropertyName attribute, as described in Recipe 7.4, to that property, which overrides the naming policy.

You might have noticed that JsonSerializerOptions, in Main, has other customizations. The AllowTrailingCommas is interesting because sometimes you receive JSON data containing a list, where the last item in the list has a trailing comma. This breaks deserialization, and setting AllowTrailingCommas to true ignores the trailing comma.

PropertyNameCaseInsensitive is an alternative that doesn't consider the property name format. It allows lowercase property names to match their uppercase equivalent when deserializing. It's useful when the incoming JSON property names might not be consistent in casing.

By default, JsonSerializer produces a single-line JSON document. Setting Write Indented formats the text for readability, as shown in the output.

One of the properties, Converters, is a collection of types that do custom conversions on properties. The PurchaseOrderStatusConverter, which derives from Json Converter<T>, allows deserialization of the Status property to the PurchaseOrder Status enum. There are two ways to apply this: in JsonSerialization options or via attribute. Adding a converter to the JsonSerializationOptions Converter collection applies the conversion for all PurchaseOrderStatus property types. Also, the PurchaseOrder class decorates the Status property with a JsonConverter attribute. I added both methods in the solution so you could see how each of them work. Adding to the Converters collection is sufficient. However, if you wanted to apply a different converter to a specific property or needed different converters for different properties, then use the JsonConverter attribute, because it has precedence over the Converters collection.

The Main method shows how to use the same JsonSerializationOptions for both deserialization and serialization.

See Also

Recipe 7.4, "Producing JSON"

7.6 Working with JSON Data

Problem

You received JSON data that doesn't cleanly deserialize into an object.

Solution

Here's what a PurchaseOrder looks like:

```
public enum PurchaseOrderStatus
{
    Received,
    Processing,
    Fulfilled
}

public class PurchaseItem
{
    public string SerialNumber { get; set; }
```

```
    public string Description { get; set; }

    public double Quantity { get; set; }

    public decimal Price { get; set; }
}

public class PurchaseOrder
{
    public string CompanyName { get; set; }
    public string Address { get; set; }
    public string Phone { get; set; }
    public string Terms { get; set; }
    public string POC { get; set; }

    public PurchaseOrderStatus Status { get; set; }

    public Dictionary<string, string> AdditionalInfo { get; set; }

    public List<PurchaseItem> Items { get; set; }
}
```

This class simulates a request that returns JSON data:

```
public class PurchaseOrderService
{
    public string Get(int poID)
    {
        // get HTTP request

        return @"{
""company_name"": ""Acme, Inc."",
""address"": ""123 4th St."",
""phone"": ""555-835-7609"",
""additional_info"": {
    ""terms"": ""Net 30"",
    ""poc"": ""J. Smith""
},
""status"": ""Processing"",
""items"": [
    {
        ""serial_number"": ""123"",
        ""description"": ""Widget"",
        ""quantity"": 5,
        ""price"": 13.95
    }
]
}";
    }
}
```

Here's a class that supports custom deserialization:

```
public static class JsonConversionExtensions
{
    public static bool IsNull(this JsonElement json)
    {
        return
            json.ValueKind == JsonValueKind.Undefined ||
            json.ValueKind == JsonValueKind.Null;
    }

    public static string GetString(
        this JsonElement json,
        string propertyName,
        string defaultValue = default)
    {
        if (!json.IsNull() &&
            json.TryGetProperty(propertyName, out JsonElement element))
            return element.GetString() ?? defaultValue;

        return defaultValue;
    }

    public static int GetInt(
        this JsonElement json,
        string propertyName,
        int defaultValue = default)
    {
        if (!json.IsNull() &&
            json.TryGetProperty(propertyName, out JsonElement element) &&
            !element.IsNull() &&
            element.TryGetInt32(out int value))
            return value;

        return defaultValue;
    }

    public static ulong GetULong(
        this string val,
        ulong defaultValue = default)
    {
        return string.IsNullOrWhiteSpace(val) ||
            !ulong.TryParse(val, out ulong result)
                ? defaultValue
                : result;
    }

    public static ulong GetUlong(
        this JsonElement json,
        string propertyName,
        ulong defaultValue = default)
    {
        if (!json.IsNull() &&
```

```
        json.TryGetProperty(propertyName, out JsonElement element) &&
        !element.IsNull() &&
        element.TryGetUInt64(out ulong value))
        return value;

    return defaultValue;
}

public static long GetLong(
    this JsonElement json,
    string propertyName,
    long defaultValue = default)
{
    if (!json.IsNull() &&
        json.TryGetProperty(propertyName, out JsonElement element) &&
        !element.IsNull() &&
        element.TryGetInt64(out long value))
        return value;

    return defaultValue;
}

public static bool GetBool(
    this JsonElement json,
    string propertyName,
    bool defaultValue = default)
{
    if (!json.IsNull() &&
        json.TryGetProperty(propertyName, out JsonElement element) &&
        !element.IsNull())
        return element.GetBoolean();

    return defaultValue;
}

public static double GetDouble(
    this string val,
    double defaultValue = default)
{
    return string.IsNullOrWhiteSpace(val) ||
        !double.TryParse(val, out double result)
            ? defaultValue
            : result;
}

public static double GetDouble(
    this JsonElement json,
    string propertyName,
    double defaultValue = default)
{
    if (!json.IsNull() &&
        json.TryGetProperty(propertyName, out JsonElement element) &&
```

```
            !element.IsNull() &&
            element.TryGetDouble(out double value))
            return value;

        return defaultValue;
    }

    public static decimal GetDecimal(
        this JsonElement json,
        string propertyName,
        decimal defaultValue = default)
    {
        if (!json.IsNull() &&
            json.TryGetProperty(propertyName, out JsonElement element) &&
            !element.IsNull() &&
            element.TryGetDecimal(out decimal value))
            return value;

        return defaultValue;
    }

    public static TEnum GetEnum<TEnum>
        (this JsonElement json,
        string propertyName,
        TEnum defaultValue = default)
        where TEnum: struct
    {
        if (!json.IsNull() &&
            json.TryGetProperty(propertyName, out JsonElement element) &&
            !element.IsNull())
        {
            string enumString = element.GetString();

            if (enumString != null &&
                Enum.TryParse(enumString, out TEnum num))
                return num;
        }

        return defaultValue;
    }
}
```

The `Main` method shows how to perform custom deserialization:

```
static void Main()
{
    string poJson =
        new PurchaseOrderService()
            .Get(poID: 123);

    JsonElement elm = JsonDocument.Parse(poJson).RootElement;

    JsonElement additional = elm.GetProperty("additional_info");
```

```
        JsonElement items = elm.GetProperty("items");

        if (additional.IsNull() || items.IsNull())
            throw new ArgumentException("incomplete PO");

        var po = new PurchaseOrder
        {
            Address = elm.GetString("address", "none"),
            CompanyName = elm.GetString("company_name", string.Empty),
            Phone = elm.GetString("phone", string.Empty),
            Status = elm.GetEnum("status", PurchaseOrderStatus.Received),
            Terms = additional.GetString("terms", string.Empty),
            POC = additional.GetString("poc", string.Empty),
            AdditionalInfo =
                (from jElem in additional.EnumerateObject()
                 select jElem)
                .ToDictionary(
                    key => key.Name,
                    val => val.Value.GetString()),
            Items =
                (from jElem in items.EnumerateArray()
                 select new PurchaseItem
                 {
                     Description = jElem.GetString("description"),
                     Price = jElem.GetDecimal("price"),
                     Quantity = jElem.GetDouble("quantity"),
                     SerialNumber = jElem.GetString("serial_number")
                 })
                .ToList()
        };

        Console.WriteLine($"{po.CompanyName}");
        Console.WriteLine($"{po.Terms}");
        Console.WriteLine($"{po.AdditionalInfo["terms"]}");
        Console.WriteLine($"{po.Items[0].Description}");
    }
```

Discussion

While using the JsonSerializer is the preferred choice in serialization and deserialization, sometimes you don't get a clean one-to-one structural match between JSON and C# objects. For example, you might need to get data from different sources with different formats and have a single C# object to populate. Other times, you might have a hierarchical JSON document and want to flatten it into your own object. Another common situation is to have objects that already work with one version, and a new version of the API changes structure. In a way, these are multiple viewpoints of the same problem, which you can solve by doing custom deserialization.

The two types from the System.Text.Json namespace for custom deserialization are JsonDocument and JsonElement. The Main method shows how to use JsonDocument to parse JSON input and obtain a JsonElement via the RootElement property. After that, we just work with JsonElement members.

JsonElement has several members, including GetString and GetInt64, for doing conversions. The problem with relying on those alone is that data is often not clean. Even if you own the consumer and producer ends of the application, obtaining perfectly clean data might be illusive. To solve this problem, I created the JsonConversion)Extensions class.

Conceptually, JsonConversionExtensions wraps a lot of boilerplate code that you need to call to ensure the data you're reading is what you expect. It also has an optional default value concept.

The first trick to work around is that a null value in JsonElement isn't represented as null. The IsNull method examines the ValueKind property, checking if either the Undefined or Null properties are true. This is an important method used by other conversion methods.

Skimming through the rest of the methods, you'll see a familiar pattern. Each of them checks for IsNull on the element and then uses one or more combinations of Try GetXxx and IsNull calls to get the value. This is safe and avoids exceptions in case the value is null or is of the wrong type. That's right, some APIs document values of one type and return another type at runtime, set numbers to null, and omit properties.

Each method has a default parameter. If the code isn't able to extract a real value, it uses defaultValue. The defaultValue parameter is optional and reverts to the C# default of the return type.

The Main method shows how to construct an object with JsonElement and the Json ConversionExtensions class. You can see how the code populates each property with a GetXxx method.

A couple of useful JsonElement methods are EnumerateObject and EnumerateArray. In previous sections, JsonSerializer deserialized the JSON additional_info object into a C# dictionary. This is how you handle an object with variable information, where you don't know what the properties of the object are. You might see this for an API that returns multiple errors in a single error JSON response, where each property is a code or description of the error. In the PurchaseOrder example, this represents a place where someone can add miscellaneous information that doesn't fit into a predesigned property. To read these properties manually, use EnumerateObject. It returns each property/value pair in the object. You can see the LINQ statement that creates a new dictionary by extracting the Key and Value from each JsonProperty that EnumerateObject returns.

`EnumerateArray` returns each element of a list. In the solution, we project each `JsonElement` returned from `EnumerateArray` into a new `PurchaseOrderItem` instance.

The `JsonConversionExtensions` is incomplete, because it doesn't include dates. Since `DateTime` processing is a special case, I separated it from this example; you can find more information about it in Recipe 7.10.

See Also

Recipe 7.10, "Flexible DateTime Reading"

7.7 Consuming XML

Problem

You need to convert an XML document to an object.

Solution

Here's what a `PurchaseOrder` looks like:

```
public enum PurchaseOrderStatus
{
    Received,
    Processing,
    Fulfilled
}

public class PurchaseItem
{
    public string SerialNumber { get; set; }

    public string Description { get; set; }

    public float Quantity { get; set; }

    public decimal Price { get; set; }
}

public class PurchaseOrder
{
    public string CompanyName { get; set; }
    public string Address { get; set; }
    public string Phone { get; set; }

    public PurchaseOrderStatus Status { get; set; }

    public Dictionary<string, string> AdditionalInfo { get; set; }
```

```
    public List<PurchaseItem> Items { get; set; }
}
```

This method simulates a request that returns XML data:

```
static string GetXml()
{
    return @"
<PurchaseOrder xmlns=""https://www.oreilly.com"">
  <Address>123 4th St.</Address>
  <CompanyName>Acme, Inc.</CompanyName>
  <Phone>555-835-7609</Phone>
  <Status>Received</Status>
  <AdditionalInfo>
    <Terms>Net 30</Terms>
    <POC>J. Smith</POC>
  </AdditionalInfo>
  <Items>
    <PurchaseItem SerialNumber=""123"">
      <Description>Widget</Description>
      <Price>13.95</Price>
      <Quantity>5</Quantity>
    </PurchaseItem>
  </Items>
</PurchaseOrder>";
}
```

The `Main` method shows how to deserialize XML into objects:

```
static void Main(string[] args)
{
    XNamespace or = "https://www.oreilly.com";

    XName address = or + nameof(PurchaseOrder.Address);
    XName company = or + nameof(PurchaseOrder.CompanyName);
    XName phone = or + nameof(PurchaseOrder.Phone);
    XName status = or + nameof(PurchaseOrder.Status);
    XName info = or + nameof(PurchaseOrder.AdditionalInfo);
    XName poItems = or + nameof(PurchaseOrder.Items);
    XName purchaseItem = or + nameof(PurchaseItem);
    XName description = or + nameof(PurchaseItem.Description);
    XName price = or + nameof(PurchaseItem.Price);
    XName quantity = or + nameof(PurchaseItem.Quantity);
    XName serialNum = nameof(PurchaseItem.SerialNumber);

    string poXml = GetXml();

    XElement poElmt = XElement.Parse(poXml);

    PurchaseOrder po =
        new PurchaseOrder
        {
```

```
                Address = (string)poElmt.Element(address),
                CompanyName = (string)poElmt.Element(company),
                Phone = (string)poElmt.Element(phone),
                Status =
                    Enum.TryParse(
                        (string)poElmt.Element(nameof(po.Status)),
                        out PurchaseOrderStatus poStatus)
                    ? poStatus
                    : PurchaseOrderStatus.Received,
                AdditionalInfo =
                    (from addInfo in poElmt.Element(info).Descendants()
                     select addInfo)
                    .ToDictionary(
                        key => key.Name.LocalName,
                        val => val.Value),
            Items =
                (from item in poElmt
                                .Element(poItems)
                                .Descendants(purchaseItem)
                 select new PurchaseItem
                 {
                     Description = (string)item.Element(description),
                     Price =
                         decimal.TryParse(
                             (string)item.Element(price),
                             out decimal itemPrice)
                         ? itemPrice
                         : 0m,
                     Quantity =
                         float.TryParse(
                             (string)item.Element(quantity),
                             out float qty)
                         ? qty
                         : 0f,
                     SerialNumber = (string)item.Attribute(serialNum)
                 })
                .ToList()
        };

    Console.WriteLine($"{po.CompanyName}");
    Console.WriteLine($"{po.AdditionalInfo["Terms"]}");
    Console.WriteLine($"{po.Items[0].Description}");
    Console.WriteLine($"{po.Items[0].SerialNumber}");
}
```

Discussion

Before JSON took over as the dominant data format, XML was ubiquitous. When working with things like configuration files, project files, or Extensible Application Markup Language (XAML), it's clear that XML is still with us. There's also a fair amount of legacy code, including Windows Communication Foundation (WCF) Web

Services, that uses XML extensively. For the time being, knowing how to work with XML is a valuable skill, and LINQ to XML is an excellent tool for that.

The solution shows how to deserialize XML into a `PurchaseOrder` object. The first thing the `Main` method does is set up the namespace. Namespaces in XML are common, and the code creates a namespace tag, or. The `XNamespace` type has a converter that transforms a string into a namespace. `XNamespace` also overloads the + operator, letting you tag elements with a specific namespace, creating a new `XName`. The code sets up an `XName` for each element to make the construction of `PurchaseOrder` easier to read.

Each element has a namespace, except for `serialNum`, which is an attribute. You don't annotate data attributes with namespaces because they're in the containing element's namespace. The exception is if you wanted to add a namespace attribute to an element, putting it into a new namespace.

After getting the XML, `Main` calls `XElement.Parse` to get a new `XElement` to work with. `XElement` has all the axis methods required to move around the document and read anything you need. This example keeps things simple by moving through the document hierarchically with the `Attribute`, `Element`, and `Descendants` axis methods.

The `Element` method helps read a subelement under the current element. The `Descendants` method goes one level deeper, accessing the children of a specified element. In the XML returned from `GetXml`, `PurchaseOrder` is the root element, represented by `poElmt`. Looking at the `PurchaseOrder`, `poElmt.Element(address)` reads the `Address` element, a subelement of `PurchaseOrder`. If you recall, `address` is a namespace-qualified `XName`.

Populating the `AdditionalInfo` and `Items` properties shows how to use `Descendants`. We use `Element` to read the subelement and `Descendants` to get a list of that element's children. For `AdditionalInfo`, `Descendants` are variable elements and values, and we don't pass an `XName` argument. In the case of `Items`, we need to pass the `purchaseItem` `XName` to `Descendants` to operate on each object.

We use the `Attribute` method to populate the `SerialNumber` property of each `PurchaseOrderItem`.

An interesting part of this object construction is the ability to declare the out parameter in `TryParse` operations. This allows us to code the assignment inline. Prior to this C# feature, we would need to declare the variable outside the object construction, which doesn't feel natural, especially when populating during a LINQ projection, like the `Items` property in the solution.

See Also

Recipe 7.8, "Producing XML"

7.8 Producing XML

Problem

You need to convert an object to XML.

Solution

Here's what a PurchaseOrder looks like:

```
public enum PurchaseOrderStatus
{
    Received,
    Processing,
    Fulfilled
}

public class PurchaseItem
{
    public string SerialNumber { get; set; }

    public string Description { get; set; }

    public float Quantity { get; set; }

    public decimal Price { get; set; }
}

public class PurchaseOrder
{
    public string CompanyName { get; set; }
    public string Address { get; set; }
    public string Phone { get; set; }

    public PurchaseOrderStatus Status { get; set; }

    public Dictionary<string, string> AdditionalInfo { get; set; }

    public List<PurchaseItem> Items { get; set; }
}
```

This method simulates a data request that returns a PurchaseOrder:

```
static PurchaseOrder GetPurchaseOrder()
{
    return new PurchaseOrder
    {
```

```
            CompanyName = "Acme, Inc.",
            Address = "123 4th St.",
            Phone = "555-835-7609",
            AdditionalInfo = new Dictionary<string, string>
            {
                { "Terms", "Net 30" },
                { "POC", "J. Smith" }
            },
            Items = new List<PurchaseItem>
            {
                new PurchaseItem
                {
                    Description = "Widget",
                    Price = 13.95m,
                    Quantity = 5,
                    SerialNumber = "123"
                }
            }
        };
    }
```

The `Main` method shows how to serialize that `PurchaseOrder` instance into XML:

```
static void Main(string[] args)
{
    PurchaseOrder po = GetPurchaseOrder();

    XNamespace or = "https://www.oreilly.com";

    XElement poXml =
        new XElement(or + nameof(PurchaseOrder),
            new XElement(
                or + nameof(PurchaseOrder.Address),
                po.Address),
            new XElement(
                or + nameof(PurchaseOrder.CompanyName),
                po.CompanyName),
            new XElement(
                or + nameof(PurchaseOrder.Phone),
                po.Phone),
            new XElement(
                or + nameof(PurchaseOrder.Status),
                po.Status),
            new XElement(
                or + nameof(PurchaseOrder.AdditionalInfo),
                (from info in po.AdditionalInfo
                 select
                    new XElement(
                        or + info.Key,
                        info.Value))
                .ToList()),
            new XElement(
                or + nameof(PurchaseOrder.Items),
```

```
                    (from item in po.Items
                     select new XElement(
                            or + nameof(PurchaseItem),
                            new XAttribute(
                                nameof(PurchaseItem.SerialNumber),
                                item.SerialNumber),
                            new XElement(
                                or + nameof(PurchaseItem.Description),
                                item.Description),
                            new XElement(
                                or + nameof(PurchaseItem.Price),
                                item.Price),
                            new XElement(
                                or + nameof(PurchaseItem.Quantity),
                                item.Quantity)))
                        .ToList()));

    Console.WriteLine(poXml);
}
```

And here's the output:

```
<PurchaseOrder xmlns="https://www.oreilly.com">
  <Address>123 4th St.</Address>
  <CompanyName>Acme, Inc.</CompanyName>
  <Phone>555-835-7609</Phone>
  <Status>Received</Status>
  <AdditionalInfo>
    <Terms>Net 30</Terms>
    <POC>J. Smith</POC>
  </AdditionalInfo>
  <Items>
    <PurchaseItem SerialNumber="123">
      <Description>Widget</Description>
      <Price>13.95</Price>
      <Quantity>5</Quantity>
    </PurchaseItem>
  </Items>
</PurchaseOrder>
```

Discussion

Recipe 7.7 deserialized an XML document into a PurchaseOrder object. This section goes in the other direction—serializing the PurchaseOrder into an XML document.

We start with the XNamespace, or, which is used as the XName parameter for each element to keep all elements in the same namespace.

The solution builds the XML document via calls to XElement and XAttribute. The only place we use XAttribute is for the SerialNumber attribute on each Purchase OrderItem element.

Visually, you can see that the LINQ to XML query clause is laid out with the same hierarchical structure as the XML output it produces. The solution uses two XEle ment constructor overloads. If an element is a bottom node, without children, the second parameter is the element value. However, if the element is a parent element, with children, the second parameter is a new XElement.

The LINQ statements for both `AdditionalInfo` and `Items` project into a new `XElement`.

See Also

Recipe 7.7, "Consuming XML"

7.9 Encoding and Decoding URL Parameters

Problem

You've working with an API that requires RFC 3986–compliant URLs.

Solution

Here's a class that properly encodes URL parameters:

```
public class Url
{
    /// <summary>
    /// Implements Percent Encoding according to RFC 3986
    /// </summary>
    /// <param name="value">string to be encoded</param>
    /// <returns>Encoded string</returns>
    public static string PercentEncode(
        string? value, bool isParam = true)
    {
        const string IsParamReservedChars = @"'`!@#$^&*+=,:;'?/|\[] ";
        const string NoParamReservedChars = @"'`!@#$^&*()+=,:;'?/|\[] ";

        var result = new StringBuilder();

        if (string.IsNullOrWhiteSpace(value))
            return string.Empty;

        var escapedValue = EncodeDataString(value);

        var reservedChars =
            isParam ? IsParamReservedChars : NoParamReservedChars;

        foreach (char symbol in escapedValue)
        {
            if (reservedChars.IndexOf(symbol) != -1)
```

```
                result.Append(
                    '%' +
                    string.Format("{0:X2}", (int)symbol).ToUpper());
            else
                result.Append(symbol);
        }

        return result.ToString();
    }

    /// <summary>
    /// URL-encode a string of any length.
    /// </summary>
    static string EncodeDataString(string data)
    {
        // the max length in .NET 4.5+ is 65520
        const int maxLength = 65519;

        if (data.Length <= maxLength)
            return Uri.EscapeDataString(data);

        var totalChunks = data.Length / maxLength;

        var builder = new StringBuilder();
        for (var i = 0; i <= totalChunks; i++)
        {
            string? chunk =
                i < totalChunks ?
                    data[(maxLength * i)..maxLength] :
                    data[(maxLength * i)..];

            builder.Append(Uri.EscapeDataString(chunk));
        }
        return builder.ToString();
    }
}
```

This method parses a URL, encodes parameters, and rebuilds the URL:

```
static string EscapeUrlParams(string originalUrl)
{
    const int Base = 0;
    const int Parms = 1;
    const int Key = 0;
    const int Val = 1;
    string[] parts = originalUrl.Split('?');
    string[] pairs = parts[Parms].Split('&');

    string escapedParms =
        string.Join('&',
            (from pair in pairs
             let keyVal = pair.Split('=')
             let encodedVal = Url.PercentEncode(keyVal[Val])
```

```
            select $"{keyVal[Key]]={encodedVal}")
            .ToList());

        return $"{parts[Base]}?{escapedParms}";
    }
```

The Main method compares different encodings:

```
static void Main()
{
    const string OriginalUrl =
        "https://myco.com/po/search?company=computers+";
    Console.WriteLine($"Original:    '{OriginalUrl}'");

    string escapedUri = Uri.EscapeUriString(OriginalUrl);
    Console.WriteLine($"Escape URI: '{escapedUri}'");

    string escapedData = Uri.EscapeDataString(OriginalUrl);
    Console.WriteLine($"Escape Data: '{escapedData}'");

    string escapedUrl = EscapeUrlParams(OriginalUrl);
    Console.WriteLine($"Escaped URL: '{escapedUrl}'");
}
```

Producing this output:

```
Original:    'https://myco.com/po/search?company=computers+'
Escape URI: 'https://myco.com/po/search?company=computers+'
Escape Data: 'https%3A%2F%2Fmyco.com%2Fpo%2Fsearch%3Fcompany
%3Dcomputers%2B'
Escaped URL: 'https://myco.com/po/search?company=computers%2B'
```

Discussion

If you're building both the consumer and producer parts of network communications, such as an internal enterprise application, getting encoding right might not matter because both parts use the same library. However, some third-party APIs require strong compliance with RFC 3986. Your first thought may be that the .NET System.Uri class has EscapeUriString and EscapeDataString methods. Unfortunately, these methods haven't always implemented RFC 3986 properly. While .NET 5+ is cross-platform and seems to have a good implementation, earlier versions of the .NET Framework for different technologies did not. To fix this, I created the Url class in the solution.

RFC 3986 is the standard defining internet URL encoding. RFC stands for "Request for Comments," and standards are generally labeled with RFC followed by some unique number.

The `PercentEncode` replaces each character of the value parameter with a two-digit hex representation with a percent (%) prefix. The first operation is to call `EscapeData String`. This method calls `Uri.EscapeDataString`. One of the issues with `Uri. EscapeDataString` is a length constraint, so this method chunks the input to ensure all the data is encoded. The approach is to allow `Uri.EscapeDataString` to take care of most of the conversion and let `PercentEncode` supplement for characters that weren't encoded.

`PercentEncode` has a second parameter, `isParam`, that indicates whether we should encode parentheses. It defaults to `true`, and users would set it to `false` to prevent encoding parentheses, which is the only difference between the `IsParamReserved Chars` and `NoParamReservedChars`. If the method finds a character that hasn't been encoded, it does the encoding manually.

We only encode query string parameter values because the base URL, segments, and parameter names are values that don't need encoding. The `EscapeUrlParameters` method does this by splitting the URL from the parameters and iterating through each parameter. For each parameter, it splits the parameter name from its value and calls `PercentEncode` on the value. After encoding values, the code rebuilds and returns the URL.

The `Main` method shows the different types of encoding, illuminating why we chose the custom encoding approach. Notice that `Uri.EscapeUriString` didn't encode the + symbol. Using `Uri.EscapeDataString` encoded the entire URL, which isn't what you want. Breaking up the URL and encoding each value worked perfectly.

Remember that you might get good results in a .NET 5+ application. However, if you're doing cross-platform work in older .NET Framework versions, the results of `Uri.EscapeUriString` and `Uri.EscapeDataString` are inconsistent and likely to cause bugs. Regardless of framework/technology version, the technique of only encoding parameter values is a common requirement.

7.10 Flexible DateTime Reading

Problem

You need to parse `DateTime` values that can be in multiple different formats.

Solution

These extension methods help in parsing dates:

```
public static class StringExtensions
{
    static readonly string[] dateFormats =
```

```
    {
        "ddd MMM dd HH:mm:ss %zzzz yyyy",
        "yyyy-MM-dd\\THH:mm:ss.000Z",
        "yyyy-MM-dd\\THH:mm:ss\\Z",
        "yyyy-MM-dd HH:mm:ss",
        "yyyy-MM-dd HH:mm"
    };

    public static DateTime GetDate(
        this string date,
        DateTime defaultValue)
    {
        return string.IsNullOrWhiteSpace(date) ||
            !DateTime.TryParseExact(
                    date,
                    dateFormats,
                    CultureInfo.InvariantCulture,
                    DateTimeStyles.AssumeUniversal |
                    DateTimeStyles.AdjustToUniversal,
                    out DateTime result)
                ? defaultValue
                : result;
    }

    public static DateTime GetDate(
        this JsonElement json,
        string propertyName,
        DateTime defaultValue = default)
    {
        string? date = json.GetString(propertyName);
        return date?.GetDate(defaultValue) ?? defaultValue;
    }

    public static string? GetString(
        this JsonElement json,
        string propertyName,
        string? defaultValue = default)
    {
        if (!json.IsNull() &&
            json.TryGetProperty(propertyName, out JsonElement element))
            return element.GetString() ?? defaultValue;

        return defaultValue;
    }

    public static bool IsNull(this JsonElement json)
    {
        return
            json.ValueKind == JsonValueKind.Undefined ||
            json.ValueKind == JsonValueKind.Null;
    }
}
```

The `Main` method shows how to extract and parse a JSON document date:

```
static void Main()
{
    const string TweetID = "1305895383260782593";
    const string CreatedDate = "created_at";

    string tweetJson = GetTweet(TweetID);

    JsonElement tweetElem = JsonDocument.Parse(tweetJson).RootElement;

    DateTime created = tweetElem.GetDate(CreatedDate);

    Console.WriteLine($"Created Date: {created}");
}

static string GetTweet(string tweetID)
{
    return @"{
        ""text"": ""Thanks @github for approving sponsorship for
            LINQ to Twitter: https://t.co/jWeDEN07HN"",
        ""id"": ""1305895383260782593"",
        ""author_id"": ""15411837"",
        ""created_at"": ""2020-09-15T15:44:56.000Z""
    }";
}
```

Discussion

When using third-party APIs, you'll encounter occasional inconsistencies in data representation. One problematic area is parsing dates. Different APIs have different date formats or even represent different date properties with separate formats in the same API. The `StringExtensions` class in the solution helps fix this problem.

I extracted `StringExtensions` members from `JsonConversion` Extensions in Recipe 7.6.

The solution includes a `dateFormats` array containing instances of date format strings. These are all the possible date formats that this code can accommodate. The `GetDate` method uses `dateFormats` in the call to `TryParseExact`. Whenever you encounter a new date format (for instance, if an API offers a new version and updates date formats), add it to `dateFormats`.

It's best practice to represent dates as UTC values, so the `DateTimeStyles` arguments reflect this assumption.

There are two overloads of GetDate, depending on whether you need to pass in a string or a JsonElement. The JsonElement overload uses the GetString extension method and forwards the result to the other GetDate method.

These methods are safe because you have to account for bad data. They check for null, use TryParse, and return default values when they can't read a valid value. The defaultValue is optional, using the default of the return type if not provided.

See Also

Recipe 7.6, "Working with JSON Data"

CHAPTER 8

Matching with Patterns

Historically, developers have implemented business rules with various logical checks and comparisons. Sometimes the rules are complex—naturally leading to code that's difficult to write, read, and maintain. Think about how often you've encountered multibranch logic with multivariate comparisons and multiple levels of nesting.

To help ease this complexity, modern programming languages have begun introducing pattern matching—features of the language that help match facts to results with declarative syntax. In C#, pattern matching manifests as a growing list of features added in each new version, especially from C# 7 and later.

The theme of this chapter revolves around hotel scheduling and using patterns for business rules. The criteria is usually around a type of customer such as Bronze, Silver, or Gold, with Gold being the highest level because those customers have more points from more frequent hotel stays.

This chapter discusses pattern matching for properties, tuples, and types. There's also a couple of sections on logical operations and how they enable and simplify multiconditional patterns. Surprisingly, C# had some form of pattern matching since v1.0. The first section of this chapter discusses the is and as operators and shows the new enhancements to the is operator.

8.1 Converting Instances Safely

Problem

Your legacy code is weakly typed, relies on procedural patterns, and needs to be refactored.

Solution

Here's an interface and implementing classes that produce results we're looking for:

```
public interface IRoomSchedule
{
    void ScheduleRoom();
}

public class GoldSchedule : IRoomSchedule
{
    public void ScheduleRoom() =>
        Console.WriteLine("Scheduling Gold Room");
}

public class SilverSchedule : IRoomSchedule
{
    public void ScheduleRoom() =>
        Console.WriteLine("Scheduling Silver Room");
}

public class BronzeSchedule : IRoomSchedule
{
    public void ScheduleRoom() =>
        Console.WriteLine("Scheduling Bronze Room");
}
```

Here's a method representing data returned in legacy nontyped instances:

```
static ArrayList GetWeakTypedSchedules()
{
    var list = new ArrayList();

    list.Add(new BronzeSchedule());
    list.Add(new SilverSchedule());
    list.Add(new GoldSchedule());

    return list;
}
```

And this code processes the legacy collection:

```
static void ProcessLegacyCode()
{
    ArrayList schedules = GetWeakTypedSchedules();

    foreach (var schedule in schedules)
    {
        if (schedule is IRoomSchedule)
        {
            IRoomSchedule roomSchedule = (IRoomSchedule)schedule;
            roomSchedule.ScheduleRoom();
        }
```

```
//
// alternatively
//

IRoomSchedule asRoomSchedule = schedule as IRoomSchedule;

if (asRoomSchedule != null)
    asRoomSchedule.ScheduleRoom();

//
// even better
//

if (schedule is IRoomSchedule isRoomSchedule)
    isRoomSchedule.ScheduleRoom();
    }
}
```

Here's more modern code that returns a strongly typed collection:

```
static List<IRoomSchedule> GetStrongTypedSchedules()
{
    return new List<IRoomSchedule>
    {
        new BronzeSchedule(),
        new SilverSchedule(),
        new GoldSchedule()
    };
}
```

And this code processes the strongly typed collection:

```
static void ProcessModernCode()
{
    List<IRoomSchedule> schedules = GetStrongTypedSchedules();

    foreach (var schedule in schedules)
    {
        schedule.ScheduleRoom();

        if (schedule is GoldSchedule gold)
            Console.WriteLine(
                $"Extra processing for {gold.GetType()}");
    }
}
```

The Main methods call both the legacy and modern versions:

```
static void Main()
{
    ProcessLegacyCode();
    ProcessModernCode();
}
```

Discussion

The `as` and `is` operators appeared in C# 1; you're probably aware of and/or have used them. To recap, the `is` operator tells whether an object's type is the same as the type being matched. The `as` operator performs a conversion of a reference type object to a specified type. The `as` operator returns `null` if the converted instance isn't the specified type. This example also demonstrates a recent C# addition that allows both type checking and conversion with the `is` operator.

Most of the code we write today uses generic collections and it's increasingly unnecessary to use weakly typed collections. I'll go out on a limb here and say that you might adopt a rule of thumb to use generic collections as a default, with the exception being when you can't avoid using weakly typed collections. One important situation where you have to use weakly typed collections is when maintaining legacy code that already uses them. Generics weren't added until C# 2, so you might encounter some old code with weakly typed collections. Another example is when you have a library you need or want to use that uses weakly typed collections. In practical terms, you might not want to rewrite that code because of the time and resources required—especially if it's already tested and working well.

In the solution, the `GetWeakTypedSchedules` method returns an `ArrayList`, which is a weakly typed collection because it only operates on instances of type `Object`. The `ProcessLegacyCode` method calls `GetWeakTypedSchedules` and shows how to use the `as` and `is` operators.

The first `if` statement in the `foreach` loop uses the `is` operator to determine whether the object is an `IRoomSchedule`. If so, it uses a cast operator to get an `IRoomSchedule` instance and calls `GetSchedule`. You might ask why the `is` operator is necessary if we already know that the collection contains `IRoomSchedule` instances—why don't we just go straight for the conversion? The problem is that there isn't a guarantee of what the types in that collection are. What if a developer accidentally loads an object that isn't `IRoomSchedule` into the collection? The `is` operator improves the reliability of the code.

An alternative to the `is` operator is the `as` operator. In the solution, the `schedule as IRoomSchedule` performs the conversion. If the result isn't `null`, the object is an `IRoomSchedule`. This approach could perform better because an `is` operation both checks the type and still requires a conversion, whereas the `as` operator only requires a conversion and a `null` check.

The final `if` statement demonstrates the newer `is` operator syntax. It does both the type check and conversion, assigning the result to the `isRoomSchedule` variable. The `isRoomSchedule` variable is `null` if `schedule` wasn't an `IRoomSchedule`, but since the `is` operator returned a `bool` result, we don't need to do the extra `null` check.

The GetStrongTypedSchedules and ProcessModernCode show how you would probably want to write the code today. Notice how it has less ceremony because of the
strong typing. Each class implements the same interface, and the collection is that
interface, allowing you to write code that operates efficiently on every object.

This example also demonstrates that the new is operator can be useful in current
code (not only legacy). In ProcessModernCode, even though all the objects implement
IRoomSchedule, the is operator lets us check for GoldSchedule and do some extra
processing.

8.2 Catching Filtered Exceptions

Problem

You need to handle logic for the same exception type with different conditions.

Solution

This is a demo class that throws exceptions:

```
public class Scheduler
{
    public void ScheduleRoom(string arg1, string arg2)
    {
        _ = arg1 ?? throw new ArgumentNullException(nameof(arg1));
        _ = arg2 ?? throw new ArgumentNullException(nameof(arg2));
    }
}
```

This Main method uses exception filters for clean processing:

```
static void Main()
{
    try
    {
        Console.Write("Choose (1) arg1 or (2) arg2? ");
        string arg = Console.ReadLine();

        var scheduler = new Scheduler();

        if (arg == "1")
            scheduler.ScheduleRoom(null, "arg2");
        else
            scheduler.ScheduleRoom("arg1", null);
    }
    catch (ArgumentNullException ex1)
        when (ex1.ParamName == "arg1")
    {
        Console.WriteLine("Invalid arg1");
    }
```

```
        catch (ArgumentNullException ex2)
            when (ex2.ParamName == "arg2")
        {
            Console.WriteLine("Invalid arg2");
        }
    }
```

Discussion

An interesting addition to C#, related to pattern matching, is the exception filter. As you know, catch blocks operate on the type of exception thrown. However, when the same exception type can be thrown for different reasons, sometimes it's useful to be able to differentiate processing for each reason. While you could add if or switch statements in the catch block, filters offer a clean way to separate and simplify the different logic.

In the solution, we're interested in filtering ArgumentNullException, depending on which parameter is null. The ScheduleRoom method checks each parameter and throws ArgumentNullException if either is null.

The Main method wraps the call to ScheduleRoom in a try/catch block. This example has two catch blocks, each of type ArgumentNullException. The difference between the two is the filter, specified by the when clause. The parameter to when is a bool expression. In the solution, the expression compares the ParamName to the parameter name it's designed to handle.

8.3 Simplifying Switch Assignments

Problem

You want to return a value, based on some criteria, but don't want to return from every switch case.

Solution

Here's an interface and implementing classes that are results we're looking for:

```
public interface IRoomSchedule
{
    void ScheduleRoom();
}

public class GoldSchedule : IRoomSchedule
{
    public void ScheduleRoom() =>
        Console.WriteLine("Scheduling Gold Room");
}
```

```
public class SilverSchedule : IRoomSchedule
{
    public void ScheduleRoom() =>
        Console.WriteLine("Scheduling Silver Room");
}

public class BronzeSchedule : IRoomSchedule
{
    public void ScheduleRoom() =>
        Console.WriteLine("Scheduling Bronze Room");
}
```

This enum is used in upcoming logic:

```
public enum ScheduleType
{
    None,
    Bronze,
    Silver,
    Gold
}
```

This class shows the switch statement and new switch expression:

```
public class Scheduler
{
    public IRoomSchedule CreateStatement(
        ScheduleType scheduleType)
    {
        switch (scheduleType)
        {
            case ScheduleType.Gold:
                return new GoldSchedule();
            case ScheduleType.Silver:
                return new SilverSchedule();
            case ScheduleType.Bronze:
            default:
                return new BronzeSchedule();
        }
    }

    public IRoomSchedule CreateExpression(
        ScheduleType scheduleType) =>
            scheduleType switch
            {
                ScheduleType.Gold => new GoldSchedule(),
                ScheduleType.Silver => new SilverSchedule(),
                ScheduleType.Bronze => new BronzeSchedule(),
                _ => new BronzeSchedule()
            };
}
```

The Main method tests the code:

```
static void Main()
{
    Console.Write(
        "Choose (1) Bronze, (2) Silver, or (3) Gold: ");
    string choice = Console.ReadLine();

    Enum.TryParse(choice, out ScheduleType scheduleType);

    var scheduler = new Scheduler();

    IRoomSchedule scheduleStatement =
        scheduler.CreateStatement(scheduleType);
    scheduleStatement.ScheduleRoom();

    IRoomSchedule scheduleExpression =
        scheduler.CreateExpression(scheduleType);
    scheduleExpression.ScheduleRoom();
}
```

Discussion

The switch statement has been around since C# 1, and a recent addition is a switch expression. The main syntactic features of the switch expression are a shorthand notation and the ability to assign a result to a variable. If you think about all the times you've used a switch statement, you might have noticed that producing a value or new instance was a common theme. The switch expression streamlines that theme and improves upon it with pattern matching.

The solution has two examples: a switch statement and a switch expression. Both rely on the ScheduleType enum for criteria and produce an IRoomSchedule type, based on that criteria.

The CreateStatement method uses a switch statement, with case clauses for each member of the ScheduleType enum. Notice how it returns the value from the method and that it requires normal block body syntax (with curly braces).

The CreateExpression method uses the new switch expression. Notice that the method can be command body (with arrow), returning the expression. Instead of a parameter in parentheses after the switch keyword, the parameter precedes the switch keyword. Also, instead of case clauses, case pattern matches precede an arrow, with the result expression after the arrow. The default case is the discard pattern, _.

Whenever the parameter matches the case pattern, the switch expression returns the result. In the solution, the patterns are the values of the ScheduleType enum. The result of the `switch` expression is the result of the method because the command syntax of the method specifies the `switch` expression.

If you have a use case where there's logic to process for each case, but don't need to return, a classic `switch` statement might make more sense. However, if you can use pattern matching and need to return a value, the `switch` expression can be an excellent choice.

8.4 Switching on Property Values

Problem

You need business rules based on strongly typed class properties.

Solution

Here's a class with properties that we need to evaluate:

```
public class Room
{
    public int Number { get; set; }
    public string RoomType { get; set; }
    public string BedSize { get; set; }
}
```

This enum is the result of the evaluation:

```
public enum ScheduleType
{
    None,
    Bronze,
    Silver,
    Gold
}
```

This method gets the data we need:

```
static List<Room> GetRooms()
{
    return new List<Room>
    {
        new Room
        {
            Number = 333,
            BedSize = "King",
            RoomType = "Suite"
        },
        new Room
        {
            Number = 222,
            BedSize = "King",
```

```
            RoomType = "Regular"
        },
        new Room
        {
            Number = 111,
            BedSize = "Queen",
            RoomType = "Regular"
        },
    };
}
```

This method uses that data and returns an enum, based on matching pattern:

```
const int RoomNotAvailable = -1;

static int AssignRoom(ScheduleType scheduleType)
{
    foreach (var room in GetRooms())
    {
        ScheduleType roomType = room switch
        {
            { BedSize: "King", RoomType: "Suite" }
                => ScheduleType.Gold,
            { BedSize: "King", RoomType: "Regular" }
                => ScheduleType.Silver,
            { BedSize: "Queen", RoomType: "Regular" }
                => ScheduleType.Bronze,
            _ => ScheduleType.Bronze
        };

        if (roomType == scheduleType)
            return room.Number;
    }

    return RoomNotAvailable;
}
```

The Main method drives the program:

```
static void Main()
{
    Console.Write(
        "Choose (1) Bronze, (2) Silver, or (3) Gold: ");
    string choice = Console.ReadLine();

    Enum.TryParse(choice, out ScheduleType scheduleType);

    int roomNumber = AssignRoom(scheduleType);

    if (roomNumber == RoomNotAvailable)
        Console.WriteLine("Room not available.");
    else
```

```
        Console.WriteLine($"The room number is {roomNumber}.");
}
```

Discussion

In the past, a switch statement matched cases with the value of a single parameter. Now, you can do parameter matching based on the values of properties in an object.

The solution uses an instance of the Room class as the parameter to a switch expression in the AssignRoom method. The pattern is an object with the properties of Room and the values to match. The result returned is based on which pattern the properties of the parameter match.

The goal of the program is to find an available room for a customer. The purpose of AssignRoom is to return the first room associated with a specific schedule type. That's why AssignRoom compares roomType and scheduleType, returning if they match.

Property pattern matching is a nice approach because it's easy to read. This potentially translates into more maintainable code. One trade-off is that it can be verbose if you're matching a lot of properties. The next recipe offers shorter syntax.

See Also

Recipe 8.5, "Switching on Tuples"

8.5 Switching on Tuples

Problem

You need business rules and prefer shorter syntax.

Solution

This class is interesting because it has a deconstructor:

```
public class Room
{
    public int Number { get; set; }
    public string RoomType { get; set; }
    public string BedSize { get; set; }

    public void Deconstruct(out string size, out string type)
    {
        size = BedSize;
        type = RoomType;
    }
}
```

Here's an enum that this program will produce:

```
public enum ScheduleType
{
    None,
    Bronze,
    Silver,
    Gold
}
```

Here's the data the program will work with:

```
static List<Room> GetRooms()
{
    return new List<Room>
    {
        new Room
        {
            Number = 333,
            BedSize = "King",
            RoomType = "Suite"
        },
        new Room
        {
            Number = 222,
            BedSize = "King",
            RoomType = "Regular"
        },
        new Room
        {
            Number = 111,
            BedSize = "Queen",
            RoomType = "Regular"
        },
    };
}
```

And this method uses the tuple returned from the class deconstructor to determine which enum to return:

```
static int AssignRoom(ScheduleType scheduleType)
{
    foreach (var room in GetRooms())
    {
        ScheduleType roomType = room switch
        {
            ("King", "Suite") => ScheduleType.Gold,
            ("King", "Regular") => ScheduleType.Silver,
            ("Queen", "Regular") => ScheduleType.Bronze,
            _ => ScheduleType.Bronze
        };

        if (roomType == scheduleType)
```

```
            return room.Number;
    }

        return RoomNotAvailable;
    }
```

The `Main` method drives the program:

```
static void Main()
{
    Console.Write(
        "Choose (1) Bronze, (2) Silver, or (3) Gold: ");
    string choice = Console.ReadLine();

    Enum.TryParse(choice, out ScheduleType scheduleType);

    int roomNumber = AssignRoom(scheduleType);

    if (roomNumber == RoomNotAvailable)
        Console.WriteLine("Room not available.");
    else
        Console.WriteLine($"The room number is {roomNumber}.");
}
```

Discussion

Throughout this book, you've seen how useful tuples are for situations where you want to manage a set of values without all the ceremony of a custom type. The quick syntax of tuples makes them ideal for simple pattern matching.

In this example, we do have a custom type, `Room`. Notice that `Room` has a custom deconstructor, which we'll use in this solution. The `GetRooms` method returns a `List<Room>`. `AssignRooms` uses that collection. However, because of the deconstructor, we can use each room as a `switch` expression parameter, which is smart enough to use the deconstructor to produce a tuple for pattern matching.

Except for using tuples through a deconstructor, this demo is the same as Recipe 8.4. In this example, the tuple offered a shorter syntax. The property pattern is more verbose but easier to read. One consideration is that if you're matching scalar values, like `bool` or `int`, the property pattern documents better. If you're matching strings or enums, a tuple might provide the best of both worlds in terms of readability and shorter syntax. Because the choice between the two approaches is situational, it's best to evaluate trade-offs in each situation to see what makes sense to you.

See Also

Recipe 8.4, "Switching on Property Values"

8.6 Switching on Position

Problem

You need business rules based on values but don't want to create a new single-use class.

Solution

This enum is the result we'll look for:

```
public enum ScheduleType
{
    None,
    Bronze,
    Silver,
    Gold
}
```

Here's a class used for specifying decision criteria:

```
public class Room
{
    public int Number { get; set; }
    public string RoomType { get; set; }
    public string BedSize { get; set; }
}
```

These methods simulate getting data from two sources:

```
static List<Room> GetHotel1Rooms()
{
    return new List<Room>
    {
        new Room
        {
            Number = 333,
            BedSize = "King",
            RoomType = "Suite"
        },
        new Room
        {
            Number = 111,
            BedSize = "Queen",
            RoomType = "Regular"
        },
    };
}

static List<Room> GetHotel2Rooms()
{
    return new List<Room>
```

```
    {
        new Room
        {
            Number = 222,
            BedSize = "King",
            RoomType = "Regular"
        },
    };
}
```

This method joins those data sources to produce a list of tuples:

```
static
    List<(int no, string size, string type)>
    GetRooms()
{
    var rooms = GetHotel1Rooms().Union(GetHotel2Rooms());
    return
        (from room in rooms
         select (
            room.Number,
            room.BedSize,
            room.RoomType
        ))
        .ToList();
}
```

This method shows the business logic based on positional pattern matching:

```
static int AssignRoom(ScheduleType scheduleType)
{
    foreach (var room in GetRooms())
    {
        ScheduleType roomType = room switch
        {
            (_, "King", "Suite") => ScheduleType.Gold,
            (_, "King", "Regular") => ScheduleType.Silver,
            (_, "Queen", "Regular") => ScheduleType.Bronze,
            _ => ScheduleType.Bronze
        };

        if (roomType == scheduleType)
            return room.no;
    }

    return RoomNotAvailable;
}
```

The Main method drives the process:

```
static void Main()
{
    Console.Write(
        "Choose (1) Bronze, (2) Silver, or (3) Gold: ");
```

```
        string choice = Console.ReadLine();

        Enum.TryParse(choice, out ScheduleType scheduleType);

        int roomNumber = AssignRoom(scheduleType);

        if (roomNumber == RoomNotAvailable)
            Console.WriteLine("Room not available.");
        else
            Console.WriteLine($"The room number is {roomNumber}.");
    }
```

Discussion

The solution here is similar to Recipe 8.5, in that it also uses tuples for pattern matching. This solution differs in that it explores the situation where you have two different sources of data, shown in GetHotel1Rooms and GetHotel2Rooms, simulating what would normally be database queries. This can happen when companies merge or form partnerships and their data is similar but not entirely alike.

The GetRooms method shows how to use the LINQ Union operator to combine the two lists. Rather than create a new type for the combination of values we need, the method builds a collection of tuples.

When AssignRooms calls GetRooms, you don't need a deconstructor on an object because you're already working with tuples. This is a useful technique if you're working with third-party types where you can't modify their members.

Inside of AssignRoom, the switch expression uses tuples for the match. What's immediately noticeable here is the first parameter, representing the Room.Number property —there's a discard symbol for each pattern. Clearly, this could have been omitted in GetRooms, but I wrote it that way to make a couple of points: value positions must match and every value is required.

Tuple patterns require values to be in the proper positions (e.g., you can't swap Number and Size). The position of each pattern value must match the corresponding tuple position. In contrast, property patterns can be in any order and differ between cases.

For tuples, you must include a value for each position of the tuple. Therefore, even if you don't use a position in a pattern, you must at least specify the discard parameter. Property patterns don't have this restriction, allowing you to add or ignore whatever properties you want for the pattern.

See Also

Recipe 8.5, "Switching on Tuples"

8.7 Switching on Value Ranges

Problem

Your business rules are continuous, rather than discrete.

Solution

Here's an interface, as well as implementing classes that are results we're looking for:

```
public interface IRoomSchedule
{
    void ScheduleRoom();
}

public class GoldSchedule : IRoomSchedule
{
    public void ScheduleRoom() =>
        Console.WriteLine("Scheduling Gold Room");
}

public class SilverSchedule : IRoomSchedule
{
    public void ScheduleRoom() =>
        Console.WriteLine("Scheduling Silver Room");
}

public class BronzeSchedule : IRoomSchedule
{
    public void ScheduleRoom() =>
        Console.WriteLine("Scheduling Bronze Room");
}
```

This method uses relational pattern matching to produce results:

```
const int SilverPoints = 5000;
const int GoldPoints = 20000;

static IRoomSchedule GetSchedule(int points) =>
    points switch
    {
        >= GoldPoints => new GoldSchedule(),
        >= SilverPoints => new SilverSchedule(),
        < SilverPoints => new BronzeSchedule()
    };
```

The `Main` method drives the process:

```
static void Main()
{
    Console.Write("How many points? ");
    string response = Console.ReadLine();
```

```
        if (!int.TryParse(response, out int points))
        {
            Console.WriteLine($"'{response}' is invalid!");
            return;
        }

        IRoomSchedule schedule = GetSchedule(points);

        schedule.ScheduleRoom();
    }
```

Discussion

Previous sections of this chapter explored pattern matching based on discrete values. The pattern had to be exact to match. However, there are a lot of situations where values are continuous, rather than discrete. An example of this is the solution in this section, where hotel customers could have a range of points in their accounts.

In the solution, customers with points from 0 to 4,999 are Bronze. Those with points from 5,000 to 19,999 are Silver. Those with 20,000 points or more are Gold. The `Sil verPoints` and `GoldPoints` constants in the solution define the boundaries.

The `Main` method asks how many points a customer has and passes that value to `Get Schedule`. This value can vary, depending on how many times a person booked a room or used other hotel services. Because of this, `GetSchedule` uses a `switch` expression based on those points. Instead of using a discrete pattern for the match, `Get Schedule` uses relational operators.

The first pattern asks if `points` is equal to or higher than `GoldPoints`. If not, `points` must be less, and the code checks to see if the points are equal to or higher than `SilverPoints`. Since we already evaluated the `GoldPoints` case, it follows that the range is between `SilverPoints` and less than `GoldPoints`. The final case, less than `SilverPoints`, documents the meaning of Bronze, but you could have easily replaced that with a discard pattern because the other two cases handled every other possibility, and Bronze is all that's left.

8.8 Switching with Complex Conditions

Problem

Your business rules are multiconditional.

Solution

Here's an interface, as well as implementing classes that are results we're looking for:

```
public interface IRoomSchedule
{
    void ScheduleRoom();
}

public class GoldSchedule : IRoomSchedule
{
    public void ScheduleRoom() =>
        Console.WriteLine("Scheduling Gold Room");
}

public class SilverSchedule : IRoomSchedule
{
    public void ScheduleRoom() =>
        Console.WriteLine("Scheduling Silver Room");
}

public class BronzeSchedule : IRoomSchedule
{
    public void ScheduleRoom() =>
        Console.WriteLine("Scheduling Bronze Room");
}
```

This class describes the criteria to use:

```
public class Customer
{
    public int Points { get; set; }

    public bool HasFreeUpgrade { get; set; }
}
```

This method generates simulated data with various values to exercise our logic:

```
static List<Customer> GetCustomers() =>
    new List<Customer>
    {
        new Customer
        {
            Points = 25000,
            HasFreeUpgrade = false
        },
        new Customer
        {
            Points = 10000,
            HasFreeUpgrade = true
        },
        new Customer
        {
            Points = 1000,
            HasFreeUpgrade = true
        },
    };
```

Here's a method using complex logic in a `switch` expression:

```
static IRoomSchedule GetSchedule(Customer customer) =>
    customer switch
    {
        Customer c
            when
                c.Points >= GoldPoints
                    ||
                (c.Points >= SilverPoints && c.HasFreeUpgrade)
            => new GoldSchedule(),

        Customer c
            when
                c.Points >= SilverPoints
                    ||
                (c.Points < SilverPoints && c.HasFreeUpgrade)
            => new SilverSchedule(),

        Customer c
            when
                c.Points < SilverPoints
            => new BronzeSchedule(),

        _ => new BronzeSchedule()
    };
```

The `Main` method iterates through results:

```
static void Main()
{
    foreach (var customer in GetCustomers())
    {
        IRoomSchedule schedule = GetSchedule(customer);
        schedule.ScheduleRoom();
    }
}
```

Discussion

Sometimes conditions are so complex that the techniques shown in earlier sections of this chapter are inadequate for solving the problem. An example is the solution in this section that requires multiple conditions involving more than one property. Here, we use a `switch` expression with when clauses to specify matches.

This scenario is based on a `Customer` type, indicating number of points and whether the customer has a free upgrade. The free upgrade could have been from a contest or hotel promotion activity. When scheduling a room, we want to make sure that the customer gets a room commensurate with their point level. Additionally, if they have the free upgrade option, they receive a room that is upgraded to the next higher level. For simplicity, we're conveniently ignoring whether Gold has a free upgrade.

The GetSchedule method operates on an instance of Customer. Both the cases for Gold and Silver result in a room at that level. Additionally, the || operator says that if customer is at the next lower level, but HasFreeUpgrade is true, then the result is a room at this higher level.

Using logic like this can get complex fast. Notice the use of newlines and other spacing to add symmetry and consistency to reading the result.

While this technique can help when the logic is a bit more complex than a discrete pattern match, you might want to consider a threshold where using if statements might be a better implementation. One consideration is maintenance, because breaking each piece of the logic out can help with debugging, whereas a single expression with multiple conditions might not be immediately obvious.

8.9 Using Logical Conditions

Problem

You want multiconditional logic to be more readable.

Solution

Here's a class to use as criteria:

```
public class Customer
{
    public int Points { get; set; }

    public int Month { get; set; }
}
```

This method simulates a data source:

```
static List<Customer> GetCustomers() =>
    new List<Customer>
    {
        new Customer
        {
            Points = 25000,
            Month = 1
        },
        new Customer
        {
            Points = 10000,
            Month = 12
        },
        new Customer
        {
            Points = 10000,
```

```
        Month = 11
    },
    new Customer
    {
        Points = 1000,
        Month = 2
    },
};
```

This method implements business rules with conditional logic in a switch expression:

```
const int SilverPoints = 5000;
const int GoldPoints = 20000;

const int May = 5;
const int Sep = 9;
const int Dec = 12;

static decimal GetDiscount(Customer customer) =>
    (customer.Points, customer.Month) switch
    {
        (>= GoldPoints, not Dec and > Sep or < May) => 0.15m,
        (>= GoldPoints, Dec) => 0.10m,
        (>= SilverPoints, not (Dec or <= Sep and >= May)) => 0.05m,
        _ => 0.0m
    };
```

The Main method drives this process:

```
static void Main()
{
    foreach (var customer in GetCustomers())
    {
        decimal discount = GetDiscount(customer);
        Console.WriteLine(discount);
    }
}
```

Discussion

Recipe 8.8 described how to add complex logic to switch expressions. By complex, I'm referring to multiple conditions involving two or more properties. This contrasts with simple pattern matching for previous sections of this chapter that used property and tuple patterns. Somewhere in between these contrasting approaches of simple and complex is a moderate approach where you need logic isolated within individual properties.

The properties of interest in this solution are the Points and Month of the Customer class. Similar to earlier sections, the Points property contributes to receiving a room for a customer that has at least a certain number of points. The other condition,

Month, is the month when the customer wants to book the room. Because of seasonal supply and demand, some months leave the hotel with more open rooms. Therefore, this application provides incentives, based on points, for customers to book rooms in the months with more open rooms.

In the solution, you can see that there are GoldPoints and SilverPoints constants to tell which level a customer is. Also, there are constants for May, Sep, and Dec—the busy months. The logic will be to give a discount in the months that are not busy.

The pattern for the switch expression in GetDiscount matches on two properties: Points and Month. Notice how this code doesn't rely on an object deconstructor and the original parameter is a class, rather than a tuple. GetDiscount creates an inline tuple for the switch expression.

The pattern itself relies on relational operators for Points, as in Recipe 8.7.

The Month pattern uses the new C# 9 logical operators: and, not, and or. The first expression ensures the customer receives a discount during the winter months, between Sep and May, except for Dec. The second pattern says that a Gold customer still gets a discount in Dec, except that it's 10% instead of 15%.

The last pattern is logically equivalent to the first and uses DeMorgan's Theorem. That is, it negates the whole result and swaps and with or. Because the last example applies not to the entire expression, it uses parentheses. In the first pattern, not applied to Dec only.

See Also

Recipe 8.7, "Switching on Value Ranges"

Recipe 8.8, "Switching with Complex Conditions"

8.10 Switching on Type

Problem

You need the type of an object for decision making.

Solution

Here's an interface, as well as implementing classes that are results we're looking for:

```
public interface IRoomSchedule
{
    void ScheduleRoom();
}
```

```
public class GoldSchedule : IRoomSchedule
{
    public void ScheduleRoom() =>
        Console.WriteLine("Scheduling Gold Room");
}

public class SilverSchedule : IRoomSchedule
{
    public void ScheduleRoom() =>
        Console.WriteLine("Scheduling Silver Room");
}

public class BronzeSchedule : IRoomSchedule
{
    public void ScheduleRoom() =>
        Console.WriteLine("Scheduling Bronze Room");
}
```

The following types represent criteria:

```
public class Customer {}

public class GoldCustomer : Customer {}

public class SilverCustomer : Customer {}

public class BronzeCustomer : Customer {}
```

This method simulates a data source:

```
static List<Customer> GetCustomers() =>
    new List<Customer>
    {
        new GoldCustomer(),
        new SilverCustomer(),
        new BronzeCustomer()
    };
```

Here's a method that implements logic based on type pattern matching:

```
static IRoomSchedule GetSchedule(Customer customer) =>
    customer switch
    {
        GoldCustomer => new GoldSchedule(),
        SilverCustomer => new SilverSchedule(),
        BronzeCustomer => new BronzeSchedule(),
        _ => new BronzeSchedule()
    };
```

The `Main` method iterates through the data to exercise the pattern matching logic:

```
static void Main()
{
    foreach (var customer in GetCustomers())
    {
        IRoomSchedule schedule = GetSchedule(customer);
        schedule.ScheduleRoom();
    }
}
```

Discussion

It used to be that the only way to make a decision on type was to either use `if` statements or convert the object's type to a `string` and use a `switch` statement with `string` cases. A popular ask for C# over the years was to allow a `switch` statement with type cases, and now we finally have it.

The solution has a set of classes for `GoldCustomer`, `SilverCustomer`, and `BronzeCustomer`, each deriving from `Customer`. Our goal in this program is to schedule a room, based on the matching class type.

The `GetSchedule` method does the scheduling by accepting an object of type `Customer`, and the `switch` expression has a pattern for each of the classes that derive from `Customer`. All you need to do is specify the name of each class and the `switch` expression matches based on the object type.

CHAPTER 9

Examining Recent C# Language Highlights

The C# programming language is continually evolving. Earlier chapters discussed subjects from C# 1 through C# 8. The exception is pattern matching in Chapter 8, where some of the patterns were introduced in C# 9. This chapter focuses primarily on C# 9, the exception being the subject of Recipe 9.9, which is a C# 8 feature.

A central concept in this chapter is immutability—the ability to create and operate on types that don't change. Immutability is important for safe multithreading as well as for the cognitive relief of knowing that code you've passed a type to won't change (mutate) the contents of the object.

The example scenario is working with addresses, such as a mailing address or a shipping address. In many contexts, an address is a value, meaning that it doesn't have an identity. The address exists as a set of data (value) associated with an entity such as a customer or company. On the other hand, an entity does have an identity, normally modeled as an ID field in a database. Because we're treating it as a value, address becomes a useful candidate for immutability because we don't want the value to change once it's set.

One interesting feature of C# 9 is called *module initialization*. Think about how we use constructors to initialize types or Main to initialize an application. Module initialization lets you write initialization code at the scope of an assembly, and you'll see how that works.

Another C# 9 theme is code simplification. You'll see a section on how to write code without namespaces or classes, eliminating the ceremony around starting an application in a Main method. Another simplification is in instantiating objects, with a new feature to infer type contextually. Let's start with simplifying application startup.

9.1 Simplifying Application Startup

Problem

You need to eliminate as much code as possible for your application entry point.

Solution

This is a top-level program:

```
using System;

Console.WriteLine("Address Info:\n");

Console.Write("Street: ");
string street = Console.ReadLine();

Console.Write("City: ");
string city = Console.ReadLine();

Console.Write("State: ");
string state = Console.ReadLine();

Console.Write("Zip: ");
string zip = Console.ReadLine();

Console.WriteLine($@"
    Your address is:

    {street}
    {city}, {state} {zip}");
```

Here's the code that the C# compiler generates:

```
using System;
using System.Runtime.CompilerServices;

[CompilerGenerated]
internal static class <Program>$
{
  private static void <Main>$(string[] args)
  {
    Console.WriteLine("Address Info:\n");
    Console.Write("Street: ");
    string street = Console.ReadLine();
    Console.Write("City: ");
    string city = Console.ReadLine();
    Console.Write("State: ");
    string state = Console.ReadLine();
    Console.Write("Zip: ");
    string zip = Console.ReadLine();
    Console.WriteLine(
```

```
            "\r\n    Your address is:\r\n\r\n    " + street +
            "\r\n    " + city + ", " + state + " " + zip);
        }
    }
```

Discussion

A lot of the code we write is boilerplate—standard syntax that we copy over and over again. In the case of a console app with a Main method, you have a namespace that generally matches the project name, a class named Program, and a Main method. While you're free to remove the namespace and rename the class, people rarely do. Developers have recognized this for years, and in C# 9, we no longer need the boilerplate code.

The solution shows the new top-level statements feature, where the code doesn't have a namespace, class, or Main method. It's the minimal amount of code required to start the app. The example code requests address details and prints out the results and works exactly as written.

 If you're teaching someone how to program in C#, top-level statements can make the task easier. You don't need to explain methods, because you're not writing a Main method. You don't need to explain a class, which is an object with members and more. You can leave out the namespace discussion and all the nuance about naming and organization. Rather than waxing lightly across (or ignoring) all of these complex details, you can discuss them later, when the student is ready.

Top-level statements serve in place of the Main method. The solution shows the code that the compiler generates. It has the CompilerGenerated attribute, class, and Main method. The naming conventions match the typical boilerplate code that Visual Studio, the .NET CLI, and other IDEs produce for console apps.

Interestingly, you can only put top-level statements in a single file. If you try putting them in multiple files, you'll encounter the following compiler error:

```
CS8802 Only one compilation unit can have top-level statements.
```

9.2 Reducing Instantiation Syntax

Problem

Object instantiation is too redundant and verbose.

Solution

We're going to instantiate this class:

```csharp
public class Address
{
    public Address() { }

    public Address(
        string street,
        string city,
        string state,
        string zip)
    {
        Street = street;
        City = city;
        State = state;
        Zip = zip;
    }

    public string Street { get; set; }
    public string City { get; set; }
    public string State { get; set; }
    public string Zip { get; set; }
}
```

Here are different ways to instantiate that class:

```csharp
class Program
{
    // doesn't work at this level
    // var address = new Address();

    // this still works
    Address addressOld = new Address();

    // new target typed field
    Address addressNew = new();

    static void Main()
    {
        // these still work
        var addressLocalVar = new Address();
        Address addressLocalOld = new Address();

        // new target typed local variable
        Address addressLocalNew = new();

        // target typed with object ini
        Address addressObjectInit = new()
        {
            Street = "123 4th St.",
            City =   "My City",
```

```
        State =  "ZZ",
        Zip =    "55555-3333"
    };

    // target typed with ctor init
    Address addressCtorInit = new(
        street: "567 8th Ave.",
        city:   "Some Place",
        state:  "YY",
        zip:    "12345-7890");
    }
}
```

Discussion

Originally, C# had a single way to instantiate a variable: declaring the type, variable name, new operator, type, and parenthesized constructor parameter list. You can see this in the solution via the addressOld field and addressLocalOld variable.

Under the C# 3 paradigm, we needed a strongly typed variable (the var keyword) to hold anonymous types, especially for LINQ queries. A var variable required assignment and became a strongly typed assigned type. Some people saw that var looked similar to the JavaScript var and were uncomfortable using it. However, as stated earlier, the C# var variable is strongly typed, meaning that you can't declare the variable to be of a different type.

Besides LINQ, a convenient use case for var emerged in type instantiation. Developers recognized the ability to eliminate redundancy in defining variables by using var. You can see how this works in the solution for the addressLocalVar variable.

Because of the popularity of var to reduce code in object instantiation, developers looked toward fields for the same experience. However, you can't use var with fields, as demonstrated in the address field in the solution, which is commented out.

C# 9 fixes the redundancy concerns with a feature called *target-typed new*. Instead of using var, target-typed new declares the type, identifier, and new keyword with a parameter list. The addressNew field and addressLocalNew variable show how this works. Now you can instantiate fields without the redundancy of specifying the same type twice in the same statement.

Target-typed new is shortcut syntax for the same type instantiation we've done forever. That means you can still use object initializers and constructor overloads, shown in addressObjectInit and addressCtorInit, respectively.

Now that we have target-typed new, there's an argument to be made for preferring that over var. The first reason is the cognitive hesitation of developers who eschew var because it's spelled the same way as the JavaScript var—even though we know the

C# var is strongly typed. The other is that since we can use target-typed new for both variables and fields, we have syntactic consistency in how we instantiate types. Some developers will view mixing var and target-typed new in the same code as distracting or messy.

 Even if you don't use var for type instantiation, it's still useful. When doing LINQ queries, you can reshape data with anonymous type projections in the same method, and that requires a var for the results.

Finally, introducing target-typed new into the language doesn't necessarily imply a preference for direct object instantiation. As explained in Recipe 1.2, IoC is a powerful mechanism for decoupling code, promoting separation of concerns, and making code more testable.

See Also

Recipe 1.2, "Removing Explicit Dependencies"

9.3 Initializing Immutable State

Problem

You need immutable properties that are populated only during instantiation.

Solution

Here's a class with immutable state:

```
public class Address
{
    public Address() { }

    public Address(
        string street,
        string city,
        string state,
        string zip)
    {
        Street = street;
        City = city;
        State = state;
        Zip = zip;
    }

    public string Street { get; init; }
```

```
    public string City { get; init; }
    public string State { get; init; }
    public string Zip { get; init; }
}
```

Here are a couple of ways to instantiate the immutable class:

```
static void Main(string[] args)
{
    Address addressObjectInit = new()
    {
        Street = "123 4th St.",
        City = "My City",
        State = "ZZ",
        Zip = "55555-3333"
    };

    // not allowed
    //addressObjectInit.City = "A Locality";

    // target typed with ctor init
    Address addressCtorInit = new(
        street: "567 8th Ave.",
        city: "Some Place",
        state: "YY",
        zip: "12345-7890");

    // not allowed
    //addressCtorInit.Zip = "98765";
}
```

Discussion

Immutability, the ability to create and operate on types that don't change, is increasingly an important feature for the quality and correctness of code. Imagine the scenario where you pass an object to a method and get the same type of object back. Assuming you don't own the code for that method, how do you know what that method did to the object you gave it? Short of decompilation or trusting documentation, you don't know. However, if the object is immutable, it can't change, and you know that the method didn't change anything.

Another use case for immutability is in multithreading. The reality of deadlocks and race conditions have plagued developers for a long time. In the deadlock scenario, separate threads wait on each other to release a resource that the other needs for changing. In the race condition scenario, you don't know which thread will modify an object first, resulting in inconsistent object state. In each case, immutability simplifies the scenario because neither thread can change an existing object—they must rely on their own copy. Multithreading is such a complex topic that it couldn't be fairly discussed here in depth, but the point is that immutability is part of the solution.

In the solution, the `Address` class is immutable. You can instantiate it with the data you need, but its contents can't change after that. Notice that the properties have a getter but not a setter. Instead, they have initters. The initters let you instantiate the object but not change it thereafter.

The `Main` method shows how this works. The `addressObjectInit` variable instantiates normally, but setting any of its properties, including `City`, won't compile. The `addressCtorInit` variable shows a similar situation.

If you have an existing class, making properties init-only can be useful. However, if you're building new types with C# 9, you can also define records, as discussed in the next recipe.

See Also

Recipe 9.4, "Creating Immutable Types"

9.4 Creating Immutable Types

Problem

You need an immutable reference type but don't want to write all the plumbing code.

Solution

Here is a C# record:

```
record Address(
    string Street,
    string City,
    string State,
    string Zip);
```

This code shows how to use that record:

```
static void Main(string[] args)
{
    var addressClassic = new Address(
        Street: "567 8th Ave.",
        City: "Some Place",
        State: "YY",
        Zip: "12345-7890");

    // or

    Address addressCtorInit = new(
        Street: "567 8th Ave.",
        City: "Some Place",
        State: "YY",
```

```
        Zip: "12345-7890");

    // not allowed
    //addressCtorInit.Street = "333 2nd St.";

    Console.WriteLine(
        $"Value Equal:      " +
        $"{addressClassic == addressCtorInit}");
    Console.WriteLine(
        $"Reference Equal: " +
        $"{ReferenceEquals(addressClassic, addressCtorInit)}");

    Console.WriteLine(
        $"{nameof(addressClassic)}: {addressClassic}");
    Console.WriteLine(
        $"{nameof(Address)}:          {addressCtorInit}");
}
```

And this is the output:

```
Value Equal:      True
Reference Equal: False
addressClassic: Address
{
    Street = 567 8th Ave., City = Some Place,
    State = YY, Zip = 12345-7890
}
Address:          Address
{
    Street = 567 8th Ave., City = Some Place,
    State = YY, Zip = 12345-7890
}
```

Here's the synthesized code that the C# compiler generates:

```
using System;
using System.Collections.Generic;
using System.Runtime.CompilerServices;
using System.Text;
using Section_09_04;

internal class Address : IEquatable<Address>
{
    protected virtual Type EqualityContract
    {
        [CompilerGenerated]
        get
        {
            return typeof(Address);
        }
    }

    public string Street { get; set; }
```

```csharp
    public string City { get; set; }

    public string State { get; set; }

    public string Zip { get; set; }

    public Address(string Street, string City, string State, string Zip)
    {
        this.Street = Street;
        this.City = City;
        this.State = State;
        this.Zip = Zip;
        base..ctor();
    }

    public override string ToString()
    {
        StringBuilder stringBuilder = new StringBuilder();
        stringBuilder.Append("Address");
        stringBuilder.Append(" { ");
        if (PrintMembers(stringBuilder))
        {
            stringBuilder.Append(" ");
        }
        stringBuilder.Append("}");
        return stringBuilder.ToString();
    }

    protected virtual bool PrintMembers(StringBuilder builder)
    {
        builder.Append("Street");
        builder.Append(" = ");
        builder.Append((object?)Street);
        builder.Append(", ");
        builder.Append("City");
        builder.Append(" = ");
        builder.Append((object?)City);
        builder.Append(", ");
        builder.Append("State");
        builder.Append(" = ");
        builder.Append((object?)State);
        builder.Append(", ");
        builder.Append("Zip");
        builder.Append(" = ");
        builder.Append((object?)Zip);
        return true;
    }

    public static bool operator !=(Address? r1, Address? r2)
    {
        return !(r1 == r2);
    }
```

```csharp
public static bool operator ==(Address? r1, Address? r2)
{
    return (object)r1 == r2 || (r1?.Equals(r2) ?? false);
}

public override int GetHashCode()
{
    return
    (((EqualityComparer<Type>.Default.GetHashCode(EqualityContract)
    * -1521134295
    + EqualityComparer<string>.Default.GetHashCode(Street))
    * -1521134295
    + EqualityComparer<string>.Default.GetHashCode(City))
    * -1521134295
    + EqualityComparer<string>.Default.GetHashCode(State))
    * -1521134295
    + EqualityComparer<string>.Default.GetHashCode(Zip);
}

public override bool Equals(object? obj)
{
    return Equals(obj as Address);
}

public virtual bool Equals(Address? other)
{
    return (object)other != null
    && EqualityContract == other!.EqualityContract
    && EqualityComparer<string>.Default.Equals(Street, other!.Street)
    && EqualityComparer<string>.Default.Equals(City, other!.City)
    && EqualityComparer<string>.Default.Equals(State, other!.State)
    && EqualityComparer<string>.Default.Equals(Zip, other!.Zip);
}

public virtual Address <Clone>$()
{
    return new Address(this);
}

protected Address(Address original)
{
    Street = original.Street;
    City = original.City;
    State = original.State;
    Zip = original.Zip;
}

public void Deconstruct(
    out string Street, out string City,
    out string State, out string Zip)
{
```

```
        Street = this.Street;
        City = this.City;
        State = this.State;
        Zip = this.Zip;
    }
}
```

Discussion

Recipe 9.3 discusses immutability and its benefits and how to create an immutable class. This works great if you have existing types and want to migrate them to being immutable. However, for new code and types that you want to make immutable, consider using a record.

Records were introduced in C# 9 as a way to create simple immutable types. The solution shows how to do this with the `Address` record. Declare the type as record, give it a type name, list the properties, and terminate with a semicolon. Although this might look similar to defining a constructor or method, the parameters define the properties of this new type, and they follow the common convention of Pascal case naming.

The solution shows how to instantiate the `Address` record. Notice how the `address CtorInit` variable doesn't allow changing its state, including the `Street` property.

An interesting fact about records is that they are reference types with value semantics. The solution shows that comparing `addressClassic` and `addressCtorInit` with `==` results in `true`. This demonstrates value equality because the properties of both records are identical. However, notice the `ReferenceEquals` comparison. It's `false` because records are reference types and each refers to separate objects in memory.

Although declaring the `Address` record was short and quick, this is a huge simplification of the real code that the C# compiler generates. The solution shows the synthesized code with many members. The type is a class and it has a constructor overload with parameters for populating each property.

The key to value equality is the implementation of `IEquatable<Address>`. The class has both a weakly typed and strongly typed `Equals` method. Recipe 2.5 showed how to implement `IEquatable<T>`, which shares some similarity to this implementation. One difference is the type being stored in the `EqualityContract` property. Since the C# generated class uses `EqualityContract` in both `Equals` and `GetHashCode`, it makes sense to eliminate the redundancy.

The `ToString` and `PrintMembers` implementations might be familiar if you've read Recipe 3.6. The implementations are nearly identical. Notice that the `PrintMembers` is `virtual`, and that allows derived types to add their values to the output.

Finally, the synthesized class includes a `Clone` method to get a shallow copy, a deconstructor for representing values as a tuple, and a copy constructor for making a copy of another record. What would also be convenient is a way to get a copy of the current object but with modifications, which is discussed next.

See Also

Recipe 2.5, "Checking for Type Equality"

Recipe 3.6, "Customizing Class String Representation"

Recipe 9.3, "Initializing Immutable State"

9.5 Simplifying Immutable Type Assignments

Problem

You need to change a property of an object but don't want to mutate the original object.

Solution

We'll use this record:

```
record Address(
    string Street,
    string City,
    string State,
    string Zip);
```

And this code shows how to make a copy of that record:

```
static void Main(string[] args)
{
    Address addressPre = new(
        Street: "567 8th Ave.",
        City: "Some Place",
        State: "YY",
        Zip: "12345-7890");

    Address addressPost =
        addressPre with
        {
            Street = "569 8th Ave."
        };

    Console.WriteLine($"Pre:  {addressPre}");
    Console.WriteLine($"Post: {addressPost}");

    Console.WriteLine(
```

```
        $"Value Equal: " +
        $"{addressPre == addressPost}");
    }
```

Discussion

As discussed in Recipe 9.4, records have a normal constructor, a copy constructor, and a clone method to create new records of the same type. There's one scenario that these options don't easily cover: getting a type with modifications. That is, what if you wanted everything on the object to be the same, except for one or two properties? This section shows a simple way to do that.

Since records are immutable, you can't modify any of their properties. You could always instantiate a new record and supply all of the properties, but that is wasteful when only a single property changes, especially if it's an object with a lot of properties.

The solution in C# 9 uses a `with` expression. You have an existing record, add a `with` expression, and only change the properties that need to change. This gives you a new instance of the record type with the changes you want.

The solution does this on the `addressPre` variable. The `with` expression uses a block of property assignments to specify the properties that need to change. This example changes a single property. You can also set multiple properties in the same way you do with object initializers, via a comma-separated list.

See Also

Recipe 9.4, "Creating Immutable Types"

9.6 Designing for Record Reuse

Problem

You need to avoid duplicating functionality.

Solution

Here's an abstract base record:

```
public abstract record AddressBase(
    string Street,
    string City,
    string State,
    string Zip);
```

These two records derive from that abstract base record:

```
public record MailingAddress(
    string Street,
    string City,
    string State,
    string Zip,
    string Email,
    bool PreferEmail)
    : AddressBase(Street, City, State, Zip);

public record ShippingAddress : AddressBase
{
    public ShippingAddress(
        string street,
        string city,
        string state,
        string zip,
        string deliveryInstructions)
        : base(street, city, state, zip)
    {
        if (street.Contains("P.O. Box"))
            throw new ArgumentException(
                "P.O. Boxes aren't allowed");

        DeliveryInstructions = deliveryInstructions;
    }

    public string DeliveryInstructions { get; init; }
}
```

Here's how you can work with those records:

```
static void Main(string[] args)
{
    MailingAddress mailAddress = new(
        Street: "567 8th Ave.",
        City: "Some Place",
        State: "YY",
        Zip: "12345-7890",
        Email: "me@example.com",
        PreferEmail: true);

    ShippingAddress shipAddress = new(
        street: "567 8th Ave.",
        city: "Some Place",
        state: "YY",
        zip: "12345-7890",
        deliveryInstructions: "Ring Doorbell");

    Console.WriteLine($"Mail: {mailAddress}");
    Console.WriteLine($"Ship: {shipAddress}");

    Console.WriteLine(
        $"Derived types equal: " +
```

```
        $"{mailAddress == shipAddress}");

    AddressBase mailBase = mailAddress;
    AddressBase shipBase = shipAddress;
    Console.WriteLine(
        $"Base types equal: " +
        $"{mailBase == shipBase}");
}
```

Discussion

One of the ways to achieve reuse in C# is via inheritance. Records support inheritance in the same manner as classes.

The solution has a record named AddressBase. As its name suggests, AddressBase is intended to be a base record. AddressBase is also abstract, preventing direct instantiation. It has properties common to all derived types.

MailingAddress and ShippingAddress derive from AddressBase, using the inheritance syntax similar to classes. The difference is that the inherited record declaration includes a parameter list, indicating which parameters from the derived record match the base record.

MailingAddress specializes AddressBase with two new properties: Email and PreferEmail. ShippingAddress specializes AddressBase with an extra Delivery Instructions property.

The definition of ShippingAddress is different because it explicitly defines members, rather than using default record syntax. It has a constructor, just like a C# class, passing parameters to the base, AddressBase. The ShippingAddress constructor implementation has validation code that throws an exception to protect against invalid initialization. In this case, it enforces the logic that a P.O. box is not a place you can deliver merchandise to. The constructor also initializes the DeliveryInstruc tions property. This demonstrates that while default record syntax simplifies the code, you still have the ability to customize records all you need.

When customizing records, you can add any member that a class could have. Additionally, you can override default implementations such as equality, ToString output, or constructors. Also, customizing as done with ShippingAddress doesn't prevent the C# compiler from generating the default record implementation.

9.7 Returning Different Method Override Types

Problem

You're overriding a base class method but need to return a more specific type.

Solution

Here are the records we want to work with:

```
public abstract record AddressBase(
    string Street,
    string City,
    string State,
    string Zip);

public record MailingAddress(
    string Street,
    string City,
    string State,
    string Zip,
    string Email,
    bool PreferEmail)
    : AddressBase(Street, City, State, Zip);

public record ShippingAddress : AddressBase
{
    public ShippingAddress(
        string street,
        string city,
        string state,
        string zip,
        string deliveryInstructions)
        : base(street, city, state, zip)
    {
        if (street.Contains("P.O. Box"))
            throw new ArgumentException(
                "P.O. Boxes aren't allowed");

        DeliveryInstructions = deliveryInstructions;
    }

    public string DeliveryInstructions { get; init; }
}
```

This base class has a method, returning a base record:

```
abstract class DeliveryBase
{
    public abstract AddressBase GetAddress(string name);
}
```

These classes have methods returning derived records:

```
class Communications : DeliveryBase
{
    public override MailingAddress GetAddress(string name)
    {
        return new(
            Street: "567 8th Ave.",
```

```
                    City: "Some Place",
                    State: "YY",
                    Zip: "12345-7890",
                    Email: "me@example.com",
                    PreferEmail: true);
        }
    }

    class Shipping : DeliveryBase
    {
        public override ShippingAddress GetAddress(string name)
        {
            return new(
                street: "567 8th Ave.",
                city: "Some Place",
                state: "YY",
                zip: "12345-7890",
                deliveryInstructions: "Ring Doorbell");
        }
    }
```

This code shows how to use those derived classes that return derived records:

```
static void Main(string[] args)
{
    Communications comm = new();
    MailingAddress mailAddr = comm.GetAddress("Person A");
    Console.WriteLine(mailAddr);

    Shipping ship = new();
    ShippingAddress shipAddr = ship.GetAddress("Person B");
    Console.WriteLine(shipAddr);
}
```

Discussion

It used to be that method overrides were required to return the same type as the base class virtual method return type. The problem was that derived classes often needed to return specialized information from their overrides. The alternatives were ugly:

1. Create a new nonpolymorphic method.

2. Return the base type.

3. Return a type derived from the base return type and expect the caller to convert.

None of these choices are optimal, and fortunately, C# 9 offers a solution through covariant return types.

The solution has two sets of type hierarchies: one for return types and one for method polymorphism. AddressBase and its two derived records, MailingAddress and ShippingAddress, represent the return types. The DeliveryBase class, with its derived classes, `Communications` and `Shipping`, have a `GetAddress` method that operates polymorphically.

 Notice how the implementation of `GetAddress` returns target-typed new instances. The compiler infers type by context, which is the return type in these examples. You can learn more about target-typed new in Recipe 9.2.

Prior to C# 9, the `GetAddress` in `Communications` and `Shipping` would be forced to return `AddressBase`. However, looking at the solution implementation, the `GetAddress` in `Communications` and `Shipping` return `MailingAddress` and `ShippingAddress`, respectively.

See Also

Recipe 9.2, "Reducing Instantiation Syntax"

9.8 Implementing Iterators as Extension Methods

Problem

You need an iterator on a third-party type for which you don't have the code.

Solution

Here's a definition to a type in a third-party library that we don't have access to:

```
public record Address(
    string Street,
    string City,
    string State,
    string Zip);
```

This class has an enumerator extension method for that type:

```
public static class AddressExtensions
{
    public static IEnumerator<string> GetEnumerator(
        this Address address)
    {
        yield return address.Street;
        yield return address.City;
        yield return address.State;
        yield return address.Zip;
        yield break;
    }
}
```

Here's how to use that enumerator:

```
class Program
{
    static void Main()
    {
        IEnumerable<Address> addresses = GetAddresses();

        foreach (var address in addresses)
        {
            foreach (var line in address)
                Console.WriteLine(line);

            Console.WriteLine();
        }
    }

    static IEnumerable<Address> GetAddresses()
    {
        return new List<Address>
        {
            new Address(
                Street: "567 8th Ave.",
                City: "Some Place",
                State: "YY",
                Zip: "12345-7890"),
            new Address(
                Street: "569 8th Ave.",
                City: "Some Place",
                State: "YY",
                Zip: "12345-7890")
        };
    }
}
```

Discussion

Sometimes, it's convenient to add an iterator to an object. Doing so lets you separate the concerns of dissecting, transforming, and returning object data from the consuming code that wants to concentrate on solving the business problem. If you own the code of an object and want to loop over its contents, add an iterator. However, if the object is from a third party and you don't have access to the code, you used to be forced to add extraneous logic to business code. In C# 9, you now have the ability to add a GetEnumerator method as an extension method.

In the solution, the Address record is the object we want to iterate over. More specifically, we want to iterate on the members of the Address record, similar to the way you can iterate over properties of a JavaScript object.

The AddressExtensions method has an extension method named GetEnumerator that takes an Address parameter and returns an IEnumerable<T>. The this parameter works just like for any other extension method, specifying the type and instance to operate on. The pattern for the iterator is that the method must be named GetEnumerator, and it must return an IEnumerator<T>. The type, T, can be any type of your choosing—whatever you need. In this example, T is string. This means that you need to convert each property to a string, which isn't a problem in Address because all properties are already a string. Consistent with C# iterator implementation, the AddressExtensions GetEnumerator method uses yield return for each value and yield break to indicate the end of iteration.

After getting a list of Address, the Main method has a nested foreach loop where the inner foreach iterates on an instance of Address. Because of the extension method, the foreach works on address the same as it does with arrays and collections—no extra syntax.

9.9 Slicing Arrays

Problem

You want to use ranges to page through data.

Solution

We're going to use this record:

```
public record Address(
    string Street,
    string City,
    string State,
    string Zip);
```

This method populates an array of records:

```
Address[] GetAddresses()
{
    int count = 15;
    List<Address> addresses = new();

    for (int i = 0; i < count; i++)
    {
        string streetSuffix =
            i switch
            {
                0 => "st",
                1 => "nd",
                2 => "rd",
                _ => "th"
```

```
        };

        addresses.Add(
            new(
            Street: $"{i+100} {i+1}{streetSuffix} St.",
            City: "My Place",
            State: "ZZ",
            Zip: "12345-7890"));
    }

    return addresses.ToArray();
}
```

This method does paging by slicing an array of records:

```
public IEnumerable<Address[]> GetAddresses(int perPage)
{
    Address[] addresses = GetAddresses();

    for (int i = 0, j = i+perPage;
        i < addresses.Length;
        i+=perPage, j+=perPage)
    {
        yield return addresses[i..j];
    }
}
```

This code iterates through pages of the record:

```
static void Main()
{
    AddressService addressSvc = new();

    foreach (var addresses in
        addressSvc.GetAddresses(perRow: 3))
    {
        foreach (var address in addresses)
        {
            Console.WriteLine(address);
        }

        Console.WriteLine("\nNew Page\n");
    }
}
```

Discussion

Since C# 8, it has been much easier to slice arrays. Specify the beginning index, concatenate two dots, and specify the last index.

This solution looks at slicing from the perspective of paging. Some of the applications we use page by number of rows or number of columns in a row. This solution pages Address instances by three per page.

There are two overloads of the GetAddresses method. The first, parameterless version, generates unique addresses.

The second GetAddresses overload is an iterator that takes an int parameter, per Page, instructing the method to return that many instances of Address at one time. After getting a list of Address instances, the for loop controls iterating through the list. The for initializer sets i to the first Address and j to one more than the last Address. Since i is the start of the range, the for condition ensures that i doesn't exceed the size of the array. The for incrementer adjusts i and j to the next set of Address instances (that is, the next page).

GetAddresses(int perPage) is an iterator, as indicated by the IEnumerable<Address[]> return type and the fact that it uses yield return on results. While Recipe 9.8 showed how to add an iterator as an extension method, this example assumes you have access to the code and adding an iterator directly to the code is preferable.

The Main method shows how to use the GetAddresses(int perPage) iterator, returning the page that was sliced out of the original Address[].

See Also

Recipe 9.8, "Implementing Iterators as Extension Methods"

9.10 Initializing Entire Modules

Problem

You need IoC to work on a class library without relying on the caller to do it right.

Solution

Here's a repository that returns records:

```
public record Address(
    string Street,
    string City,
    string State,
    string Zip);

public interface IAddressRepository
{
    List<Address> GetAddresses();
```

```
    }

    public class AddressRepository : IAddressRepository
    {
        public List<Address> GetAddresses() =>
            new List<Address>
            {
                new (
                    Street: "123 4th St.",
                    City: "My Place",
                    State: "ZZ",
                    Zip: "12345-7890"),
                new (
                    Street: "567 8th Ave.",
                    City: "Some Place",
                    State: "YY",
                    Zip: "12345-7890"),
                new (
                    Street: "567 8th Ave.",
                    City: "Some Place",
                    State: "YY",
                    Zip: "12345-7890")
            };
    }
```

This module initializer configures an IoC container:

```
class Initializer
{
    internal static ServiceProvider Container { get; set; }

    [ModuleInitializer]
    internal static void InitAddressUtilities()
    {
        var services = new ServiceCollection();
        services.AddTransient<AddressService>();
        services.AddTransient<IAddressRepository, AddressRepository>();
        Container = services.BuildServiceProvider();
    }
}
```

This service relies on the IoC container:

```
public class AddressService
{
    readonly IAddressRepository addressRep;

    public AddressService(IAddressRepository addressRep) =>
        this.addressRep = addressRep;

    public static AddressService Create() =>
        Initializer.Container.GetRequiredService<AddressService>();

    public List<Address> GetAddresses() =>
```

```
        (from address in addressRep.GetAddresses()
         select address)
        .Distinct()
        .ToList();
}
```

This `Main` method is a client that consumes the service:

```
static void Main()
{
    AddressService addressSvc = AddressService.Create();

    addressSvc
        .GetAddresses()
        .ForEach(address =>
            Console.WriteLine(address));
}
```

Discussion

C# 9 added a feature called module initialization. Essentially, this allows you to add any kind of initialization code for an assembly. This initialization code runs before any other code in the assembly.

At first glance, this might sound strange because console, Windows Forms, and WPF apps have `Main` methods. Even all versions of ASP.NET and Web API have startup code. I'm not saying that there isn't a use case for those technologies, though it seems like a rare event for the average professional developer.

 Another initialization technique that has existed since C# 1 is the use of static constructors. A static constructor only runs whenever code accesses class members, either via type or instance. So, a static constructor isn't a valid substitute for module initialization because it's possible that calling code will never access a member of that class, and the static constructor will never run.

That said, there is a set of use cases that involve class libraries. The problem has always been that you don't know how consuming code will use your library. You can document and set a contract that says the user must call some method or start the library a certain way, and that's as close as you get to guaranteeing any type of control over initialization.

Module initialization changes that because now you have more control over how to initialize library code, regardless of what the user does. The solution solves the problem of ensuring that IoC gets initialized before any code runs.

The `AddressService` class offers two ways to instantiate an instance of itself, via IoC or with the `Create` method. The user has a choice of whether to use IoC or not. The benefit is that IoC becomes an option for the library developer too for making it easy to write unit tests and write maintainable code.

Recipe 1.2 explains how IoC works, using `Microsoft.Extensions.Dependency Injection`, and this solution uses the same library and technique. The main difference is where the IoC container gets configured.

The `Initializer` class has a method named `InitAddressUtilities`. The `Module Initializer` attribute indicates that `InitAddressUtilities` is the module initialization code for this class library. The `InitAddressUtilities` method will run before any other code in the class library.

 In the early days of .NET, a module was a way to group code into a single file, for modularization. You could combine modules into an assembly, where the assembly was defined as being one or more modules with an additional manifest. The manifest contains metadata for the CLR, the details of which are voluminous and unimportant for the current focus.

Using modules was largely a theoretical capability, as most code is compiled as a single module in an assembly. This is the default behavior for the C# compiler and Visual Studio. In fact, you had to go out of your way to create a module that was potentially useful. While it's interesting that the `ModuleInitializer` has the word "module" in it, the practical reality is that it applies toward initialization at the level of the assembly.

Because the `InitAddressUtilities` method has already run, the `Create` method in `AddressService` can rely on `Initializer.Container` having a valid container reference for resolving an `AddressService` instance.

See Also

Recipe 1.2, "Removing Explicit Dependencies"

Summary

In many ways, this book has been a reflection of my own career. In one form or another, each recipe represents solutions to problems that I and others have encountered over the years. However, it's more than that because the thought process that goes into each recipe, chapter, and the entire book has been illuminating. The way we write code today has changed a lot. So have the types of applications we write.

C# was born in an era of the internet coming of age, when the .com bust of the early 2000s was barely conceivable. The impetus behind its creation was the legal battles between Microsoft and Sun Microsystems over the Java programming language. Microsoft needed a component-based programming language for its new .NET platform. It was the early days of distributed computing, and visions of proprietary remoting technology and XML Web services have come and gone. Today is a different world.

In the intervening years, we've seen revolutions that changed the entire face of computing. Mobile phones evolved into smart phones with more computing power than the original IBM PC. Applications and entire businesses moved from hosted services to the cloud. Client/server and nascent distributed computing models became massive world-scale native cloud applications using microservice architectures and serverless computing. The types of applications we build are different.

So, as the computing world has evolved, the programming languages and tools we use must embrace that change. That was the goal with this book, and I hope it helps you. I'm honored to have shared this journey with you and wish you the best in your C# development career.

Index

About the Author

Joe Mayo is an author, instructor, and independent consultant who has been working with C# and .NET since their announcement in the summer of the year 2000. As an independent consultant, he's worked with a variety of organizations, from startups to Fortune 500 enterprises. His experience in this journey includes desktop, web, mobile, cloud, and AI technologies. In addition to practical hands-on application, he's also taught C# and .NET for many years via in-person, live video, and recorded video courses. His top open source project is LINQ to Twitter (*https://oreil.ly/1YEZ8*), with over 1.5 million NuGet downloads. When Joe isn't serving valued customers, he contributes to the community through Q&A forums, presenting, and (one of his favorite pastimes) writing.

Colophon

The animal on the cover of *C# Cookbook* is a northern copperhead snake (*Agkistrodon contortrix*), a poisonous snake native to North America. Their range includes most of the United States east of the Mississippi River. Northern copperheads live in rocky, forested, and wetland environments.

Young northern copperheads cannot count on their parents' support after they're born, and they have adapted a bright yellow tail tip to help them lure prey as they grow. Mature northern copperheads are sexually dimorphic; females are larger than males, and males have longer tails. They grow to 24–37 inches long and live, on average, about 18 years. Their coloring is copper or reddish brown, with an hourglass pattern in darker shades down their back. Northern copperhead snakes have spade-shaped heads with a heat-sensing organ common to all pit vipers, as well as tongues that help them "smell" prey.

These snakes eat small mammals, small birds, other reptiles, amphibians, and insects. They will strike humans if they feel threatened, but the attacks are rarely fatal. Northern copperheads prefer to hide, waiting to surprise their prey. In winter, they hibernate with large groups of other snakes—sometimes other species of snakes.

Many of the animals on O'Reilly's covers are endangered; all of them are important to the world.

The cover illustration is by Jose Marzan, based on a black and white engraving from *Lydekker's Royal Natural History*. The cover fonts are Gilroy Semibold and Guardian Sans. The text font is Adobe Minion Pro; the heading font is Adobe Myriad Condensed; and the code font is Dalton Maag's Ubuntu Mono.